Learning Ceph

Second Edition

Unified, scalable, and reliable open source storage solution

Anthony D'Atri
Vaibhav Bhembre
Karan Singh

BIRMINGHAM - MUMBAI

Learning Ceph

Second Edition

First published: January 2015

Second edition: October 2017

Production reference: 1121017

Published by Packt Publishing Ltd.
Livery Place
35 Livery Street
Birmingham
B3 2PB, UK.

ISBN: 978-1-78712-791-3

www.packtpub.com

Credits

Authors
Anthony D'Atri
Vaibhav Bhembre
Karan Singh

Reviewer
Christian Kauhaus

Acquisition Editor
Meeta Rajani

Content Development Editor
Abhishek Jadhav

Technical Editor
Manish D Shanbhag

Copy Editors
Safis Editing
Juliana Nair

Project Coordinator
Judie Jose

Proofreader
Safis Editing

Indexer
Tejal Soni Daruwala

Graphics
Kirk D'Penha
Vaibhav Bhembre
Anthony D'Atri
Suzanne D'Atri

Production Coordinator
Aparna Bhagat

About the Authors

Anthony D'Atri's career in system administration has spanned laptops to vector supercomputers. He has brought his passion for fleet management and the underlying server components to bear on a holistic yet, detailed approach to deployment and operations. Experience with architecture, operation, and troubleshooting of NetApp, ZFS, SVM, and other storage systems dovetailed neatly into Ceph. Three years with Ceph as a petabyte-scale object and block backend to multiple OpenStack clouds at Cisco, additionally built on Anthony's depth. Now helping deliver awesome storage to DigitalOcean's droplet customers, Anthony aims to help the growing community build success with Ceph.

Anthony would like to thank everyone whose technical and professional support have contributed to his success with Ceph, including Cisco, Digital Ocean, Michael Kidd, Tupper Cole, James Donohoe, Louis Watta, Jade Lester, Narendra Trivedi, Weiguo Sun, Richard "Fuzzy" Miller, Damon Hsu-Hung, Satish Sangapu, Shweta Saraf, Swati Gaikwad, Yi Chen, Ryan Roemmich, Sebastian Sobolewski, Stan Ayzenberg, Sébastien Han, Adam Wolfe Gordon, Vaibhav Bhembre, William Lehman, and Dan van der Ster. Paramount thanks to his wife Suzanne for her support, patience, and support of his long hours.

Vaibhav Bhembre is a systems programmer working currently as a Technical Lead for cloud storage products at DigitalOcean. Before joining DigitalOcean, Vaibhav wore multiple hats leading backend engineering and reliability engineering teams at Sailthru Inc. From helping scale dynamically generated campaign sends to be delivered to over tens of millions of users on time, to architecting a cloud-scale compute and storage platform, Vaibhav has years of experience writing software across all layers of the stack.

Vaibhav holds a bachelor's degree in Computer Engineering from the University of Mumbai and a master's degree in Computer Science from the State University of New York in Buffalo. During his time in academia, Vaibhav co-published a novel graph algorithm that optimally computed closeness and betweeness in an incrementally updating social network. He also had the fortune of committing changes to a highly available distributed file-system built on top of iRODs data management framework as his master's project. This system, that was actively used across 10+ educational institutions live, was his foray into large-scale distributed storage and his transition into using Ceph professionally was only natural.

Vaibhav is forever indebted to his parents Dileep and Vandana Bhembre for devoting incalculable amount of time and effort into making him who he is today. He cannot thank his beautiful wife, Harshita, enough for her constant support, encouragement and most of all, her incredible heart. Vaibhav wholeheartedly thanks all the individuals who have contributed directly or indirectly to his successful career, the list which includes but is not limited to, Prof. Rakesh Nagi, Prof. Murat Demirbas, Sushant Khopkar, Ian White, Moisey Uretsky, Joonas Bergius, and Anthony D'Atri. And finally, Vaibhav is deeply grateful to the Ceph community for designing and building a remarkable piece of software and forming a diverse and open community around it.

Karan Singh is a senior storage architect working with Red Hat and living with his charming wife Monika in Finland. In his current role, Karan is doing solution engineering on Ceph together with partners, customers and exploring new avenues for software defined storage.

Karan devotes a part of his time in learning emerging technologies and enjoys the challenges that comes with it.. He also authored the first edition of Learning Ceph and Ceph Cookbook, Packt Publishing. You can reach him on Twitter @karansingh010.

I'd like to thank my wife, Monika for being the perfect better half. I'd also like to thank my employer Red Hat for giving me an opportunity to work on some cutting-edge technologies and use cases. Finally, special thanks to Vikhyat and Michael for putting great efforts to help in the continued success of Learning Ceph.

About the Reviewer

Christian Kauhaus set up his first Ceph cluster using the *Argonaut* release back in 2012. He got hooked on sysadmin stuff since helping out to set up his school's computer room back in the nineties. After studying Computer Science in Rostock and Jena, he spent a few years with the High Performance Computing group at the University of Jena. Currently, he is working as a systems engineer at Flying Circus Internet Operations GmbH, a small company providing managed hosting and data center related services located in Halle (Saale), Germany.

Apart from that, Christian likes to program in Python and Rust and is an active member of the NixOS community. He loves to play Jazz piano in his leisure time. He currently lives in Jena, Germany.

I want to thank my wife Hanna for bearing with me while I repeatedly sat half the night in front of the computer trying out code examples. And I would like to thank everyone involved in this project for their patience and helpfulness.

www.PacktPub.com

For support files and downloads related to your book, please visit `www.PacktPub.com`. Did you know that Packt offers eBook versions of every book published, with PDF and ePub files available? You can upgrade to the eBook version at `www.PacktPub.com` and as a print book customer, you are entitled to a discount on the eBook copy. Get in touch with us at `service@packtpub.com` for more details. At `www.PacktPub.com`, you can also read a collection of free technical articles, sign up for a range of free newsletters and receive exclusive discounts and offers on Packt books and eBooks.

`https://www.packtpub.com/mapt`

Get the most in-demand software skills with Mapt. Mapt gives you full access to all Packt books and video courses, as well as industry-leading tools to help you plan your personal development and advance your career.

Why subscribe?

- Fully searchable across every book published by Packt
- Copy and paste, print, and bookmark content
- On demand and accessible via a web browser

Customer Feedback

Thanks for purchasing this Packt book. At Packt, quality is at the heart of our editorial process. To help us improve, please leave us an honest review on this book's Amazon page at https://www.amazon.com/dp/1787127915. If you'd like to join our team of regular reviewers, you can email us at customerreviews@packtpub.com. We award our regular reviewers with free eBooks and videos in exchange for their valuable feedback. Help us be relentless in improving our products!

Table of Contents

Preface

Learning Ceph, Second Edition will give you all the skills you need to plan, deploy, and effectively manage Ceph clusters. You will begin with an introduction to Ceph use cases and components, then progress through advice on selecting and planning servers and components. We then cover a number of important decisions to make before provisioning your servers and clusters and walk through hands-on deployment of a fully functional virtualized sandbox cluster. A wide range of common (and not so common) management tasks are explored. A discussion of monitoring is followed by a deep dive into the inner workings of Ceph, a selection of topics related to provisioning storage, and an overview of Ceph's role as an OpenStack storage solution. Rounding out our chapters is advice on benchmarking and tuning for performance and stability.

By the end of the book you will have learned to deploy and use Ceph effectively for your data storage requirements.

What this book covers

Chapter 1, *Introducing Ceph Storage*, here we explore Ceph's role as storage needs evolve and embrace cloud computing. Also covered are Ceph's release cycle and history including changes since the first edition of Learning Ceph .

Chapter 2, *Ceph Components and Services*, a tour through Ceph's major components and the services they implement. Examples of each service's use cases are given.

Chapter 3, *Hardware and Network Selection*, is a comprehensive journey through the maze of hardware choices that one faces when provisioning Ceph infrastructure. While Ceph is highly adaptable to diverse server components, prudent planning can help you optimize your choices for today and tomorrow.

Chapter 4, *Planning Your Deployment*, is the software complement to Chapter 3, *Hardware and Network Selection*. We guide the reader through deployment and provisioning decisions for both Ceph and the underlying operating system.

Chapter 5, *Deploying a Virtual Sandbox Cluster*, is an automated, fully functional Ceph deployment on virtual machines. This provides opportunities for hands-on experience within minutes.

Chapter 6, *Ceph Operations and Maintenance*, is a deep and wide inventory of day to day operations. We cover management of Ceph topologies, services, and configuration settings as well as, maintenance and debugging.

Chapter 7, *Monitoring Ceph*, a comprehensive collection of commands, practices, and dashboard software to help keep a close eye on the health of Ceph clusters.

Chapter 8, *Ceph Architecture: Under the Hood*, deep-dives into the inner workings of Ceph with low-level architecture, processes, and data flow.

Chapter 9, *Storage Provisioning with Ceph*, here we practice the client side of provisioning and managing each of Ceph's major services.

Chapter 10, *Integrating Ceph with OpenStack*, explores the components of the OpenStack cloud infrastructure platform and how they can exploit Ceph for resilient and scalable storage.

Chapter 11, *Performance and Stability Tuning*, provides a collection of Ceph, networks, filesystems, and underlying operating system settings to optimize cluster performance and stability. Benchmarking of cluster performance is also explored.

What you need for this book

A basic knowledge of storage terms, server hardware, and networking will help digest the wealth of information provided. The virtual deployment sandbox was tested on macOS with specified software versions. It should work readily on Linux or other desktop operating systems. While execution of the virtual deployment is valuable, it is not strictly required to reap the benefits of this book.

Who this book is for

A basic knowledge of GNU/Linux, storage systems, and server components is assumed. If you have no experience with software-defined storage solutions and Ceph, but are eager to learn about them, this is the book for you. Those already managing Ceph deployments will also find value in the breadth and depth of the material presented.

Conventions

In this book, you will find a number of text styles that distinguish between different kinds of information. Here are some examples of these styles and an explanation of their meaning. Code words in text, database table names, folder names, filenames, file extensions, pathnames, dummy URLs, user input, and Twitter handles are shown as follows: "Create a new user for JIRA in the database and grant the user access to the `jiradb` database that we just created using the following command:" A block of code is set as follows:

```
glance-api.conf:
[glance_store]
 stores = rbd
 default_store = rbd
 rbd_store_pool = images
 rbd_store_user = glance-user
 rbd_store_ceph_conf = /etc/ceph/ceph.conf
 rbd_store_chunk_size = 8
```

Any command-line input or output is written as follows:

```
instance$ ls /dev/vd*
/dev/vda /dev/vda1 /dev/vdb
instance$ lsblk
```

New terms and **important words** are shown in bold.

Warnings or important notes appear like this.

Tips and tricks appear like this.

Reader feedback

Feedback from our readers is always welcome. Let us know what you think about this book-what you liked or disliked. Reader feedback is important for us as it helps us develop titles that you will really get the most out of. To send us general feedback, simply e-mail feedback@packtpub.com, and mention the book's title in the subject of your message. If there is a topic that you have expertise in and you are interested in either writing or contributing to a book, see our author guide at www.packtpub.com/authors.

Customer support

Now that you are the proud owner of a Packt book, we have a number of things to help you to get the most from your purchase.

Downloading the example code

You can download the example code files for this book from your account at http://www. packtpub.com. If you purchased this book elsewhere, you can visit http://www.packtpub. com/support and register to have the files e-mailed directly to you. You can download the code files by following these steps:

1. Log in or register to our website using your e-mail address and password.
2. Hover the mouse pointer on the **SUPPORT** tab at the top.
3. Click on **Code Downloads & Errata**.
4. Enter the name of the book in the **Search** box.
5. Select the book for which you're looking to download the code files.
6. Choose from the drop-down menu where you purchased this book from.
7. Click on **Code Download**.

You can also download the code files by clicking on the **Code Files** button on the book's webpage at the Packt Publishing website. This page can be accessed by entering the book's name in the **Search** box. Please note that you need to be logged in to your Packt account. Once the file is downloaded, please make sure that you unzip or extract the folder using the latest version of:

- WinRAR / 7-Zip for Windows
- Zipeg / iZip / UnRarX for Mac
- 7-Zip / PeaZip for Linux

The code bundle for the book is also hosted on GitHub at https://github.com/ PacktPublishing/Learning-Ceph-Second-Edition. We also have other code bundles from our rich catalog of books and videos available at https://github.com/PacktPublishing/. Check them out!

Downloading the color images of this book

We also provide you with a PDF file that has color images of the screenshots/diagrams used in this book. The color images will help you better understand the changes in the output. You can download this file from `https://www.packtpub.com/sites/default/files/downloads/LearningCephSecondEdition_ColorImages.pdf`.

Errata

Although we have taken every care to ensure the accuracy of our content, mistakes do happen. If you find a mistake in one of our books-maybe a mistake in the text or the code-we would be grateful if you could report this to us. By doing so, you can save other readers from frustration and help us improve subsequent versions of this book. If you find any errata, please report them by visiting `http://www.packtpub.com/submit-errata`, selecting your book, clicking on the **Errata Submission Form** link, and entering the details of your errata. Once your errata is verified, your submission will be accepted and the errata will be uploaded to our website or added to any list of existing errata under the Errata section of that title. To view the previously submitted errata, go to `https://www.packtpub.com/books/content/support` and enter the name of the book in the search field. The required information will appear under the **Errata** section.

Piracy

Piracy of copyrighted material on the Internet is an ongoing problem across all media. At Packt, we take the protection of our copyright and licenses very seriously. If you come across any illegal copies of our works in any form on the Internet, please provide us with the location address or website name immediately so that we can pursue a remedy. Please contact us at `copyright@packtpub.com` with a link to the suspected pirated material. We appreciate your help in protecting our authors and our ability to bring you valuable content.

Questions

If you have a problem with any aspect of this book, you can contact us at `questions@packtpub.com`, and we will do our best to address the problem.

1
Introducing Ceph Storage

Ceph is an open source project that provides a solution for software-defined, network-available storage with high performance and no single point of failure. It is designed to be highly scalable to the exabyte level and beyond while running on general-purpose commodity hardware.

In this chapter, we will cover the following topics:

- The history and evolution of Ceph
- What's new since the first edition of *Learning Ceph*
- The future of storage
- Ceph compared with other storage solutions

Ceph garners much of the buzz in the storage industry due to its open, scalable, and distributed nature. Today public, private, and hybrid cloud models are dominant strategies for scalable and scale-out infrastructure. Ceph's design and features including multi-tenancy are a natural fit for cloud **Infrastructure as a Service (IaaS)** and **Platform as a Service (PaaS)** deployments: at least 60% of OpenStack deployments leverage Ceph.

For more information regarding the use of Ceph within OpenStack deployments, visit
`https://keithtenzer.com/2017/03/30/openstack-swift-integration-w`
`ith-ceph`.

Ceph is architected deliberately to deliver enterprise-quality services on a variety of commodity hardware. Ceph's architectural philosophy includes the following:

- Every component must be scalable
- No individual process, server, or other component can be a single point of failure
- The solution must be software-based, open source, and adaptable
- Ceph software should run on readily available commodity hardware without vendor lock-in
- Everything must be self-manageable wherever possible

Ceph provides great performance, limitless scalability, power, and flexibility to enterprises, helping them move on from expensive proprietary storage silos. The Ceph universal storage system provides block, file, and object storage from a single, unified back-end, enabling customers to access storage as their needs evolve and grow.

The foundation of Ceph is *objects*, building blocks from which complex services are assembled. Any flavor of data, be it a block, object, or file, is represented by objects within the Ceph backend. Object storage is the flexible solution for unstructured data storage needs today and in the future. An object-based storage system offers advantages over traditional file-based storage solutions that include platform and hardware independence. Ceph manages data carefully, replicating across storage devices, servers, data center racks, and even data centers to ensure reliability, availability, and durability. Within Ceph objects are not tied to a physical path, making objects flexible and location-independent. This enables Ceph to scale linearly from the petabyte level to an exabyte level.

The history and evolution of Ceph

Ceph was developed at University of California, Santa Cruz, by Sage Weil in 2003 as a part of his PhD project. The initial implementation provided the **Ceph Filesystem (CephFS)** in approximately 40,000 lines of C++ code. This was open sourced in 2006 under a **Lesser GNU Public License (LGPL)** to serve as a reference implementation and research platform. Lawrence Livermore National Laboratory supported Sage's early followup work from 2003 to 2007.

DreamHost, a Los-Angeles-based web hosting and domain registrar company also co-founded by Sage Weil, supported Ceph development from 2007 to 2011. During this period Ceph as we know it took shape: the core components gained stability and reliability, new features were implemented, and the road map for the future was drawn. During this time a number of key developers began contributing, including Yehuda Sadeh-Weinraub, Gregory Farnum, Josh Durgin, Samuel Just, Wido den Hollander, and Loïc Dachary.

In 2012 Sage Weil founded Inktank to enable the widespread adoption of Ceph. Their expertise, processes, tools, and support enabled enterprise-subscription customers to effectively implement and manage Ceph storage systems. In 2014 Red Hat, Inc.,the world's leading provider of open source solutions, agreed to acquire Inktank.

 For more information, visit `https://www.redhat.com/en/technologies/storage/ceph`.

The term Ceph is a common nickname given to pet octopuses; Ceph and is an abbreviation of cephalopod, marine animals belonging to the Cephalopoda class of molluscs. Ceph's mascot is an octopus,referencing the highly parallel behavior of an octopus and was chosen to connect the file system with UCSC's mascot, a banana slug named *Sammy*. Banana slugs are gastropods,which are also a class of molluscs. As Ceph is not an acronym, it should not be uppercased as CEPH.

 For additional information about Ceph in general, please visit `https://en.wikipedia.org/wiki/Ceph_(software)`

Ceph releases

Each release of Ceph has a numeric version. Major releases also receive cephalopod code-names in alphabetical order. Through the Luminous release the Ceph community tagged a new major version about twice a year, alternating between Long Term Support (LTS) and stable releases. The latest two LTS releases were officially supported, but only the single latest stable release.

 For more information on Ceph releases please visit `https://ceph.com/category/releases`.

The release numbering scheme has changed since the first edition of *Learning Ceph* was published. Earlier major releases were tagged initially with a version number (0.87) and were followed by multiple point releases (0.87.1, 0.87.2, ...). Releases beginning with Infernalis however are numbered as shown:

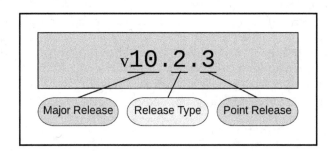

The major release number matches the letter of the alphabet of its code name (for example **I** is the ninth letter of the English alphabet, so 9.2.1 was named Infernalis). As we write, there have been four releases following this numbering convention: Infernalis, Jewel, Kraken, and Luminous.

The early versions of each major release have a type of 0 in the second field, which indicates active pre-release development status for early testers and the brave of heart. Later release candidates have a type of 1 and are targeted at test clusters and brave users. A type of 2 represents a general-availability, production-ready release. Point releases mostly contain security and bug fixes, but sometimes offer functionality improvements as well.

Ceph release name	Ceph package version	Release date
Argonaut	0.48 (LTS)	July 2012
Bobtail	0.56 (LTS)	January 2013
Cuttlefish	0.61	May 2013
Dumpling	0.67 (LTS)	August 2013
Emperor	0.72	November 2013
Firefly	0.80 (LTS)	May 2014
Giant	0.87	October 2014
Hammer	0.94 (LTS)	April 2015
Infernalis	9.2.1	November 2015
Jewel	10.2.3 (LTS)	April 2016

Kraken	11.2.0	January 2017
Luminous	12.2.0 (LTS)	August 2017
Mimic	13.2.0	2018
Nautilus	14.2.0	2019

Note that as this book was being readied for publication in October 2017 Sage announced that the release cycle has changed. Starting with Mimic there will no longer be alternating LTS and stable releases. Each release henceforth will be LTS at a roughly 9 month cadence. For the details visit

https://github.com/ceph/ceph/pull/18117/files

New since the first edition

The Jewel LTS release brought a number of significant changes:

- Unified queue of client I/O, recovery, scrubs, and snapshot trimming
- Daemons now run as the **ceph** user, which must be addressed when upgrading
- Cache tier improvements
- SHEC erasure coding is no longer experimental
- The SWIFT API now supports object expiration
- RBD improvements (now supports suffixes)
- `rbd du` shows actual and provisioned usage quickly via `object-map` and `fast-diff` features
- New `rbd status` command
- `deep-flatten` now handles snapshots
- CephFS snapshots can now be renamed
- And CephFS is considered stable!
- Scrubbing improvements
- TCMalloc improvements
- Multisite functionality in RGW significantly improved
- OpenStack Keystone v3 support
- Swift per-tenant namespace
- Async RBD mirroring
- A new look for `ceph status`

More details on the Jewel release can be found at `http://ceph.com/releases/v10-2-0-jewel-released`.

As we write, the major Luminous LTS release has *just* reached general availability. Early experiences are positive and it is the best choice for new deployments. Much-anticipated features in Luminous include:

- The BlueStore back end is supported
- In-line compression and read checksums
- Erasure coding for RBD volumes
- Better tools for uniform OSD utilization
- Improved tools for the OSD lifecycle
- Enhanced CLI
- Multiple active CephFS MDS servers are supported

The release notes for Luminous 12.2.0 can be found at `https://ceph.com/releases/v12-2-0-luminous-released/`.

The future of storage

Enterprise storage requirements have grown explosively over the last decade. Research has shown that data in large enterprises is growing at a rate of 40 to 60 percent annually, and many companies are doubling their data footprint each year. IDC analysts estimated that there were 54.4 exabytes of total digital data worldwide in the year 2000. By 2007, this reached 295 exabytes, by 2012 2,596 exabytes, and by the end of 2020 it's expected to reach 40,000 exabytes worldwide

`https://www.emc.com/leadership/digital-universe/2012iview/executive-summary-a-universe-of.htm`

Traditional and proprietary storage solutions often suffer from breathtaking cost, limited scalability and functionality, and vendor lock-in. Each of these factors confounds seamless growth and upgrades for speed and capacity.

Closed source software and proprietary hardware leave one between a rock and a hard place when a product line is discontinued, often requiring a lengthy, costly, and disruptive forklift-style total replacement of EOL deployments.

Modern storage demands a system that is unified, distributed, reliable, highly performant, and most importantly, massively scalable to the exabyte level and beyond. Ceph is a true solution for the world's growing data explosion. A key factor in Ceph's growth and adoption at lightning pace is the vibrant community of users who truly believe in the power of Ceph. Data generation is a never-ending process and we need to evolve storage to accommodate the burgeoning volume.

Ceph is the perfect solution for modern, growing storage: its unified, distributed, cost-effective, and scalable nature is the solution to today's and the future's data storage needs. The open source Linux community saw Ceph's potential as early as 2008, and added support for Ceph into the mainline Linux kernel.

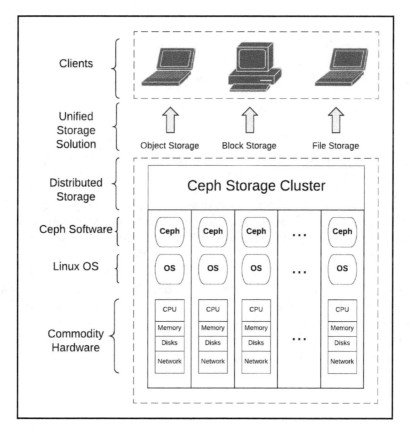

Ceph as the cloud storage solution

One of the most problematic yet crucial components of cloud infrastructure development is storage. A cloud environment needs storage that can scale up and out at low cost and that integrates well with other components. Such a storage system is a key contributor to the **total cost of ownership** (**TCO**) of the entire cloud platform. There are traditional storage vendors who claim to provide integration to cloud frameworks, but we need additional features beyond just integration support. Traditional storage solutions may have proven adequate in the past, but today they are not ideal candidates for a unified cloud storage solution. Traditional storage systems are expensive to deploy and support in the long term, and scaling up and out is uncharted territory. We need a storage solution designed to fulfill current and future needs, a system built upon open source software and commodity hardware that can provide the required scalability in a cost-effective way.

Ceph has rapidly evolved in this space to fill the need for a true cloud storage backend. It is favored by major open source cloud platforms including as OpenStack, CloudStack, and OpenNebula. Ceph has built partnerships with Canonical, Red Hat, and SUSE, the giants in Linux space who favor distributed, reliable, and scalable Ceph storage clusters for their Linux and cloud software distributions. The Ceph community is working closely with these Linux giants to provide a reliable multi-featured storage backend for their cloud platforms.

Public and private clouds have gained momentum with to the OpenStack platform. OpenStack has proven itself as an end-to-end cloud solution. It includes two core storage components: Swift, which provides object-based storage, and Cinder, which provides block storage volumes to instances. Ceph excels as the back end for both object and block storage in OpenStack deployments.

Swift is limited to object storage. Ceph is a unified storage solution for block, file, and object storage and benefits OpenStack deployments by serving multiple storage modalities from a single backend cluster. The OpenStack and Ceph communities have worked together for many years to develop a fully supported Ceph storage backend for the OpenStack cloud. From OpenStack's Folsom release Ceph has been fully integrated. Ceph's developers ensure that Ceph works well with each new release of OpenStack, contributing new features and bug fixes. OpenStack's Cinder and Glance components utilize Ceph's key **RADOS Block Device** (**RBD**) service. Ceph RBD enables OpenStack deployments to rapidly provision of hundreds of virtual machine instances by providing thin-provisioned snapshot and cloned volumes that are quickly and efficiently created.

Cloud platforms with Ceph as a storage backend provide much needed flexibility to service providers who build **Storage as a Service (SaaS)** and **Infrastructure-as-a-Service (IaaS)** solutions that they cannot realize with traditional enterprise storage solutions. By leveraging Ceph as a backend for cloud platforms, service providers can offer low-cost cloud services to their customers. Ceph enables them to offer relatively low storage prices with enterprise features when compared to other storage solutions.

Dell, SUSE, Redhat, and Canonical offer and support deployment and configuration management tools such as Dell Crowbar, Red Hat's Ansible, and Juju for automated and easy deployment of Ceph storage for their OpenStack cloud solutions. Other configuration management tools such as Puppet, Chef, and SaltStack are popular for automated Ceph deployment. Each of these tools has open source, ready made Ceph modules available that can be easily leveraged for Ceph deployment. With Red Hat's acquisition of Ansible the open source **ceph-ansible** suite is becoming a favored deployment and management tool. In distributed cloud (and other) environments, every component must scale. These configuration management tools are essential to quickly scale up your infrastructure. Ceph is fully compatible with these tools, allowing customers to deploy and extend a Ceph cluster instantly.

> More information about Ansible and **ceph-ansible** can be found at
> `https://www.redhat.com/en/about/blog/why-red-hat-acquired-ansible`
> and
> `https://github.com/ceph/ceph-ansible/wiki`.

Ceph is software-defined

Storage infrastructure architects increasingly favor **Software-defined Storage (SDS)** solutions. SDS offers an attractive solution to organizations with a large investment in legacy storage who are not getting the flexibility and scalability they need for evolving needs. Ceph is a true SDS solution:

- Open source software
- Runs on commodity hardware
- No vendor lock in
- Low cost per GB

An SDS solution provides much-needed flexibility with respect to hardware selection. Customers can choose commodity hardware from any manufacturer and are free to design a heterogeneous hardware solution that evolves over time to meet their specific needs and constraints. Ceph's software-defined storage built from commodity hardware flexibly provides agile enterprise storage features from the software layer.

In Chapter 3, *Hardware and Network Selection* we'll explore a variety of factors that influence the hardware choices you make for your Ceph deployments.

Ceph is a unified storage solution

Unified storage from a storage vendor's perspective is defined as file-based **Network-Attached Storage** (**NAS**) and block-based **Storage Area Network(SAN)** access from a single platform. NAS and SAN technologies became popular in the late 1990's and early 2000's, but when we look to the future are we sure that traditional, proprietary NAS and SAN technologies can manage storage needs 50 years down the line? Do they have what it takes to handle exabytes of data?

With Ceph, the term unified storage means much more than just what traditional storage vendors claim to provide. Ceph is designed from the ground up to be future-ready; its building blocks are scalable to handle enormous amounts of data and the open source model ensures that we are not bound to the whim or fortunes of any single vendor. Ceph is a true unified storage solution that provides block, file, and object services from a single unified software defined backend. Object storage is a better fit for today's mix of unstructured data strategies than are blocks and files. Access is through a well-defined RESTful network interface, freeing application architects and software engineers from the nuances and vagaries of operating system kernels and filesystems. Moreover, object-backed applications scale readily by freeing users from managing the limits of discrete-sized block volumes. Block volumes can sometimes be expanded in-place, but this rarely a simple, fast, or non-disruptive operation. Applications can be written to access multiple volumes, either natively or through layers such as the Linux LVM (Logical Volume Manager), but these also can be awkward to manage and scaling can still be painful. Object storage from the client perspective does not require management of fixed-size volumes or devices.

Rather than managing the complexity blocks and files behind the scenes, Ceph manages low-level RADOS objects and defines block- and file-based storage on top of them. If you think of a traditional file-based storage system, files are addressed via a directory and file path, and in a similar way, objects in Ceph are addressed by a unique identifier and are stored in a flat namespace.

 It is important to distinguish between the RADOS objects that Ceph manages internally and the user-visible objects available via Ceph's S3 / Swift RGW service. In most cases, objects refer to the latter.

The next-generation architecture

Traditional storage systems lack an efficient way to managing metadata. Metadata is information (data) *about* the actual user payload data, including where the data will be written to and read from. Traditional storage systems maintain a central lookup table to track of their metadata. Every time a client sends a request for a read or write operation, the storage system first performs a lookup to the huge metadata table. After receiving the results it performs the client operation. For a smaller storage system, you might not notice the performance impact of this centralized bottleneck, but as storage domains grow large the performance and scalability limits of this approach become increasingly problematic.

Ceph does not follow the traditional storage architecture; it has been totally reinvented for the next generation. Rather than centrally storing, manipulating, and accessing metadata, Ceph introduces a new approach, the **Controlled Replication Under Scalable Hashing (CRUSH)** algorithm.

 For a wealth of whitepapers and other documents on Ceph-related topics, visit
`http://ceph.com/resources/publications`

Instead of performing a lookup in the metadata table for every client request, the CRUSH algorithm enables the client to independently computes where data should be written to or read from. By deriving this metadata dynamically, there is no need to manage a centralized table. Modern computers can perform a CRUSH lookup very quickly; moreover, a smaller computing load can be distributed across cluster nodes, leveraging the power of distributed storage.

CRUSH accomplishes this via infrastructure awareness. It understands the hierarchy and capacities of the various components of your logical and physical infrastructure: drives, nodes, chassis, datacenter racks, pools, network switch domains, datacenter rows, even datacenter rooms and buildings as local requirements dictate. These are the failure domains for any infrastructure. CRUSH stores data safely replicated so that data will be protected (durability) and accessible (availability) even if multiple components fail within or across failure domains. Ceph managers define these failure domains for their infrastructure within the topology of Ceph's CRUSH map. The Ceph backend and clients share a copy of the CRUSH map, and clients are thus able to derive the location, drive, server, datacenter, and so on, of desired data and access it directly without a centralized lookup bottleneck.

CRUSH enables Ceph's self-management and self-healing. In the event of component failure, the CRUSH map is updated to reflect the down component. The back end transparently determines the effect of the failure on the cluster according to defined placement and replication rules. Without administrative intervention, the Ceph back end performs behind-the-scenes recovery to ensure data durability and availability. The back end creates replicas of data from surviving copies on other, unaffected components to restore the desired degree of safety. A properly designed CRUSH map and CRUSH rule set ensure that the cluster will maintain more than one copy of data distributed across the cluster on diverse components, avoiding data loss from single or multiple component failures.

RAID: the end of an era

Redundant Array of Independent Disks (RAID) has been a fundamental storage technology for the last 30 years. However, as data volume and component capacities scale dramatically, RAID-based storage systems are increasingly showing their limitations and fall short of today's and tomorrow's storage needs.

Disk technology has matured over time. Manufacturers are now producing enterprise-quality magnetic disks with immense capacities at ever lower prices. We no longer speak of 450 GB, 600 GB, or even 1 TB disks as drive capacity and performance has grown. As we write, modern enterprise drives offer up to 12 TB of storage; by the time you read these words capacities of 14 or more TB may well be available. **Solid State Drives** (**SSDs**) were formerly an expensive solution for small-capacity high-performance segments of larger systems or niches requiring shock resistance or minimal power and cooling. In recent years SSD capacities have increased dramatically as prices have plummeted. Since the publication of the first edition of *Learning Ceph*, SSDs have become increasingly viable for bulk storage as well.

Consider an enterprise RAID-based storage system built from numerous 4 or 8 TB disk drives; in the event of disk failure, RAID will take many hours or even days to recover from a single failed drive. If another drive fails during recovery, chaos will ensue and data may be lost. Recovering from the failure or replacement of multiple large disk drives using RAID is a cumbersome process that can significantly degrade client performance.

Traditional RAID technologies include RAID 1 (mirroring), RAID 10 (mirroring plus striping), and RAID 5 (parity).

Effective RAID implementations require entire dedicated drives to be provisioned as hot spares. This impacts TCO, and running out of spare drives can be fatal. Most RAID strategies assume a set of identically-sized disks, so you will suffer efficiency and speed penalties or even failure to recover if you mix in drives of differing speeds and sizes. Often a RAID system will be unable to use a spare or replacement drive that is very slightly smaller than the original, and if the replacement drive is larger, the additional capacity is usually wasted.

Another shortcoming of traditional RAID-based storage systems is that they rarely offer any detection or correction of latent or bit-flip errors, aka *bit-rot*. The microscopic footprint of data on modern storage media means that sooner or later what you read from the storage device won't match what you wrote, and you may not have any way to know when this happens. Ceph runs periodic scrubs that compare checksums and remove altered copies of data from service. With the Luminous release Ceph also gains the ZFS-like ability to checksum data at every read, additionally improving the reliability of your critical data.

Enterprise RAID-based systems often require expensive, complex, and fussy RAID-capable HBA cards that increase management overhead, complicate monitoring, and increase the overall cost. RAID can hit the wall when size limits are reached. This author has repeatedly encountered systems that cannot expand a storage pool past 64TB. Parity RAID implementations including RAID 5 and RAID 6 also suffer from write throughput penalties, and require complex and finicky caching strategies to enable tolerable performance for most applications. Often the most limiting shortcoming of traditional RAID is that it only protects against disk failure; it cannot protect against switch and network failures, those of server hardware and operating systems, or even regional disaster. Depending on strategy, the maximum protection you may realize from RAID is surviving through one or at most two drive failures. Strategies such as RAID 60 can somewhat mitigate this risk, though they are not universally available, are inefficient, may require additional licensing, and still deliver incomplete protection against certain failure patterns.

For modern storage capacity, performance, and durability needs, we need a system that can overcome all these limitations in a performance- and cost-effective way. Back in the day a common *solution* for component failure was a backup system, which itself could be slow, expensive, capacity-limited, and subject to vendor lock-in. Modern data volumes are such that traditional backup strategies are often infeasible due to scale and volatility.

A Ceph storage system is the best solution available today to address these problems. For data reliability, Ceph makes use of data replication (including erasure coding). It does not use traditional RAID, and because of this, it is free of the limitations and vulnerabilities of a traditional RAID-based enterprise storage system. Since Ceph is software-defined and exploits commodity components we do not require specialized hardware for data replication. Moreover, the replication level is highly configurable by Ceph managers, who can easily manage data protection strategies according to local needs and underlying infrastructure. Ceph's flexibility even allows managers to define multiple types and levels of protection to address the needs of differing types and populations of data within the same back end.

 By replication we mean that Ceph stores complete, independent copies of all data on multiple, disjoint drives and servers. By default Ceph will store three copies, yielding a usable capacity that is 1/3 the aggregate raw drive space, but other configurations are possible and a single cluster can accommodate multiple strategies for varying needs.

Ceph's replication is superior to traditional RAID when components fail. Unlike RAID, when a drive (or server!) fails, the data that was held by that drive is recovered from a large number of surviving drives. Since Ceph is a distributed system driven by the CRUSH map, the replicated copies of data are scattered across many drives. By design no primary and replicated copies reside on the same drive or server; they are placed within different failure domains. A large number of cluster drives participate in data recovery, distributing the workload and minimizing the contention with and impact on ongoing client operations. This makes recovery operations amazingly fast without performance bottlenecks.

Moreover, recovery does not require spare drives; data is replicated to unallocated space on other drives within the cluster. Ceph implements a weighting mechanism for drives and sorts data independently at a granularity smaller than any single drive's capacity. This avoids the limitations and inefficiencies that RAID suffers with non-uniform drive sizes. Ceph stores data based on each drive's and each server's weight, which is adaptively managed via the CRUSH map. Replacing a failed drive with a smaller drive results in a slight reduction of cluster aggregate capacity, but unlike traditional RAID it still works. If a replacement drive is larger than the original, even many times larger, the cluster's aggregate capacity increases accordingly. Ceph does the right thing with whatever you throw at it.

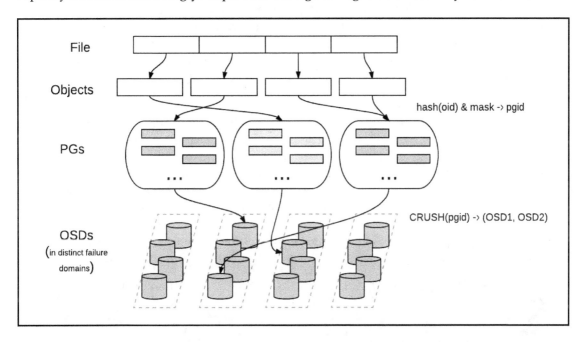

In addition to replication, Ceph also supports another advanced method of ensuring data durability: erasure coding, which is a type of **Forward Error Correction (FEC)**. Erasure-coded pools require less storage space than replicated pools, resulting in a greater ratio of usable to raw capacity. In this process, data on failed components is regenerated algorithmically. You can use both replication and erasure coding on different pools with the same Ceph cluster. We will explore the benefits and drawbacks of erasure-coding versus replication in coming chapters.

Ceph Block Storage

Block storage will be familiar to those who have worked with traditional SAN (Storage Area Network) technologies. Allocations of desired capacity are provisioned on demand and presented as contiguous statically-sized volumes (sometimes referred to as *images*). Ceph RBD supports volumes up to 16 exabytes in size. These volumes are attached to the client operating system as virtualized disk drives that can be utilized much like local physical drives. In virtualized environments the attachment point is often at the hypervisor level (eg. QEMU / KVM). The hypervisor then presents volumes to the guest operating system via the **virtio** driver or as an emulated IDE or SCSI disk.Usually a filesystem is then created on the volume for traditional file storage. This strategy has the appeal that guest operating systems do not need to know about Ceph, which is especially useful for software delivered as an appliance image. Client operating systems running on bare metal can also directly map volumes using a Ceph kernel driver.

Ceph's block storage component is RBD, the RADOS Block Device. We will discuss RADOS in depth in the following chapters, but for now we'll note that RADOS is the underlying technology on which RBD is built. RBD provides reliable, distributed, and high performance block storage volumes to clients. RBD volumes are effectively striped over numerous objects scattered throughout the entire Ceph cluster, a strategy that is key for providing availability, durability, and performance to clients. The Linux kernel bundles a native RBD driver; thus clients need not install layered software to enjoy Ceph's block service. RBD also provides enterprise features including incremental (diff) and full-volume snapshots, thin provisioning, copy-on-write (COW) cloning, layering, and others. RBD clients also support in-memory caching, which can dramatically improve performance.

 An exabyte is one quintillion (1018) bytes, or one billion gigabytes (GB).

The Ceph RBD service is exploited by cloud platforms including OpenStack and CloudStack to provision both primary / boot devices and supplemental volumes. Within OpenStack, Ceph's RBD service is configured as a backend for the abstracted Cinder (block) and Glance (base image) components. RBD's copy-on-write functionality enables one to quickly spin up hundreds or even thousands of thin-provisioned instances (virtual machines).

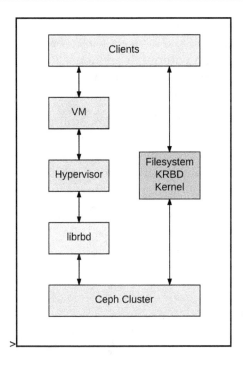

Ceph compared to other storage solutions

The enterprise storage market is experiencing a fundamental realignment. Traditional proprietary storage systems are incapable of meeting future data storage needs, especially within a reasonable budget. Appliance-based storage is declining even as data usage grows by leaps and bounds.

The high TCO of proprietary systems does not end with hardware procurement: nickle-and-dime feature licenses, yearly support, and management add up to a breathtakingly expensive bottom line. One would previously purchase a pallet-load of hardware, pay for a few years of support, then find that the initial deployment has been EOL'd and thus can't be expanded or even maintained. This perpetuates a cycle of successive rounds of en-masse hardware acquisition. Concomitant support contracts to receive bug fixes and security updates often come at spiraling cost. After a few years (or even sooner) your once-snazzy solution becomes unsupported scrap metal, and the cycle repeats. Pay, rinse, lather, repeat. When the time comes to add a second deployment, the same product line may not even be available, forcing you to implement, document, and support a growing number of incompatible, one-off solutions. I daresay your organization's money and your time can be better spent elsewhere, like giving you a well-deserved raise.

With Ceph new software releases are always available, no licenses expire, and you're welcome to read the code yourself and even contribute. You can also expand your solution along many axes, compatibly and without disruption. Unlike one-size-fits-none proprietary solutions, you can pick exactly the scale, speed, and components that make sense today while effortlessly growing tomorrow, with the highest levels of control and customization.

Open source storage technologies however have demonstrated performance, reliability, scalability, and lower TCO (Total Cost of Ownership) without fear of product line or model phase-outs or vendor lock-in. Many corporations as well as government, universities, research, healthcare, and HPC (High Performance Computing) organizations are already successfully exploiting open source storage solutions.

Ceph is garnering tremendous interest and gaining popularity, increasingly winning over other open source as well as proprietary storage solutions. In the remainder of this chapter we'll compare Ceph to other open source storage solutions.

GPFS

General Parallel File System (**GPFS**) is a distributed filesystem developed and owned by IBM. This is a proprietary and closed source storage system, which limits its appeal and adaptability. Licensing and support cost added to that of storage hardware add up to an expensive solution. Moreover, it has a very limited set of storage interfaces: it provides neither block storage (like RBD) nor RESTful (like RGW) access to the storage system, limiting the constellation of use-cases that can be served by a single backend.

In 2015 GPFS was rebranded as IBM Spectrum Scale.

iRODS

iRODS stands for Integrated Rule-Oriented Data System, an open source data-management system released with a 3-clause BSD license. iRODS is not highly available and can be bottlenecked. Its iCAT metadata server is a single point of failure (SPoF) without true high availability (HA) or scalability. Moreover, it implements a very limited set of storage interfaces, providing neither block storage nor RESTful access modalities. iRODS is more effective at storing a relatively small number of large files than both a large number of mixed small and large files. iRODS implements a traditional metadata architecture, maintaining an index of the physical location of each filename.

HDFS

HDFS is a distributed scalable filesystem written in Java for the Hadoop processing framework. HDFS is not a fully POSIX-compliant filesystem and does not offer a block interface. The reliability of HDFS is of concern as it lacks high availability. The single NameNode in HDFS is a SPoF and performance bottleneck. HDFS is again suitable, primarily storing a small number of large files rather than the mix of small and large files at scale that modern deployments demand.

Lustre

Lustre is a parallel-distributed filesystem driven by the open source community and is available under GNU **General Public License** (**GPL**). Lustre relies on a single server for storing and managing metadata. Thus, I/O requests from the client are totally dependent on a single server's computing power, which can be a bottleneck for enterprise-level consumption. Like iRODS and HDFS, Lustre is better suited to a small number of large files than to a more typical mix of numbers files of various sizes. Like iRODS, Lustre manages an index file that maps filenames to physical addresses, which makes its traditional architecture prone to performance bottlenecks. Lustre lacks a mechanism for failure detection and correction: when a node fails clients must connect to another node.

Gluster

GlusterFS was originally developed by Gluster Inc., which was acquired by Red Hat in 2011. GlusterFS is a scale-out network-attached filesystem in which administrators must determine the placement strategy to use to store data replicas on geographically spread racks. Gluster does not provide block access, filesystem, or remote replication as intrinsic functions; rather, it provides these features as add-ons.

Ceph

Ceph stands out from the storage solution crowd by virtue of its feature set. It has been designed to overcome the limitations of existing storage systems, and effectively replaces old and expensive proprietary solutions. Ceph is economical by being open source and software-defined and by running on most any commodity hardware. Clients enjoy the flexibility of Ceph's variety of client access modalities with a single backend.

Every Ceph component is reliable and supports high availability and scaling. A properly configured Ceph cluster is free from single points of failure and accepts an arbitrary mix of file types and sizes without performance penalties.

Ceph by virtue of being distributed does not follow the traditional centralized metadata method of placing and accessing data. Rather, it introduces a new paradigm in which clients independently calculate the locations of their data then access storage nodes directly. This is a significant performance win for clients as they need not queue up to get data locations and payloads from a central metadata server. Moreover, data placement inside a Ceph cluster is transparent and automatic; neither the client nor the administrators need manually or consciously spread data across failure domains.

Ceph is self-healing and self-managing. In the event of disaster, when other storage systems cannot survive multiple failures, Ceph remains rock solid. Ceph detects and corrects failure at every level, managing component loss automatically and healing without impacting data availability or durability. Other storage solutions can only provide reliability at drive or at node granularity.

Ceph also scales easily from as little as one server to thousands, and unlike many proprietary solutions, your initial investment at modest scale will not be discarded when you need to expand. A major advantage of Ceph over proprietary solutions is that you will have performed your last ever forklift upgrade. Ceph's redundant and distributed design allow individual components to be replaced or updated piecemeal in a rolling fashion. Neither components nor entire hosts need to be from the same manufacturer.

Examples of upgrades that the authors have performed on entire petabyte-scale production clusters, without clients skipping a beat, are as follows:

- Migrate from from one Linux distribution to another
- Upgrade within a given Linux distribution, for example, RHEL 7.1 to RHEL 7.3
- Replace all payload data drives
- Update firmware
- Migrate between journal strategies and devices
- Hardware repairs, including entire chasses
- Capacity expansion by swapping small drives for new
- Capacity expansion by adding additional servers

Unlike many RAID and other traditional storage solutions, Ceph is highly adaptable and does not require storage drives or hosts to be identical in type or size. A cluster that begins with 4TB drives can readily expand either by adding 6TB or 8TB drives either as replacements for smaller drives, or in incrementally added servers. A single Ceph cluster can also contain a mix of storage drive types, sizes, and speeds, either for differing workloads or to implement tiering to leverage both cost-effective slower drives for bulk storage and faster drives for reads or caching.

While there are certain administrative conveniences to a uniform set of servers and drives, it is also quite feasible to mix and match server models, generations, and even brands within a cluster.

Summary

Ceph is an open source software-defined storage solution that runs on commodity hardware, freeing organizations from expensive, restrictive, proprietary storage systems. It provides a unified, distributed, highly scalable, and reliable object storage solution, crucial for today's and tomorrow's unstructured data needs. The world's demand for storage is exploding, so we need a storage system that is scalable to the exabyte level without compromising reliability and performance. By virtue of being open source, extensible, adaptable, and built from commodity hardware, Ceph is future-proof. You can readily replace your entire cluster's hardware, operating system, and Ceph version without your users noticing.

In the next chapter, we will discuss the core components of Ceph and the services they provide.

2
Ceph Components and Services

Introduction

This chapter covers Ceph's components, services, and how they work together:

- The daemons and components that make up the Ceph backend:
    - RADOS
    - **Monitors (MONs)**
    - OSDs
    - Ceph Manager
    - RGW
- The services presented to users:
    - Block
    - Object
    - File

We'll describe each in turn, and what they mean to Ceph admins and users. This sets the stage for topics covered in the following chapters:

Core components

One of Ceph's advantages over other storage solutions is the wide and extensible range of services that can be offered with a single backend to manage.

Reliable Autonomic Distributed Object Store (RADOS)

Ceph's foundation is a low-level data store named RADOS that provides a common backend for multiple user-consumable services.

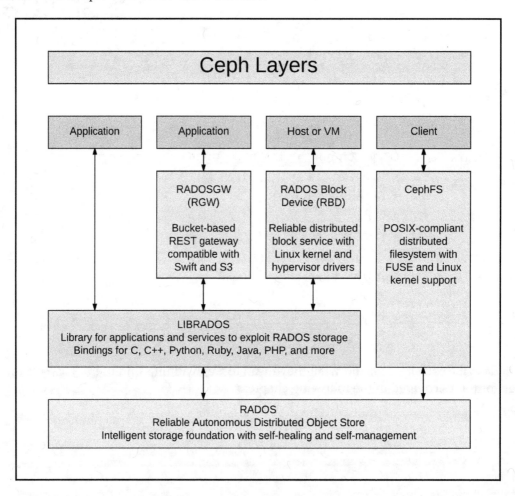

RADOS is an object storage system layer that provides a data durability and availability framework that all user-facing Ceph services are layered atop. RADOS is:

- Highly available with no **single point of failure (SPoF)**
- Reliable and resilient
- Self-healing
- Self-managing
- Adaptive
- Scalable
- Not found on the Galactica

RADOS manages the distribution of data within Ceph. Durability and availability of data are adaptively maintained by initiating operations as needed to recover from component failures and to balance the cluster when capacity is added or removed. Fundamental to this task is the CRUSH algorithm, which we will discuss in depth later. RADOS ensures that multiple copies of data are maintained at all times across defined failure zones so that when drives, hosts, or even entire racks of equipment fail, data integrity and client services are preserved.

MONs

Of all the nomenclature and jargon within the Ceph ecosystem, Ceph MONs are perhaps the most misleadingly named. While MONs do *monitor* cluster status, they are much more as well. They act as arbiters, traffic cops, and physicians for the cluster as a whole. As with OSDs, a Ceph MON is, strictly speaking, a daemon process (`ceph-mon`) that communicates with peer MONs, OSDs, and users, maintaining and distributing various information vital to cluster operations. In practice, the term is also used to refer to the servers on which these daemons run, that is *Monitor nodes, mon nodes,* or simply *mons.*

As with all other Ceph components, MONs need to be distributed, redundant, and highly available while also ensuring strict data consistency at all times. MONs accomplish this by participating in a sophisticated *quorum* that utilizes an algorithm called PAXOS. It is recommended to provision at least three for production clusters, but always an odd number to avoid a problematic situation known as *split brain* where network issues prevent some members from talking to each other, with the potential for more than one believing it is in charged and, worse yet, data divergence. Readers familiar with other clustering technologies such Oracle Solaris Cluster (™) may already be familiar with some of these concepts.

Among the data managed by Ceph MONs are *maps* of OSDs, other MONs, placement groups, and the CRUSH map,which describes where data should be placed and found. MONs are thus distributors of this data: they distribute initial state and updates to each other, Ceph OSDs, and Ceph clients. Alert readers might ask at this point, *Hey, you said Ceph doesn't have a bottlenecked centralized metadata store, who are you trying to kid?* The answer is that while these maps may be considered a type of metadata, they are data concerning the Ceph cluster itself, not actual user data. The secret sauce here is CRUSH, which will be described in more detail later in this chapter. The CRUSH algorithm operates on the CRUSH map and PG map so that both clients and the Ceph backend can *independently* determine where given data lives. Clients thus are kept up-to-date with all they need to perform their own calculations that direct them to their data within the cluster's constellation of OSDs. By enabling clients to dynamically determine where their data resides, Ceph enables scaling without choke points or bottlenecks

Object Storage Daemons (OSDs)

OSDs provide bulk storage of all user data within Ceph. Strictly speaking, an OSD is the operating system process (`ceph-osd`) running on a storage host that manages data reads, writes, and integrity. In practice, however, OSD is also used to refer to the underlying collection of data, the object storage device, that a given OSD manages. As the two are intimately linked, one can also quite reasonably think of an OSD as the logical combination of the process and underlying storage. At times, one may see OSD also used to refer to the entire server/host that houses these processes and data, though it is much better practice to refer to the server/host as an *OSD node* that houses as many as dozens of individual OSDs.

Each OSD within a Ceph cluster stores a subset of data. As we explored in Chapter 1, *Introduction to Ceph Storage,* Ceph is a distributed system without a centralized access bottleneck. Many traditional storage solutions contain one or two *head units* that are the only components that users interact with, a chokepoint of both control and data planes, which leads to performance bottlenecks and scaling limitations. Ceph clients, however—virtual machines, applications, and so on—communicate directly with the cluster's OSDs. **Create, Read, Update, and Delete (CRUD)** operations are sent by clients and performed by the OSD processes that manage the underlying storage.

The object storage device that a given OSD manages is usually a single **Hard Disk Drive (HDD)** or **Solid State Device (SSD)**. Exotic architectures for the storage underlying a single OSD are uncommon but not unknown, and range from simple software or an HBA RAID volume to LUNs or iSCSI targets on external storage arrays, SanDisk's InfiniFlash, or even a ZFS ZVOL.

Ceph organizes data into units known as **Placement Groups (PGs)**. A PG serves as the granularity at which various decisions and operations within the cluster operate. A well-utilized Ceph cluster will contain *millions* of low-level objects, a population that is unwieldy for high-level operations. PGs are collections of objects that are grouped together and typically number in the thousands to tens of thousands. Each PG maintains multiple copies on disjoint OSDs, nodes, racks, or even data centers as a key part of Ceph's passion for high availability and data durability. PGs are distributed according to defined constraints that avoid creating hotspots and to minimize the impact of server and infrastructure failures. By default, Ceph maintains three replicas of data, realized by placing a copy of each PG on three different OSDs located on three different servers. For additional fault tolerance, configuration can be added to ensure that those servers are located within three separate data center racks.

At any given time, one OSDs copy of a PG is designated the primary and the others as secondaries; one important distinction is that at this time, all client read and write operations are directed at the primary OSD. The additional OSDs containing copies of a PG may be thought of as slaves or secondaries; the latter term is more frequently used. Recent releases of Ceph include an alternative known as *erasure coding;* we will explore that in later chapters.

Ceph's constellation of OSDs maintain periodic contact with each other both to ensure consistency, and also to take steps if a given OSD becomes unavailable. When a given OSDs process or host crashes, experiences hardware or network issues, or in other ways becomes unresponsive, other OSDs in the cluster will report it as down and initiate recovery to maintain adequate redundant copies of data.

A complete glossary of Ceph terms may be found here:
`http://docs.ceph.com/docs/master/glossary`

Ceph manager

The Kraken release brought the debut of the Ceph Manager daemon (`ceph-mgr`), which runs alongside the MONs to provide cluster-wide services via a plugin architecture. While exploitation of `ceph-mgr` is still nascent, it has much potential:

- Management of drive and chassis status/locator LEDs
- Creating and managing a map of clients such as `rbd-mirror` and RADOS Gateway, which were previously less well-integrated

- Holistic management of Ceph's scrubs
- Richer management of reweighting and rebalancing operations.
- Integration with external inventory systems such as RackTables, NetBox, HP SIM, and Cisco UCS Manager
- Interface for monitoring/metrics systems such as Nagios, Icinga, Graphite, and Prometheus

More information may be found at :
`http://docs.ceph.com/docs/master/mgr`

RADOS GateWay (RGW)

Ceph RGW servers offer a highly scalable API-style interface to data organized as objects contained within buckets. RESTful services compatible with both Amazon's S3 and OpenStack's Swift can be enabled, including direct integration with Keystone for multitenancy.

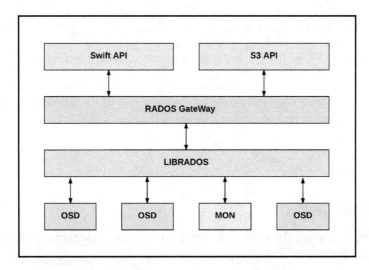

As with MDS, Ceph RGW components are optional; you do not need to provision them onto clusters that are intended to only provide block or file service.

Admin host

Management of Ceph clusters is usually done via a set of **command-line interface** (**CLI**) tools. While some Ceph managers perform these actions from one or more MON hosts, others choose to provision one or more dedicated, standalone servers for the purpose. These admin hosts require very few resources and are easily implemented as **Virtual Machines** (**VMs**) or even piggybacked onto bastion, jump, gateway, or other infrastructure services. One choice might be to share an existing Puppet or Ansible master host, which is likely set up in a conducive fashion. Be careful, though, to not provision Admin hosts with circular dependencies. If you use an OpenStack instance with a boot drive that lives on a Ceph cluster, sooner or later you'll find that cluster issues that require action prevent the admin host itself from working properly!

Another factor to consider when piggybacking the admin host role onto one or more Ceph MON nodes is that during cluster software upgrades and server hardware maintenance, each may in turn be rebooted or otherwise experience interrupted unavailability. While this does not impact cluster operations, it does prevent the continuity that is required of an admin host. For this reason as well, it is suggested to provision one or more admin hosts that are not hosted on or dependent on any other Ceph components.

CephFS MetaData server (MDS)

In order to manage and provide the hierarchy of data as presented in the context of a familiar tree-organized filesystem, Ceph needs to store additional metadata given the semantics expected:

- Permissions
- Hierarchy
- Names
- Timestamps
- Owners
- Mostly POSIX compliant. mostly.

Unlike legacy systems, the CephFS MDS is designed to facilitate scaling. It is important to note that actual file data does not flow through the Ceph MDS: as with RBD volumes, CephFS clients use the RADOS system to perform bulk data operations directly against a scalable number of distributed OSD storage daemons. In a loose sense, the MDS implements a control plane while RADOS implements the data plane; in fact, the metadata managed by Ceph's MDS also resides on the OSDs via RADOS alongside payload data / file contents:

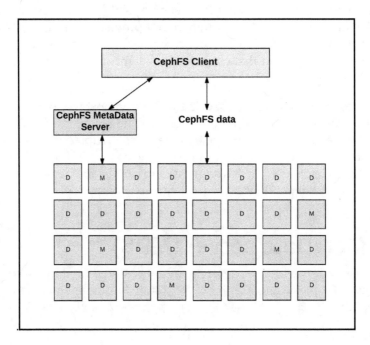

It is important to note that MDS servers are only required if you're going to use the CephFS file-based interface; the majority of clusters that provide only block and / or object user-facing services do not need to provision them at all. It is also important to note that CephFS is best limited to use among servers—a B2B service if you will—as opposed to B2C. Some Ceph operators have experimented with running NFS or Samba (SMB/CIFS) to provide services directly to workstation clients, but this should be considered as advanced.

Although CephFS is the oldest of Ceph's user-facing interfaces, it has not received as much user and developer attention as have the RBD block service and the common RADOS core. CephFS in fact was not considered ready for production until the Jewel release in early 2016, and as I write still has certain limitations, notably, running multiple MDSes in parallel for scaling and high availability is still problematic. While one can and should run multiple MDSes, with the Kraken release only one can safely be active at any time. Additional MDSes instances are advised to operate in a standby role for failover in case the primary fails. With the Luminous release, multiple active MDS instances are supported. It is expected that future releases will continue to improve the availability and scaling of the MDS services.

More and updated information on CephFS best practices and limitations can be found at
`http://docs.ceph.com/docs/master/cephfs/best-practices`
and
`http://docs.ceph.com/docs/master/cephfs/posix`

The community

The Ceph community is an active, growing, and vital part of the Ceph ecosystem. Contributions of code, expertise, and invaluable experience with running Ceph in a variety of hardware and network contexts for myriad purposes continually help refine and improve the Ceph experience for everyone.

Those interested in deploying or exploring Ceph are especially encouraged to check out the `ceph-announce` and `ceph-users` mailing lists.

Ceph mailing lists and other community resources can be found at the following sites:
`http://ceph.com/irc/#mailing-lists`
`http://ceph.com/cephdays`
`http://ceph.com/meetups`
`http://ceph.com/ceph-tech-talks`
`http://ceph.com/irc`

And, of course reference documentation for Ceph is available at
`http://docs.ceph.com`

Core services

Ceph provides four distinct interfaces to its common storage back end, each designed for a specific type of use case. In this section, we'll describe each and offer a real-world example of how it is used.

RADOS Block Device (RBD)

The RBD service is perhaps the most familiar, and at many sites is the primary or even only application of Ceph. It presents block (also known as volume) storage in a fashion that with traditional HDD/SDD applications can consume with little or no adjustment. In this way, it is somewhat analogous with facets of VxVM (™), Solaris Disk Suite (SVM)(™), the Linux MD/LVM system, ISCSI or Fibre Channel (™) appliance, or even a ZFS (™) ZVOL. RBD volumes, however, are natively available to multiple servers across the network.

One can build a filesystem directly upon an RBD volume, often as the boot device of a virtual machine in which case the hypervisor is the client of the RBD service and presents the volume to the guest operating system via the `virtio` or emulation driver. Other uses include direct *raw* use by databases, direct attachment to a physical or virtual machine via a kernel driver. Some users find value in building logical volumes within their operating system instance on top of multiple RBD volumes in order to achieve performance or expansion goals. Block storage is appropriate when a disk-like resource is desired, and provides consistent performance and latency. Capacity is provisioned in discrete, disjointed chunks, so scaling up or down can be awkward and complex. Tools such as ZFS or a volume manager such as Linux LVM can mitigate this somewhat, but applications with highly variable volumes of data—think fluctuation of orders of magnitude—may be better suited to an object storage model.

RBD volume operations include the usual data reads and writes as well as creation and deletion. Snapshots can be managed for archival, checkpointing, and deriving related volumes. OpenStack's Nova, Cinder, and Glance services (Chapter 11, *Performance and Stability Tuning*) utilize RBD snapshots for instances, abstracted volumes, and guest OS images respectively. There is a facility to replicate/mirror RBD volumes between clusters or even sites for high availability and disaster recovery.

RBD volumes are often used transparently by virtual machines and abstractions including OpenStack Cinder and Glance, but applications and users can exploit them as well via the `rbd` command line and programmatically via `librbd`.

The following is an example use case:

The author of this chapter needed to deploy a system of `yum` repo mirrors within OpenStack clouds for tenant use. CPU and RAM requirements were low, but a fair amount of storage was needed to mirror the growing collections of upstream rpm and metadata files for multiple versions of two Linux distributions. A small instance flavor was chosen with 4 GB RAM and one vCPU, but only a 50 GB virtual disk volume. That 50 GB volume, which itself mapped to an RBD volume, quickly filled up as new package versions and new distributions were added. The OpenStack Cinder interface to RBD was used to provision a 500 GB volume that was then attached to the instance, where the virtio driver presented it as `/dev/vdb`. An EXT4 filesystem was created on that device and an entry added to `/etc/fstab` to mount it at each boot, and the payload data was moved over to its capacious new home.

Alert readers might suggest simply resizing the original volume. This may be possible in some environments, but is more complex and requires additional steps.

RADOS Gateway (RGW)

Ceph natively manages *objects*, but it is crucial to not confuse this with other uses of the name, especially in relation to object storage in the vein of OpenStack Swift or Amazon's S3() service. The Ceph RGW service can be used to provide object storage compatible with both Swift and S3. Note that when used, the Ceph RGW service utilizes one or more dedicated *pools* (see `Chapter 2`, *Ceph Components and Services*) and cannot be used to access RBD volumes or other types of data that may live within your cluster in their own pools. This service is provided RESTfully with a familiar HTTP/HTTPS interface.

The Ceph RGW service can reside on the same servers as the OSD and their devices in a *converged architecture*, but it is more common to dedicate servers or even virtual machines to RGW services. Environments with very light usage may co-locate them with MON daemons on physical Ceph servers, but there pitfalls, and this must be done carefully, perhaps even using containers and cgroups. Small, lightly used, or **proof-of-concept** (PoC) installations may choose a virtual machine for ease of provisioning and to contain costs and space. Larger, production-class installations often provision RGW servers on bare metal servers for performance and to limit dependencies and avoid cascading failures. The author of this chapter has run but does not recommend a combination of dedicated RGW servers and ones co-located with Ceph MONs on modest servers.

Typically, one uses `haproxy` or another load balancer solution, perhaps in conjunction with `keepalived`, to achieve balanced and high availability service across multiple RGW instances. The number of RGW servers can be scaled up and down according to workload requirements, independently of other Ceph resources including OSDs and MONs. This flexibility is one of Ceph's many salient advantages over traditional storage solutions, including appliances. Ceph can readily utilize server resources that you already know how to manage, without one-off differences in chassis management, support contracts, or component sparing. It is even straightforward to migrate an entire Ceph cluster from one operating system and server vendor to another without users noticing. Ceph also allows one to architect and expand for changing requirements of usable bytes, IOPS, and workload mix without having to over-provision one component in order to scale another.

In releases of Ceph prior to Hammer, the RGW service was provided by a discrete daemon to interact with the cluster, coupled with the traditional Apache / httpd as the client frontend. This was subtle and fiddly to manage, and with the Ceph Hammer release, the service has been reworked to utilize a single `ceph.radowsgw` application with an embedded Civetweb web server.

Some large Ceph installations are run purely for the RGW service, without any RBD or other clients. Ceph's flexibility is among its strengths.

Object storage does not offer the low operation latency and predictable performance that block storage boasts, but capacity can scale up or down effortlessly.

A potential use case can be a collection of web servers using a **Content Management System (CMS)** to store an unstructured mix of HTML, JavaScript, image, and other content that may grow considerably over time.

CephFS

CephFS, the Ceph filesystem, has been around for quite some time and was, in fact, the first use case of Ceph back-end storage. While certain installations have successfully used CephFS in production for years, only with the 2016 release of Jewel did we gain official support versus the former *tech preview* status, and a complete set of management/ maintenance tools.

CephFS is *somewhat* akin to NFS (™) but not directly analogous. In fact, one can even run NFS *on top* of CephFS! CephFS is designed for use on well-behaved servers, and is not intended to be ubiquitously mounted on user desktops. You can use an operating system kernel driver to mount a CephFS filesystem as one would a local device or Gluster network filesystem. There is also the option of a userspace FUSE driver. Each installation must weigh the two mount methods: FUSE is easier to update, but the native kernel driver may provide measurably better performance.

Client mounts are directed to the cluster's Ceph MON servers, but CephFS requires one or more **MDS** instances to store filenames, directories, and other traditional metadata, as well as managing access to Ceph's OSDs. As with RGW servers, small and lightly utilized installations may elect to run MDS daemons on virtual machines, though most will choose dedicated physical servers performance, stability, and simplified dependency management.

A potential use case is an established archival system built around an aging fileserver that requires POSIX filesystem permissions and behavior. The legacy fileserver can be replaced by a CephFS mount with little or no adjustment.

Librados

`Librados` is the common underpinning of which other Ceph services behind the scenes. It is also possible for applications to interface directly with RADOS in ways that are not an ideal fit with the higher level RBD, RGW, or CephFS interfaces, but wish to exploit the scalability, networking, and data protection that Ceph offers instead of reinventing the wheel. There are RADOS API bindings for multiple programming languages, including C, C++, Ruby, PHP, Java, Erlang, Go, Haskell, and Python.

A potential use case is the Vaultaire **Time Series Database (TSDB)**. Vaultaire is described as a massively scalable metrics database, in the vein of RRDtool and Whisper (part of Graphite):

```
http://www.anchor.com.au/blog/2014/06/vaultaire-ceph-based-immutable-tsdb/
```

There is also a plugin for the popular Dovecot mail system that stores email messages as RADOS objects:

```
https://github.com/ceph-dovecot/dovecot-ceph-plugin
```

```
https://www.mail-archive.com/ceph-users@lists.ceph.com/msg40429.html
```

Summary

In this chapter we have touched on the required and optional components of your Ceph cluster, and the services they provide. In the following chapters, we'll help you select the right hardware for your own deployment, explore a number of crucial decisions and dependencies, and proceed through virtual deployment and common maintenance and monitoring tasks.

3
Hardware and Network Selection

Introduction

Traditional large-scale storage solutions often feature expensive, proprietary hardware that presents physical, management, security, and even electrical challenges when integrating into a data center populated with familiar network and server gear. Ceph, by design, does not prescribe specific hardware component types or models. Hardware vendor lock-in is avoided, and the architect is able to choose server and network components that meet individual cost, standards, performance, and physical criteria. Ceph's distributed design also affords tremendous flexibility over time as needs change and hardware product lines cycle and evolve. You may build your cluster from one set of gear today only to find that tomorrow's needs, constraints, and budget are distinctly different. With Ceph, you can seamlessly add capacity or refresh aging gear with very different models, completely transparently to your users. It is entirely straightforward to perform a 100% replacement of a cluster's hardware without users experiencing so much as a hiccup.

Ceph clusters have been built successfully from the gamut of server classes, from 90-drive 4RU monsters all the way down to minimal systems integrated directly into the storage drive's logic board (`http://ceph.com/community/500-osd-ceph-cluster`).

That said, it *is* still important to choose equipment that meets organizational, supportability, financial, and performance needs. In the next section, we explore a number of criteria; your situation may well present others as well. Ceph is designed for Linux systems and can run on a wide variety of distributions. Most clusters are deployed on x64 systems, but 32-bit and ARM architectures are possible as well.

Today's servers and components offer a dizzying array of choices; if they seem overwhelming, one may seek configurations pre-configured for Ceph usage by brands such as Quanta and Supermicro.

These links to examples are informational and are not endorsements for any vendor:
`https://www.qct.io/solution/index/Storage-Virtualization/QxStor-Red-Hat-Ceph-Storage-Edition`
`https://www.supermicro.com/solutions/storage_ceph.cfm`
`https://www.supermicro.com/solutions/storage_ceph.cfm`

It is highly valuable, nonetheless, to be conversant with the ideas presented in the rest of this chapter. These examples are provided to illustrate this idea and are not to be construed as recommendations for any specific vendor.

Hardware selection criteria

There is a dizzying amount of hardware for today's x64 servers. In this section, we'll explore a number of these choices to help you navigate the selection process for your local conditions and requirements. We'll discuss the ramifications of each and offer thoughts on trade-offs, limitations, and opportunities.

Corporate procurement policies

Hardware choice may be constrained by organizational policy. Perhaps your company enjoys a volume discount from HP, or has an umbrella support contract with IBM. You may even work *for* a company that sells servers and are thus urged or compelled to keep it in the family, dogfood style: `https://en.wikipedia.org/wiki/Eating_your_own_dog_food`.

In most cases, this will not crimp your Ceph-stacking style substantially, though this author has seen three problematic instances.

- On occasion, procurement policies are so draconian that it is nearly impossible to order a custom hardware configuration, with the only choices a small handful of ill-fitting models on an anachronistic menu, for example, a 1U chassis with only 4 x 300 GB LFF drives. Situations such as this are fortunately rare, but you must weigh how creative you can be with the options provided against the difficulty of escalating to source a configuration that makes sense. One strategy might be to order a bare-bones chassis and add appropriate drives and adapters as additional line items.

- Another was a division compelled to use only a certain brand of servers, without the ability to add even out-of-sight these internal third-party components. This resulted in an initial architecture using co-located journals (see `Chapter 2`, *Ceph Components and Services*) on **Large Form Factor** (**LFF**) rotating disks. Aggregate cluster performance was cut in half right from the start, and the intense seek pattern tickled a flaw in one manufacturer's firmware, resulting in frequent read errors. Remediation costs far more in service degradation, engineer time, and drive replacement than lobbying for appropriate third-party components up front would have.

- A major customer of another division within the company suddenly in-sourced, abandoning nearly three thousand servers with considerable time left on their leases. Other business units were compelled to take over these one- to two-generation old systems, with small and tired HDDs, instead of buying new ones.

Consider carefully your compromises in these areas, as they set precedents and may be difficult, expensive, or impossible to recover from when unsuitable gear is deployed.

Power requirements-amps, volts, and outlets

In the US, standard outlets are 110-120V, 60 Hz, with NEMA 5-15 plugs, rated at ~ 1,875 watts. Other parts of the world use different standards, but the ideas apply. Many (but by no means all) small to medium and even large data centers and server installations use the local common standard. Servers today often incorporate power supplies that can handle a range of input voltages and frequencies, requiring only a localized power cable to adapt to the proper plug/socket type.

Some larger storage appliances, disk arrays, and even certain dense servers, however, may require (US) 240V power that may not be readily available in your data center. Even servers that accept conventional power may pull so much current that you cannot fill a rack with them. Say you have 40 U of rack space available, and chose a 4 U server that pulls 800 watts. If your data center racks are only provisioned for 5,000 watts each, then you would only be able to stack six of these servers per rack, and might be paying dearly for space occupied only by blanking panels or 26 RU of expensive air.

Some data centers similarly provide only a limited number of outlets per rack, and with lightweight servers—say a 1 RU model using SSDs—you may run out of outlets long before you use up the power budget for a given rack. Some data centers, especially those that favor telco gear, offer 48V DC power. Major server vendors usually offer models or power supplies compatible with 48V power, but that may not extend across the entire product line. Some data centers favor DC power for efficiency, avoiding the losses inherent in one or more AC-DC or DC-AC conversion steps through the stages of building power, conditioning, **uninterruptible power supply batteries** (**UPS**), and server power supplies. Often, this is an all-or-nothing proposition for an entire data center; do not assume that yours can accommodate these niche servers without consulting your data center management people.

In practice, one often balances voracious and leaner gear within a rack to accommodate outlet and current budgets, say, mixing IDF/ODF panels and network gear to average out. Factor these layout decisions into your Ceph cluster's logical topology to avoid crippling failure domains.

Within the server itself, you may have multiple options for the power supplies you order. You must evaluate the tradeoffs among the following factors:

- Local datacenter standards
- Startup, peak, and steady-state server wattage requirements
- Power supply efficiency
- Redundancy

Many Ceph installations find that a 2RU server is the sweet spot or best fit; this may or may not be true for your data center and use case. It is also very common in an enterprise setting to provision servers and other gear with redundant power supplies to both guard against component failure and to allow electrical maintenance without disrupting operations. Some data center managers even require redundant power.

 This author experienced the meltdown of a power inductor within a Ceph OSD server, which caused the entire server to shut down. The monitoring system alerted the on-call team to the failure of that node, and the cluster was rebalanced to remove it from service. It was not until the next day that I learned that the failure had also taken down half of the power for the entire row of 20 racks. The servers were all provisioned with dual power supplies, which allowed them to survive the outage.

Server vendors often allow one to select from an array of **power supply unit (PSU)** choices:

- Single, dual, or quad
- Multiple levels of efficiency
- Multiple current ratings
- Voltage compatibility

Your choice can significantly affect your cluster's reliability and data center infrastructure costs. Dual power supplies also mean dual power sockets, which may be in short supply in your racks. They also mean dual power cords, a commodity on which server vendors may enjoy considerable markup. Always ensure that your power cords are rated for enough current.

A single PSU architecture simplifies cabling and often costs less than a dual solution. The downside is that the failure of that PSU, of the power circuit/PSU takes down the entire server or the entire rack/row. It is also vulnerable to the cable becoming unseated by a technician brushing while walking down the aisle or working on a nearby server, or even trucks rumbling down the street. In large clusters of smaller servers, distributed among multiple racks, rows, or even rooms, this may be an acceptable risk with careful logical topology choices and settings. This author, however, suggests that the operational cost of failure or a protracted outage usually outweighs the additional cost and layer 1 complexity.

With any PSU architecture, you must ensure that you provision adequate capacity for the server's present—and future—needs. For example, as I wrote, one prominent server vendor offers no fewer than ten PSU options, with ratings of 495, 750, and 1,100 watts. Server specs and configurators often provide a sum of the current / wattage needs of the selected chassis and components. Be careful that the startup, peak, and typical power consumption of components—especially rotational drives—can vary considerably. Drive spin-up in some cases can be staggered to de-align the peaks.

Plan also for future upgrades. If you order a chassis model with 24 drive bays but only populate 12 today, you will want to provision a power infrastructure that can accommodate the additional load. Two years from now you may also wish to replace your 4 TB drives with 8 TB models, which itself may require additional RAM. Those adjustments may add non-trivially to your power needs. That said, if your foreseeable power needs per server add up to say 600 watts, dual 1000 watt PSU's may be overkill, and dual 750 watt units would serve just as well. Incremental price increases or savings per unit add up rapidly in clusters with dozens or even hundreds of servers.

Also, be sure that if you lose a single power supply, those that remain have enough capacity to run the server properly. In the preceding example, this is why dual 495 watt units would not be a wise choice. These days, many servers used for Ceph offer only single or dual PSU configurations, but there are still those where you may have the option of four or even three. Say you need for 900 watts of power and four slots for PSUs. You might provision a single or dual 1,000 watts PSU configuration, three 495 watt units, or even four 300 watt units. With any multi-PSU choice, if the loss of one unit does not allow the server to run, you've actually decreased reliability compared to a single-PSU architecture.

Some server vendors offer multiple power supply efficiencies. A PSU with a greater efficiency rating may result in lower overall costs for data center power and cooling, at the trade-off of a higher price. Consider household natural gas furnaces: a traditional model may be rated at 80% efficiency. A condensing model recovers heat from effluent, saving on monthly gas bills, but at the expense of more expensive up-front cost and installation. For example, as I write one prominent server vendor offers Silver PSUs at 90% efficiency, Gold at 92%, and Platinum at 94%. Consider your local CapEx and OpEx trade-offs as well as corporate green guidance and data center standards.

Compatibility with management infrastructure

Your organization may be heavily invested in cross-system server management systems such as Cisco UCS, HP's SIM, or Dell's CMC. There may be a tradition of remote management via serial consoles, which can be problematic with many types of x64-based servers. Compatibility in these respects must be considered when choosing servers.

Compatibility with physical infrastructure

Decades ago, computers were large and standards were few; each might demand a dedicated room with unique physical requirements. These days, we enjoy considerable benefits from standards and convergent designs, yet there can still be surprises. Just within the preceding five years this author has encountered the following:

- Serial console infrastructure defaulting to 9,600 bps but equipment defaulting to 19,200 bps
- Atypical DTE/DCE pinouts incompatible with common RJ45 adapters
- Gear that still uses 1990s-style DB9 connectors or even an audio-type 3.5mm round jack for management access

- One server model out of a larger product line with an unusual onboard network interface whose PXE code for network boots would inexplicably switch the system's serial console to 115,200 bps.
- A server vendor whose mounting hardware was designed for 19" racks with square holes. These rails, in theory, were usable with common round hole racks, yet had to be attacked with a power drill due to differing hole/screw sizes.

Chances are that you are well versed in your local server practices, but these are among the gotchas that can still arise when considering new brands or product generations.

Take care as well that your server choices will fit into your data center racks! Some very dense servers, such as 90-drive 4U beasts, can be so deep that they do not fit well into racks, and may block aisles or prevent doors from closing. Gather your dimensional constraints in advance and pay careful attention to spec tables.

Configuring options for one-stop shopping

Corporate procurement systems can be, well, corporate. Your organization might allow you to only select only from a set menu of pre-configured systems, which may even be years obsolete. Perhaps the purchasing people get a deal on a certain product line and resist ordering from others that may be better suited to your Ceph aspirations. Say only a 12-bay LFF server is offered, but your IOPS needs favor a 25-bay SFF server. Or only configurations with a single 300 GB disk are offered, as a legacy of a proprietary SAN or NAS strategy. Perhaps your warehouse is full of expensive high-speed 24-core overkill servers with only four disk bays, or 1.2 GHz 4-core weaklings. Or you are charged for a bay-robbing optical drive that you have no use for.

In some cases, you might be able to order a bare-bones system and additional line items to grow it to your needs, but beware of significant compromises that can hinder the success, capacity, and stability of your Ceph clusters.

Memory

In the past, **Random Access Memory (RAM)** was very expensive and admins were tightly constrained by budget and server slots when provisioning out infrastructure. Today's technologies, however, afford us very large capacity modules and sufficient slots to often provision as much as a **terabyte (TB)** or even more for each server.

Ceph components vary in their memory needs; in this section, we'll help you chose the right size for your servers to fulfill both operational and financial goals.

RAM capacity and speed

Consider the total RAM capacity of your servers. This is not nearly the quandary it once was, but it is still vital to plan carefully. If your server model accepts say at most 16 memory modules and your initial calculations are that 64 GB of RAM is what you need, resist the urge to save a few bucks on 4 GB DIMMs. Any future upgrades would require removing installed modules to make way for newer, larger DIMMs. Situations that could increase your RAM needs include:

- Adding more storage drives per server
- Swapping in larger storage drives for smaller
- Cluster expansion via additional servers may increase per-process memory requirements
- Future use of caching software
- Operating system or Ceph setting tweaks
- Conversion to a converged storage/compute architecture

It is often the case that the largest available memory modules carry a hefty per-GB price premium, so one step down may be the sweet spot of preserving both CapEx and expandability.

Servers today are typically able to use memory of multiple speeds, though mixing modules will generally step operation down to the lowest common denominator. Your server vendor may offer memory at multiple speeds, technologies, and price points, and the choice of module size, count, and layout may influence the speed at which the entire memory system is able to run. Certain CPU choices within a product line may also have memory or QPI channel differences that affect configuration options, total configurable memory, and speed. These concerns may increase with larger system configurations, for example, a 72-bay four-socket system where meticulous tuning may be required to extract the last 20% of performance.

Many factors influence RAM requirements. A suggested rule-of-thumb was once a base of 16 GB plus at least 2 GB for each Ceph daemon (MON, RGW, MDS), and at least 2 GB per OSD. With 16 GB DIMMs common and affordable today, we suggest that for any Ceph server role you provision a minimum of 64 GB, with dense OSD nodes adding 2 GB for each OSD after the first ten. Again, when selecting memory module sizes ensure that you count available slots and provision DIMMs in a way that allows future expansion without throwing away your initial investment. However, at any given time the very latest and densest module size is often disproportionately expensive, making the modules a step down the sweet spot. Take care on multi-socket systems that each CPU socket has its own memory slots that are ideally filled in a balanced fashion.

Storage drives

Each Ceph cluster comprises a large number of individual storage drives that house both Ceph's internal metadata and the bulk data entrusted to us by users. By habit, many resources refer to these as *disks*, an artifact of the times when SSDs were not capacious or affordable, and even before they existed. Throughout this book we use the more expansive term *drives* to include other technologies. In practice and out in the community you will encounter the terms used interchangeably, though imprecisely.

Storage drive capacity

Less capacious drive models are often attractive from a price/GB (or price/TB) angle than each generation's densest monsters, but there are other factors. Every drive needs a bay to live in and a controller / HBA / expander channel. Cheap drives are no bargain if you have to acquire, manage, rack, power, and cool double the number of servers in order to house them.

You may also find that the awesomeness of your Ceph cluster draws users and applications out of the woodwork, and the capacity you initially thought adequate might be severely taxed in the next fiscal year or even quarter. Clusters can be expanded by adding additional servers or swapping larger existing drives for smaller ones. The former can be a considerable undertaking from financial and logistical angles, if you can even go back to the data center well for additional racks in a suitable location. The latter can be done piecemeal, but will probably require significant engineer and logistical resources. Care is also needed to not disrupt ongoing client operations as your cluster rebalances.

One might then decide to provision the largest drives available up front. This can be an effective strategy, but with several critical caveats:

As we write, the spinning drives with the largest capacities often utilize a technology known as *SMR* to achieve stunning densities. SMR unfortunately presents a substantial write operation penalty, which often means they are unsuitable for Ceph deployment, especially in latency-sensitive block-storage applications. Elaborate caching may somewhat mitigate this drawback, but this author asserts that *these are not the drives you're looking for*.

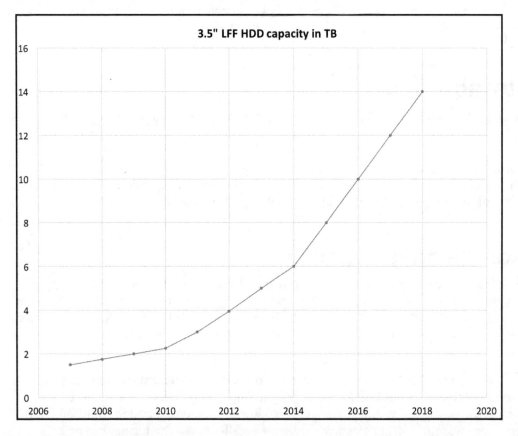

Fewer, more-capacious drives also present a trade-off against more, less-capacious drives, in classic terms, *more spindles are faster*. With traditional rotating drives (also known as *spinning rust*) drive throughput tends to not nearly keep pace with drive capacity. Thus, a cluster built with 300 8 TB drives may offer much less aggregate speed (IOPS) than a cluster of the same raw capacity constructed from 600 4 TB drives.

Newer technologies may conversely present the opposite: often larger models of SAS, SATA, or NVMe drives are multiples faster than smaller models due to internal parallelism: internally, operations are distributed across multiple, smaller electronic components.

Thus, it is a crucial to plan ahead for the capacity you will need next month, next year, and three years from now. There are multiple paths to growth, but you will save yourself indescribable grief if you prepare a plan of some sort in advance. You may even choose to not fully populate the drive bays in your Ceph OSD servers. Say you choose a 12-bay chassis but only populate eight of those bays initially with 6TB drives. Next year, when you need additional capacity, you might populate those remaining four bays per server with eight or 10 TB drives at the same unit cost as today's smaller drives. Deployment would not require lockstep removal of those smaller drives, though that would still be possible down the road.

> When calculating and comparing capacities as reported by Ceph or tools such as df and lsblk, it's also important to note the distinction between power of ten marketing units (TB) and the power of two units (TiB) that software nearly always uses. Storage and especially drive component vendors tend to use the former as it inflates capacities.

> `https://www.gbmb.org/tb-to-tib` is a useful calculator for converting between the two. It shows us for example that a nominal 8 TB drive is in truth a 7.28 TiB drive. When a filesystem such as XFS is laid down, the structural overhead and the small percentage of space reserved for the root user additionally decrease the capacity reported by df especially. This distinction is widely known, but it's still quite easy to get tripped up by it.

> That said, we primarily write TB and PB throughout this book, both because they are more familiar to readers, and to with the unit labels that Ceph and other tools display.

Storage drive form factor

While it is possible to mix use cases, server strategies, and storage technologies within a single cluster, for clarity here we'll focus on uniform deployments.

The most common physical sizes of storage drives in use today are 3.5" LFF and 2.5" Small. You may also occasionally find the 1.8" form factor that never caught on in a big way. Recent and emerging technologies include PCI-e and hot-pluggable U.2 NVMe solid-state devices.

Major server vendors usually offer both LFF and SFF chassis models. LFF models and rotating drives often offer greater TB/**RU** (**Rack Unit**) and TB/unit cost. SFF models and rotating drives typically provide more but smaller drives, and the greater number of spindles presents increased parallelism and aggregate performance at the expense of (usually) lesser rack density and cost per unit of storage. The form factor is thus part of your decision process. Clusters designed for latency-sensitive block storage may favor SFF drives, while those optimized for cost, large capacity, and/or object storage lean toward stalwart LFF drives.

Solid State Disk (**SSD**) storage is rarely available natively in an LFF form factor; SFF drives are the norm. While SFF drives can be fitted into many LFF bays and carriers via inexpensive adapters and interposers, it is more common to select SFF-native server models. That said, server shoppers today face an embarrassment of options; one popular approach is a server chassis that presents 12 or as many as 72 LFF drives for high TB/RU density while providing a pair of internal or rear-panel SFF bays for boot / operating system use. This avoids a reduction of the cluster capacity by having to divert precious front-panel LFF bays from bulk data service.

In it's early years, SSD storage was mainly used for specialized cases due to the very high cost relative to rotating drives, for example, caching, hot databases, and as an option in laptops where battery power is at a premium and physical shocks are all too common.

Storage drive durability and speed

The durability of a given drive model is generally not a concern for traditional spinning drives, claims about enterprise versus consumer drives notwithstanding. Flash / SSD drives do, however, vary considerably. In the past, conventional wisdom held that **Single-Level Cell** (**SLC**) flash devices would last longer than denser/less-expensive **Multi-Level Cell** (**MLC**) models, though more recently this has been questioned. So long as you avoid the lowest-end consumer/desktop SATA drives, this distinction should not be a significant concern.

Modern enterprise-class drives incorporate greater over-provisioning, which means that a fraction of the storage cells are reserved so that the drive's on-board controller can more effectively balance writes evenly across storage cells, and as needed bring spare blocks into service over time to replace aging sectors. For example, you might see an inexpensive consumer drive advertised as 480 GB, but an enterprise model from the same manufacturer rated at *only* 400 GB.

Certain drive characteristics also affect how well a given model can serve Ceph OSD journals. Here is an excellent article on evaluating them for this purpose:

```
https://www.sebastien-han.fr/blog/2014/10/10/ceph-how-to-test-
if-your-ssd-is-suitable-as-a-journal-device/
```

Even among *enterprise* SSDs, the durability—the number of data writes of the device's entire capacity is rated for over its lifetime—can vary considerably. This is often measured in **Drive Writes Per Day (DWPD)**—over the drive's rated lifetime, which is often five-years but sometimes as little as three years. Say a 1TB device has a five year warranty and is rated at 3.65 PB of writes over its lifetime. This works out to ~ 2 DWPD.

Consider this example of an SSD product line with three tiers.

Tier 1:

Capacity	Random 4KB 70/30 read/write IOPS	DWPD
400 GB	65,000	0.3
1.2 TB	65,000	0.3
2.0 TB	80,000	0.3

Tier 2:

Capacity	Random 4KB 70/30 read/write IOPS	DWPD
400 GB	80,000	3
800 GB	110,000	3
1.2 TB	130,000	3
1.6 TB	160,000	3
2.0 TB	160,000	3

Tier 3:

Capacity	Random 4KB 70/30 read/write IOPS	DWPD
400 GB	150,000	10
800 GB	200,000	10
1.6 TB	240,000	15
2.0 TB	265,000	17

You can see that durability within even a single product line can vary by a factor of more than 30, and that speeds vary considerably as well. Attend carefully to both ratings especially for drives intended for journal use, as they will dictate how many OSD journal partitions each can host before becoming a bottleneck. As a rule of thumb, divide the journal device's write rating by the OSD device's write rating. For example, if your journal device is rated at writing 1GB/s, and your OSDs are rated at 100MB/s, you would not want to pack more than 10 journals onto each journal device. As journals are relatively small, at most a set-and-forget size of 10GB each, it is not uncommon to run out of speed before capacity.

Choosing a durability target for your cluster's journal and OSD devices can be complex and rely on difficult-to-predict future traffic. This author's personal philosophy is that the peace of mind gained from top-tier durability tends to outweigh the incremental cost of upselling from a middle-tier, but your constraints may vary. Many clusters do fine with 3 DWPD-class drives, but this author would not recommend going any lower on the price/durability curve. Note also that SSDs used for Ceph Monitor DBs can easily experience 2 DPWD or more in a cluster with hundreds of OSDs. For this reason, you are strongly encouraged to provision MON SSDs rated at least 3 DWPD, with 10 DWPD better yet. The authors have experienced multiple near-simultaneous MON failures due to lesser drives wearing out; we want you to avoid suffering the same anguish.

Circumstances sometimes force us to deploy pre-loved servers. In the past, used HDDs could be an ongoing headache, but today's drives enjoy substantially improved longevity. Used SSDs, however, can be a (silently) ticking time bomb. At the very least, you would need to examine each drive's remaining lifetime counter with a tool such as `smartctl` or `isdct` to avoid a (literal) rude awakening.

The `isdct` tool provides management, monitoring, and firmware capabilities for Intel SSD drives, including both SAS/SATA and NVMe. It may be found at
`https://www.intel.com/content/www/us/en/support/memory-and-stora`
`ge/000006289.html`

The `smartctl` utility is part of `smartmontools` packaged with many Linux distributions and can also be found at
`https://www.smartmontools.org`.

Storage drive type

Fibre channel drives, while once popular in enterprise data centers, are increasingly uncommon in new deployments, and in most cases aren't a good fit for Ceph's design of operating on commodity hardware. Most clusters today will be built from drives with SAS or SATA interfaces. Opinions vary regarding the merits of SAS versus SATA; with modern HBA, drive and OS driver technologies the gap between the two may be smaller than it used to be. Successful clusters have been built on SATA drives, but many admins feel that SAS drives tend to perform better especially under heavy load. Neither choice is likely to be disastrous, especially as Ceph is built to ensure redundancy and data availability.

The more important choice is between traditional rotating magnetic drives, also known as *spinning rust* or simply *spinners*, versus SSDs. Modern SSD speed, capacity, and pricing has been dropping steadily year over year. Magnetic drive progress has been less dramatic: capacities creep progressively higher, but speed/throughput are largely limited by physics. In the past, the cost per GB of an SSD was dramatically higher than that for magnetic drives, limiting their use to certain performance-critical and other applications, but as the costs continue to fall, they are increasingly price-competitive. Considering TCO and not just up-front CapEx, the fact that rotational drives consume more power and thus also require more cooling additionally narrows the financial gap. Today's enterprise SSDs are also more reliable than magnetic drives, which must be considered as well.

Your constraints may vary, but for many the choice between SSD and magnetic drives is now driven by use case. If your cluster's role is to supply block storage to thousands of virtual machines running a variety of applications, your users may not be satisfied with the performance limitations of magnetic drives and you stand a good chance of running out of IOPS long before the cluster fills up. If, however, your use case is purely for REST-style object service using the RADOS Gateway, or long- term archival, density and capacity requirements may favor larger but slower rotating drives for the OSD service.

NVMe drives are a fairly new technology that is rapidly gaining acceptance as an alternative to SAS/SATA - based SSD drives. Most NVMe drives available today take the form of conventional PCIe cards, though there are interesting emerging designs for hot-swappable drives in the style of traditional front-panel-bay rotational drives. Pricing of NVMe drives has fallen significantly in recent years, which with their impressive speed finds them an increasingly popular choice for Ceph journal service. The traditional SAS and SATA interfaces were designed in an era of much slower media, compared to a multi-lane PCIe bus.

NVMe was designed for modern, fast media without the physical seek limitations of rotating drives, and offers a more efficient protocol. The blazing speed thus achieved by NVMe drives increasingly finds them selected for Ceph journal services: you can often pack ten or more OSD journals onto a single NVMe device. While they do today cost more per GB than a traditional SSD, dramatic increases in capacity are coming, and we should expect to see NVMe becoming common place for journals. Most servers offer a handful at most of available traditional PCIe slots, which today usually limits NVMe use to journal versus bulk OSD storage, but as server and chassis designs evolve, we are are beginning to see products offering hot-swappable NVMe drives utilizing novel PCIe connection types and in coming years entire scale-out clusters may enjoy NVMe speeds.

Regardless of drive type, you may consider provisioning drives from at least two manufacturers, to minimize the degree to which supply problems, disparate failure rates, and the potential for design or firmware flaws can impact your clusters. Some go so far as to source drives from separate VARs or at different times, the idea being to have drives from multiple manufacturing runs to avoid the *bad batch* phenomenon.

Number of storage drive bays per chassis

One of the key factors when choosing your server models is the number of drives that can be provisioned within each. In the past, servers often could house as few as two drives, requiring external JBOD or RAID arrays for bulk storage, but today the entire front-panel and in some cases much of the rear panel, is available for storage.

Ceph MON, RGW, and MDS servers do not need much local storage, and are often realized with basic 1 U servers, blades, or twin models offering two server modules in a single 1 U chassis. Two or four drives are probably all that you will need. Beware, though, the failure domain: with twin or blade systems, you must take care that the loss or temporary downtime of a chassis does not decimate your cluster. For this reason, many Ceph designers use modest but standalone 1U servers for these applications.

For Ceph OSD servers, drive bays are often the limiting factor. As optical media have become increasingly less relevant, the utility of them in a server has largely disappeared, and the space they once occupied is better used to provide more drive bays. For example, a 1U server with an optical drive might offer eight SFF bays, but one without will usually offer 10, a 25% bump in density. For 2U servers, it is common to find models offering 24 or 25 SFF or 12 LFF front-accessible bays. Models are also available from some vendors with drive bays in the rear, accommodating as many as 24 or 32 drives in 2U or 3U chassis. Consider cooling and mounting constraints when pondering these models to avoid embarrassment. A data center designed with hot and cold aisles, for example, may not be an ideal environment for rear-mounted drives.

Mirroring of operating system / boot drives is common, and with some server models a pair of rear-panel or even internal bays can be provisioned for this use, freeing precious front-panel drive bays for bulk data drives. Exercise caution when using internal bays that require the server to be taken down for drive replacement.

As data center space is often limited or charged per-rack or per-RU, servers offering more slots per rack unit appeal from density/RU and cost/RU angles. They may also offer financial advantages in that fewer total CPUs and switch ports need to be provisioned. Thus, except for very small or lab / test clusters, 1U servers with a limited number of drive bays are seldom—but not never—favored for OSD systems.

One may be tempted to thus design a cluster around dense servers providing 36, 72, or even 90 drive bays, but there are significant dangers to this approach, notably the size of failure domains. A failure domain is a set of resources that may fail together or otherwise be unavailable. With Ceph, there are two important factors here. First, you must ensure that no failure domain will take down a majority of your MON nodes, or more than one copy of data on OSD nodes. Thus, MONs are best provisioned no more than one per physical rack. Second, for OSD nodes, consider the percentage of the total cluster contained within a single rack, or more crucially within a single chassis.

This is where some twin/quad systems present a hidden danger: if they share power supplies, failure may take down multiple servers. Any server chassis type will need periodic maintenance to replace failing or failed components, to insert more RAM, to upgrade firmware, or make other fleet and architectural changes. While Ceph is designed with redundancy to ensure that data is not lost, a large failure domain can temporarily but significantly reduce your cluster's aggregate performance during a failure, maintenance, or even simple reboot to update your kernel. More dangerous yet is a catastrophic hardware failure: the larger the fraction of your cluster in a single chassis—or even single rack—the greater the impact to service, especially as your cluster madly rebalances data to ensure data safety. This rebalancing may substantially impact normal user operations or even result in the remaining, operational drives filling up as they rapidly accept additional data.

Consider the example of a cluster with 450 OSDs, spread across three physical and logical racks.

Number of OSDs per server / chassis	Server share of one rack	Server share of the entire cluster
10	6.66%	2.22%
25	16.66%	5.55%
50	33.33%	11.11%
75	50%	16.66%

In this case, the loss of just one 75-bay server would mean that to preserve data safety the cluster will need to shift double the volume of data stored on the remaining server in that rack. If that server's OSDs are already more than 40% full, they will now be hammered by recovery writes, starving user operations. As data pours in, many OSDs will also cross capacity thresholds and the cluster will grind to a halt. Your users will have a very bad day and you will have an even worse day as they storm your workspace with torches and pitchforks. Even if the OSDs are less full, object service performance will degrade, and block service will slow down to the point that hundreds or thousands of VMs may crash.

At the other extreme are twin, quad, or blade systems. These feature a single chassis that houses two, four, or more compact blade / tray servers. Some organizations favor these for density and other reasons, though sometimes the advantage there is marginal at best. These systems generally are not good choices for Ceph OSDs:

- They often are not designed to accommodate more than two or three storage drives, which confounds density and cost/TB.
- They prevent a favorable ratio of OSDs to journals for efficient usage of fast but expensive journal devices.
- The chassis is a failure domain: failure or maintenance will take down all of the servers contained therein. Some models have limited or no PSU redundancy or even share network connections, which increases the exposure surface to power issues.

Since Ceph MON, RGW, and MDS nodes do not require much local storage, these systems, however, have a certain appeal for these applications with narrow hardware complement requirements. This can be a trap, however, again given the failure domain. If your cluster has five MONs, four of which are in a quad chassis, a single failure can take your entire operation offline.

Server density is thus a trade-off of multiple factors, but the failure domain *must* be considered. For block storage use cases a 24- to 25-bay chassis is often considered a sweet spot. For object service where latency is less critical, denser systems may be tolerable in order to maximize GB/RU and cost/RU.

You probably have a target capacity in mind for your cluster, carefully extrapolated from existing data, user requirements, and forecasts. You can easily do the math and plan for how many drive bays and OSDs you need to provide that capacity. Consider, though, that the future is unpredictable; you may win yourself considerable gratitude by planning up front for additional drive bay capacity that is initially unfilled, to accommodate later incremental expansion without having to find budget or rack space for new servers. This also facilitates organic migration to larger storage drives without having to first compress the cluster onto fewer existing drives or discarding some to free bays.

Controllers

Today's servers utilize *controllers* to connect storage drives, networks, and other technologies we used to call peripherals. These are often separate add-in cards utilizing PCI-e or other standards, though some server motherboards and chassis may offer built-in choices as well. Built-in controllers are convenient but may offer modest capacities and performance. They also are less readily upgraded to exploit technology improvements.

In this section, we will explore a number of choices for your Ceph servers' controllers.

Storage HBA / controller type

HBA, synonymous with *controller*, describes a server component that attaches storage drives to the rest of the server. If that functionality is embedded in your motherboard versus being implemented with a discrete card, it is still an HBA. Carefully consider using embedded HBA's for Ceph data; their performance may be lackluster at best.

There are two main types of HBA: basic controllers, and ones that offer onboard RAID functionality. Some refer to the former as a JBOD card and the latter as an HBA, though this inaccurate and misleading.

RAID-capable HBAs usually contain a RAID **System on Chip** (**SoC**) along with a GB or more of cache memory. As that memory is volatile, it is customary to include a **battery backup unit** (**BBU**) to preserve contents across reboots and power events, so they can be flushed to drives as the system is restored. These cards can be used to organize drives into mirror, stripe, or other volumes, which are then presented to the operating system as a single drive. This can reduce complexity on the software side at the expense of considerable management overhead and operational drawbacks:

- Increased cost.
- Increased complexity and opportunity for firmware bugs result in decreased reliability.
- Increased deployment complexity.
- Increased latency in some cases.
- Increased maintenance: traditional batteries are often rated for just one year; expensive supercapacitor alternatives for perhaps three years. As these fail, become unseated, or manifest firmware issues, performance drops and they must be replaced or updated.
- Decreased monitorability: single drives presented as OSDs may need to pass through or be wrapped in a single-drive RAID0 volume; this complicates or prevents the use of utilities such as `iostat` and `smartctl`.

This author has found RAID HBA's to be the *single most troublesome component* of his Ceph clusters and vehemently encourages the use of plain, non-RAID HBA models. The financial and operational cost savings can support improvements elsewhere in the system. This approach, however, often means that one may need to choose the vulnerability of an unmirrored boot volume or the complexity of software mirroring. Some admins run Ceph systems with unmirrored boot volumes, but failure here can be painful to recover from, so this author strongly favors mirroring.

Networking options

Improved networking is perhaps the single most effective use of money within your Ceph cluster, and at times the most easily overlooked. This is the worst part of your architecture for penny-pinching, and the most difficult to fix later. Don't do it. Just don't.

Most Ceph clusters are deployed with Ethernet networking, though Infiniband and other technologies are not unknown. As Ceph uses TCP/IP, it can use most types of network infrastructure. Lab, **Proof of Concept (PoC)**, and very small clusters may get by with 1Gb/s links, but most sizeable production clusters demand at least 10 Gb/s. Larger and SSD-based installations are increasingly utilizing emerging 25 Gb/s, 40 Gb/s, and 100 Gb/s networks.

While Ceph does not require LACP or other link bonding / trunking / aggregation strategy, employing one is standard practice. As Ceph is typically utilized by a larger number of clients hitting each server, this effectively increases available user bandwidth. The ability to ride out NIC / switch failures and network maintenance is however even more important, and alone is worth the cost. This author suggests active/active LACP bonding.

It is customary to provision two networks for Ceph:

- A **public** network over which clients access data. MON and OSD nodes also communicate across the public network.
- A **private** network used only for replication and recovery among OSD nodes, also known as the *cluster*, *backend*, or *replication* network. It is advised for this network to not have a gateway.

It is possible to configure Ceph to use only a single network, but for production-scale deployments this is discouraged to help ensure that replication and client traffic do not compete with or DoS each other. A split architecture also simplifies trending of bandwidth utilization and facilitates future speed increases and capacity expansions as needed.

The public and private networks may be implemented with separate network switches, or they may use VLANs or other partitioning strategies. Consult your network team for preferred approaches, but do ensure that the network design chosen can deliver full bandwidth and permit future growth by adding additional OSD, RGW, or MDS hosts.

If your budget, infrastructure, or server components do not permit fast implementations of *both* the public and private replication networks, your best strategy will be to favor the private backend replication network, for example, bonded 40 Gb/s links for replication and bonded 10 Gb/s links for the public network. During periods of backfill / recovery, the replication network can easily be saturated and become a bottleneck.

One common strategy is to provision each server with two identical dual-port NICs, bonding one port from each card for the replication network, and one from each for the public network. This way, the failure of a single NIC is tolerated as well as the failure of a single upstream switch.

Network versus serial versus KVM management

In the past, servers were primarily managed via serial consoles, with CLI or menu interfaces. Today, even inexpensive beige-box commodity servers usually offer a network management interface as well, with SSH and HTTP UI's. Examples include Oracle's ILOM, Dell's iDRAC, and HP's iLO.

Some servers may offer neither, though a network KVM unit from brands such as Lantronix or Raritan can retrofit some of the management functionality. This author is old-school and likes servers to have at least basic power control and bootstrap ability via serial console, though this does require dedicated infrastructure. Network management interfaces offer a variety of management and monitoring functionality. Whichever way you go, this author strongly advises that you ensure that you can bring up a server console that functions both pre-boot (BIOS and setup), and post-boot (operating system). This ability is invaluable for troubleshooting network and hardware issues, and saves sending someone to the DC at 3am to figure out what's broken.

Adapter slots

Servers today often offer a wealth of built-in resources:

- Network interfaces
- Management interfaces
- Storage controllers
- Keyboard / video / mouse (KVM)
- Multi-purpose USB ports

Chances are that you will need to add additional network and storage controllers for bonding or because embedded interfaces may only be 1 Gb/s. Depending on your server model, these may take the form of:

- Standard PCI-e cards
- Custom mezzanine cards that do not consume a PCI slot
- Proprietary **LAN On Board** (**LOM**) modules

With Ceph systems—especially OSD servers—it is common to need to add as many as four network interfaces and at least one storage adapter, easily consuming three PCI-e slots. Carefully examine your server model diagrams and spec sheets to ensure that you can provision what you need. Some server models may need optional PCI-e risers to accommodate enough slots; examine your server models' specs closely to ensure that the number and length/height of slots are sufficient. Some systems also define an order for populating PCI-e slots and may restrict the cards that are supported in certain slots due to cooling or clearance limitations. The speed of available slots may vary; it is not unusual for a server to provide both x8 and x16 slots. Hungry cards including NICs may be bottlenecked if installed in a slot that provides fewer PCI-e lanes than they can utilize.

This author strongly advises planning for at least one empty PCI-e slot: you may well find yourself in a year wishing to add NVMe journals or other retrofits as your needs and workload change. This is far less hassle and cost than replacing an entire inadequate server, and your foresight will be lauded.

Processors

The first decision for server planning is often the choice of **Central Processor Unit (CPU)** model. In the past, you often had only a handful or even one choice, but today's x64 servers offer dozens of options, including core count and clock rate. In this section, we'll explore these options and help you make the right choices for your Ceph deployment. This is an area where overkill is all too possible, but as we'll see it is not necessarily the best place to blow your budget.

CPU socket count

Most servers used for Ceph today are either single-socket or dual-socket designs. Large four-socket servers are usually overkill for Ceph, and present increased cost and operational complexity. MON and RGW servers often can get away with only a single socket filled with at least a four-core CPU, though this will limit memory capacity as well.

CPU model

It is natural to feel that more, faster CPU cores are better, but with Ceph this is usually the *least effective* place to spend extra money. The first and largest bottlenecks a cluster faces under load are usually saturating the storage drives or the replication network. Ceph daemons are multi threaded, so solving for core count is usually better than throwing money up the price/GHz curve. Rules of thumb can be tricky and opinions here vary, especially as CPUs evolve, but as a minimum this author suggests the following:

- MON nodes: four cores
- RGW nodes: eight cores
- MDS nodes: four-eight cores at a higher clock rate
- OSD nodes: one core-GHz per HDD, two per SSD, five per NVMe. Round up if using dmcrypt or compression.

OSD systems with fast SSD / NVMe storage need more CPU per unit of storage to avoid CPU saturation.

Within some CPU product lines, different models may support differing numbers of inter-socket QPI links or differing numbers of memory channels. This can affect your total memory capacity or impact speed. Given a choice, choose a model with more channels rather than fewer channels.

That said, having *too much* CPU may actually hurt performance. Modern processors utilize a technology called *C-states* to slow down or even turn off selected cores in order to conserve power and heat. There is some evidence that transitions between C-states can impact interrupt processing, especially when using high-speed NICs. Thus, the highest-end CPUs with as many as 18 cores per may actually be detrimental to performance for MON nodes, or even OSD nodes with a modest number of drives. This can perhaps be mitigated after the fact by disabling C-states both in BIOS and via the kernel's command line arguments, but it underscores the importance of not gratuitously provisioning CPU cycles.

Real world example: OSD nodes with dual E5-2680 v2 Xeon processors driving 10 OSDs of 3-4TB LFF rotational drives each. These 10 core, 2.8GHz CPUs were mostly idle. Selecting E5-2630 v2 Xeons instead would have saved ~$2600 per system (list price) and mitigated C-state issues.

Real world example: OSD nodes with dual E5-2683 v4 Xeon processors driving 24 OSDs of 1.6 to 3.8 B SSD drives each. These 16 core, 2.1GHz CPUs are 10-20% utilized under load. The E5-2630 with 10 cores at 2.2GHz would save $2200 off the list price of each server and still provide sufficient cycles.

It's long been true that within a CPU generation, incremental performance gains come at increasingly higher prices. For all but the most dense servers, the fastest available CPU models -- be it measured by core count or by clock rate -- are generally overkill and not cost-effective for Ceph. It is however prudent to not cut it too close; you want burst capacity for times when the cluster is hammered or under other stress. We also never know what awesome yet computationally-expensive feature the next release will bring (including the compression newly available in Luminous), so there is also value in a prudent margin of safety. Running your CPUs consistently at 90% utilization won't do wonders for your latency and ability to weather stress. As erasure coding (see Chapters 4 and 8) becomes more common in Ceph installations, the CPU resources required increase, which is another reason to provision a reasonable amount of extra CPU cycles today.

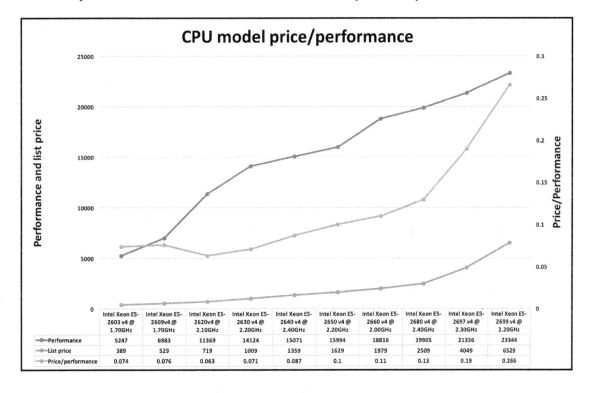

	Intel Xeon E5-2603 v4 @ 1.70GHz	Intel Xeon E5-2609v4 @ 1.70GHz	Intel Xeon E5-2620v4 @ 2.10GHz	Intel Xeon E5-2630 v4 @ 2.20GHz	Intel Xeon E5-2640 v4 @ 2.40GHz	Intel Xeon E5-2650 v4 @ 2.20GHz	Intel Xeon E5-2660 v4 @ 2.00GHz	Intel Xeon E5-2680 v4 @ 2.40GHz	Intel Xeon E5-2697 v4 @ 2.30GHz	Intel Xeon E5-2699 v4 @ 2.20GHz
Performance	5247	6983	11369	14124	15071	15994	18816	19905	21356	23344
List price	389	529	719	1009	1359	1629	1979	2509	4049	6529
Price/performance	0.074	0.076	0.063	0.071	0.087	0.1	0.11	0.13	0.19	0.266

Emerging technologies

Today conventional servers are generally used for Ceph deployments, but an interesting emerging technology is that of embedding a compact system right onto a drive's electronics board, including dual Ethernet interfaces. One can think of these novel assemblies as disk drives that run Linux onboard. As each only needs to power a single OSD, their modest processors and bandwidth are sufficient. An OSD chassis, instead of being an expensive general-purpose computer, becomes effectively a disk array with an embedded network switch. These microserver drives are not yet widely available or implemented, but hold promise for interesting, scalable, modular Ceph systems of tomorrow.

Read more about microserver drives here

`http://ceph.com/community/500-osd-ceph-cluster`

Another novel technology that one can purchase and deploy today is SanDisk's InfiniFlash, a dense SSD technology that can be used as the underlying storage for Ceph OSDs.

`https://www.sandisk.com/business/datacenter/products/flash-syste
ms/infiniflash`

Additional hardware selection resources can be found at the following sites:

- `https://access.redhat.com/documentation/en-us/red_hat_ceph_storage/1.3/html-single/hardware_guide`
- `https://www.redhat.com/cms/managed-files/st-rhcs-config-guide-technology-detail-inc0387897-201604-en.pdf`
- `http://docs.ceph.com/docs/wip-17440/start/hardware-recommendations`
- `https://www.slideshare.net/mirantis/ceph-talk-vancouver-20`
- `http://tracker.ceph.com/projects/ceph/wiki/Tuning_for_All_Flash_Deployments`

Summary

There are many factors that influence selection of server hardware for Ceph clusters, and each type of node has different requirements and constraints. Among the most important points to consider are network speed and failure domains. When planning for Ceph capacity, it is important to remember that one cannot run the OSD drives right up to 99% full; it is prudent to plan for a cluster to not exceed 70% utilization of raw OSD space.

4
Planning Your Deployment

This chapter describes a number of architectural and administrative decisions to make when planning your own Ceph deployment. Chapter 3, *Hardware and Network Selection* outlines many of the hardware choices one has when architecting a production Ceph storage solution. Here we'll concentrate on a number of decisions one must make as well when realizing production clusters:

- Layout Decisions
- Architectural Decisions
- Operating System Decisions
- Networking Decisions

We suggest that you read through this chapter now, then return after digesting Chapter 8: *Ceph Architecture - Under the Hood,* which elaborates on many of the ideas we will touch upon. That deeper understanding of the processes and dynamics of a production Ceph deployment will stand you well when making decisions regarding your deployments.

Layout decisions

In this section we'll explore strategies for placing your Ceph servers within a data center. Consider in advance each of these factors to prevent potentially expensive (and embarrassing) rude awakenings after you deploy your production clusters.

Convergence: Wisdom or Hype?

Literature and the media have been buzzing for a few years about Converged Infrastructure and as if that weren't catchy enough, *Hyper*converged Infrastructure. Perhaps, next year we'll see Ultraconverged Infrastructure that also makes julienne fries. The distinction between the two is mostly marketing. Traditional cloud and server farm designs have typically featured servers / chassis dedicated to each role: Compute, Storage, Networking. Convergence however is all the rage today: provisioning all services onto the same servers. The touted advantages of this approach are savings in management costs and maintenance (read: headcount), in DC footprint recurring operational costs, and in hardware up front capital costs. There is also an expectation of incremental and linear growth on demand.

The assumptions of a SuperMegaConverged+ architecture include that servers are up to the task and that all components readily scale horizontally. Sometimes this works out. In OpenStack deployments example, Nova services are typically bound by CPU and memory, but do not necessarily saturate the full complement of local storage that can be provisioned. Ceph on the other hand is not voracious when it comes to CPU cycles, and its memory requirements are fairly constrained during steady-state operation. It is perhaps natural to view the services as complementary and thus compatible with a converged architecture. Indeed some people are successfully doing this, for example, Cisco's Metacloud. This can work well for modestly-sized deployments, but as utilization grows one may find that one part of the equation—say, storage—becomes saturated in advance of another. One may then need to expand all components across the board, rather than focusing capital expenditure and effort only where needed.

For more info on OpenStack, see `Chapter 10`, *Integrating Ceph with OpenStack*. Sixty or more percent of OpenStack deployments rely on Ceph for block and object storage.

A less-obvious pitfall of convergence is also the complication of maintenance and the intertwining of failure domains. Within a dedicated Ceph infrastructure one routinely takes down individual nodes for firmware or kernel upgrades transparently to users, but with convergence such operations would also take down a number of virtual machines. Live migration can help with this problem, but it is not always feasible, and it does require that one maintain enough spare capacity to support a dance of hypervisor musical-chairs.Contention between competing services is also a concern that grows with scale and utilization. Within a converged system Ceph OSD RAM usage can climb, contending with compute and other services.

A spike in Nova/QEMU CPU hunger or a prolonged burst in Neutron network traffic might impinge enough on Ceph services to result in OSDs being marked down. During heavy backfill or recovery Ceph OSD RAM usage can climb, then everyone has a bad day. New technologies including containers and Linux cgroups hold potential for mitigating this *noisy neighbor* effect, but may entail additional management effort and ongoing tweaking as one strives for the perfect—or perhaps least painful—balance.

This is not to say that converged infrastructure is inherently flawed or never the right approach, but the pros and cons must be carefully weighed along with use-case and foreseeable growth. For smaller **Proof of Concept** (**PoC**) implementations or those for a targeted purpose it may work well, but many Ceph installations find compelling value in independent scaling along multiple axes (Compute, Network, Storage) and decoupling of failure domains.

Concentrating then on servers dedicated to Ceph, consider the components we explored in `Chapter 2`, *Ceph Components and Services*. Systems must be allocated to serve each role: multiple OSDs, MONs, `ceph-mgr`, potentially CephFS MDS and **RADOS Gateway** (**RGW**) as well. Even within the Ceph ecosystem it is natural to consider a measure of convergence to minimize CapEx, server count, RUs, and so on. This must be considered carefully.

Planning Ceph component servers

As Ceph OSDs are tightly coupled to underlying storage, in almost any production-scale system they rate dedicated servers. This approach allows scaling up and out at will, along with a degree of rolling or ad-hoc maintenance flexibility that will turn your Compute and Network colleagues green with envy.

Ceph **Monitor** (**MON**) services have very different needs. They typically do not demand much in the way of CPU, and their RAM requirements are not considerable by modern standards. MONs do not require considerable local storage capacity either but they need it to be durable. As we described in `Chapter 3`, *Hardware and Network Selection*, SSDs used for Ceph Monitor DBs receive steady traffic. MON DBs in larger clusters write at a steady rate of as much as 20 MB/s and can thus easily incur two **Drive Writes Per Day** (**DWPD**) when provisioned on 1 TB drives. For this reason, you are strongly encouraged to provision highly durable drives. If using SSDs, choose a model with a higher endurance rating, at least three DWPD or higher for 1 TB drives. The authors have experienced multiple near-simultaneous MON failures due to lesser drives wearing out; we wish to spare you that kind of anguish.

Durability can additionally be increased by *overprovisioning*. A 100 GB SSD may be *large* enough to fit the MON DB, or even the operating system as well, but a 240 GB model with the same DWPD rating will *last* much longer before failure. And of course a 480 GB unit will provide service for an even longer period. The SSD's onboard controller distributes write operations across all storage cells at its disposal so that write-heavy hot spots do not prematurely exhaust their lifetime supply of write cycles. This strategy is known as *wear leveling*. SSDs can be queried via SMART to keep tabs on their remaining service life. Incorporating longevity counter alerts into your monitoring system can alert you to refresh SSDs before they fail.

It is strongly advised to deploy an odd number of MONs so that the Paxos consensus algorithm can always ensure an unambiguous majority quorum. This avoids the split-brain phenomenon where a fault in network connectivity leaves two subsets of Monitors able to communicate among themselves but not to the other subset. In this scenario each could think that it's authoritative, and no OSD can serve two masters. While a cluster may operate for a time with no available MONs, it's a rather precarious state and thus provisioning only a single MON in production deployments is not acceptable. A healthy Ceph cluster requires *(n/2)+1* Monitor daemons to be up and participate in what is known as the *mon quorum*. Many small to moderate sized clusters do well with three as a single MON can be down for maintenance or upgrade without disrupting Ceph operations.

Larger clusters like the 900+ OSD deployments the authors manage typically include five MONs. Provisioning five allows for one at a time to undergo maintenance while tolerating the failure of second.

Few if any clusters require seven MONs. At a recent OpenStack Summit a group of seasoned Ceph operators asked the question of whether seven was ever called for; the consensus is that that nobody had found justification for doing so. Since each Ceph MON is in constant contact with all other MONs serving the same cluster, the volume and overhead of intercommunication among MONs grows considerably as MONs are added. This is one reason why 7, 9, or even higher numbers are usually not advised.

The provisioning of multiple MONs does help spread out network traffic and the transactional workload, but our primary motivation is fault tolerance. MON scalability has improved dramatically in the last several Ceph LTS releases, and each properly equipped daemon can adequately service a very large number of clients. See the info box in the Rack Strategy section below for additional information regarding scalability.

Thus, for your deployments you should target three or five MONs.

Given their relatively modest requirements, it is common to wish to piggyback MON service onto OSD nodes. This works for dev or PoC deployments like the ones we'll explore in the next chapter, but don't succumb to this temptation in production:

- Since it's undesirable to deploy more than a handful of MONs, some OSD nodes would host a MON and some wouldn't. This asymmetry can be confusing and it complicates system management.
- Ceph MONs form a resilient cluster of their own using the Paxos consensus algorithm, but frequent disruption can be problematic. For example, it is straightforward to temporarily take a single OSD node out of service for maintenance or even just a reboot. If a MON is deployed on the same server, downtime must consider more than just OSD health as it takes both OSD and MON services down at the same time.
- OSDs readily lend themselves to rolling maintenance, but MONs need more time to settle and recover. A rolling upgrade that dedicated OSDs weather just fine may seriously degrade MON performance if the next OSD MON server is taken down before the quorum has fully recovered from the previous downtime. This author has personally experienced outages due to cycling MONs too quickly.
- Heavy OSD utilization may starve MONs for resources, slowing them down considerably, which may cascade into problems for OSDs.

Judicious use of cgroups may mitigate this last concern, but for most production deployments the risks of converging MONs with OSDs on the same chassis outweigh the potential incremental CapEx savings. For this reason the reader is strongly encouraged to dedicate servers to MON usage. They do not have to be big, buff nodes; a modest, relatively inexpensive 1U single-socket system with a basic CPU is generally plenty. In fact over provisioning CPU sockets and cores for MONs may result in network and performance issues due to c-state hunting. They should however be fully standalone in order to minimize the failure domain, for example, blade servers may not be a good choice, especially if more than one MON blade were to reside in the same chassis, as chassis maintenance may cause unforeseen service degradation. This author has seen enough grief caused by complicated and flaky blade chassis to eschew them entirely; your mileage as they say may vary.

As **virtual machine** (**VM**) performance can be somewhat unpredictable, they are also not recommended for Ceph MON service. If VMs rely on Ceph for their storage, circular dependency would be a very real problem since MONs are a crucial part of the Ceph back end.

Ceph's RGW services however are Ceph clients, not part of the core back end. They have looser latency and performance demands than backend components and readily scale horizontally when abstracted behind a load balancer. If your use cases include object service it may be reasonable to provision some or all RGW servers as virtual machines.

As the Ceph Manager (`ceph-mgr`) service is new (and required) with the Luminous release, best practices for it are still evolving, but colocating them on MON nodes seems to be today's strategy.

Some Ceph deployments and documents refer to one or more *admin nodes*, which provide no services of their own but serve solely as a place to run administrative and cluster monitoring commands. As such they are excellent candidates for virtualization provided that the VMs used boot from storage local to their hypervisors (also known as ephemeral) and thus do not themselves rely on the Ceph cluster for their health and operation. When things go bad, the last thing you need is to realize that a circular dependency is preventing you from troubleshooting or fixing problems.

One or more dedicated admin nodes are not required, and in fact MON nodes can be simply used as admin nodes. This author has experienced both strategies. Using MONs affords an incremental measure of complexity reduction, but separating admin and MON nodes appeals to many organizations. You might even utilize an existing *jump* or *bastion* host as a Ceph admin node, though there are the usual concerns of accessibility and dependencies. One or more admin nodes also obviate the need for NOC, support, billing, or other personnel to log into the actual production cluster back end nodes, satisfying the demands of your Information Security department for compartmentalization of access.

Rack strategy

Rack and stack strategies and policies vary across organizations and even among datacenters (DCs) within a given organization. In this section, we'll explore considerations for placing your Ceph servers, especially as regards to failure domains, a topic that we'll discuss in greater detail in `Chapter 8`, *Ceph Architecture: Under the Hood*.

Small to modest Ceph clusters may not comprise enough servers to fill multiple datacenter racks, especially with today's dense 1U and 2U chassis. For these there are two classes of layout strategies:

1. Place everything within a single rack
2. Spread the servers over multiple racks

Single rack deployments offer simplicity: networking can be fulfilled with fewer switches and you never have to think which rack to which remote hands must be directed. However, one is putting one's proverbial OSDs all in one basket and a failure at the switch or PDU level can be catastrophic. In such deployments we configure Ceph to regard each host as a failure domain, and to ensure that no single host has more than one copy of replicated data. It is especially important in single-rack layouts to leverage redundant networking and power supplies, as explored below and in the previous chapter.

Multiple rack deployments add a strong measure of fault tolerance to even small clusters as with careful planning the failure of an entire rack does not compromise the cluster as a whole. This can however mean a more complex networking strategy and demands that the logical topology closely mirror the physical topology, we'll also explore in `Chapter 8`, *Ceph Architecture: Under the Hood*. With the default replication factor of three set on a cluster's pools it's highly desirable to spread the nodes across at least three racks so that the CRUSH failure domain can enforce no more than one copy of data in each. With **Erasure Coded (EC)** pools, a larger number of racks may be best to ensure that the cluster as a whole can weather the loss of one without a service outage or data loss.

In a small to medium multiple rack deployment one will not entirely fill each rack with Ceph servers. Common datacenter racks offer 42 U of space, some of which is often consumed by networking gear. A modest cluster might then fill as little as a third of the available mounting space, which often has significant financial concerns. Your datacenter folks may thus pressure you to either condense into a single rack deployment, or share your racks with other services. Sharing is often entirely feasible, though with such a layout you must realistically consider and plan for in advance a number of concerns:

- Room to grow as your most excellent Ceph cluster requires additional servers to increase capacity to slake users' never-ending thirst for data storage. This includes both rack space aka RUs as well as available power amps and sockets as we discussed in the previous chapter.
- Room for the *other* services to grow, which can potentially prevent your Ceph cluster from expanding, or even displace it into other racks.
- If networking gear is shared, insist on dedicated switches for at least Ceph's replication aka private network—or at the very very least a dedicated VLAN. Contention for bandwidth with other services can lead to service degradation or outages, that is noisy neighbors are the pits.

In larger deployments we often have dedicated racks, which can obviate the noisy neighbor factor, and allows us desirable networking and topological failure domains.

Here is an example layout that this author has managed. We'll discuss below several important points regarding the design goals, benefits, and concerns.

Rack 1	Rack 2	Rack 3
ToR	ToR	ToR
ToR	ToR	ToR
MON	MON	MON
MON	Empty (you don't want to know)	MON
OSD	OSD	OSD
OSD	OSD	OSD
OSD	OSD	OSD
OSD	OSD	OSD
OSD	OSD	OSD
OSD	OSD	OSD
PDU	PDU	PDU
OSD	OSD	OSD
OSD	OSD	OSD
OSD	OSD	OSD
OSD	OSD	OSD
OSD	OSD	OSD
OSD	OSD	OSD
OSD	OSD	OSD
OSD	OSD	OSD
OSD	OSD	OSD

In this cluster, we had multiple replicated pools each with three-way replication. Thus, each rack held exactly one copy of data. The MONs were provisioned with 1U servers; the OSD servers were 2 U. With networking and patch panel overhead, this filled the available racks completely for zero unused space. With dual Top of Rack (ToR) switches all Ceph systems enjoyed network redundancy, which will we explore in more detail later in this chapter. The OSD nodes each served 10 drives, for a cluster total of 450.

With conventional Ceph replication, the placement of one copy of data in each rack informs equal OSD capacity in each rack. If, say, the servers in rack 3 above were to house larger OSD drives than the first two racks, their additional delta of capacity would be wasted. Racks 1 and 2 would fill up first, and the requirement for replication would prohibit the cluster from using the balance of Rack 3. For this reason it is highly advised to provision the initial complement of racks (of servers) with equal capacity.

If circumstances (availability, fire sale, pre-loved gear, etc.) present you with a mix of server or drive capacities, it is best to distribute components so that each rack's complement adds up to a roughly equal total. This is especially important when using a failure domain of rack as described in Chapter 8, *Ceph Architecture: Under the Hood*, as is common in larger, multi-rack deployments. When summing drive or server capacities be sure to use the actual size presented by each device, for example, 3.84 TB, rather than nominal marketing figures like 4 TB. The rounding and (ahem) exaggeration inherent in the latter can result in embarrassing mistakes.

The provisioning of a pair of ToR (Top of Rack) switches in each rack means that a failure does not affect other racks and avoids cross-rack cabling. Five MON nodes is very typical for a cluster of this size. They are carefully spread across racks so that the cluster can survive the catastrophic failure of any single rack (say, when someone backs a forklift into it).

Financial, efficiency, and organizational concerns dictated that when expansion was needed, one or more full racks of OSD servers with associated networking were provisioned. As we discussed previously, the number of Ceph MONs does not need to be scaled linearly as the OSD farm grows, so these expansion racks did not not include additional MON nodes. Alert readers might observe that this could allow the provisioning of a sixteenth OSD node in their space, or for existing MONs to spread for increased resilience. We totally should have done one or the other.

For a fascinating discussion of real-world tests that push the envelope of Ceph at scale, this CERN article is highly recommended. It's a perfect example of the Ceph community is a priceless resource for Ceph admins.

`http://ceph.com/community/new-luminous-scalability/`

With any rack layout, single or multiple, it is advised to plan for future expansion. This may mean pre-allocating additional rack space to ensure that it's available when needed, or it might inform one's network device choice or topology in order to accommodate growth in switch chassis or port count. The addition of a fourth rack to a replicated cluster somewhat relaxes the need to strictly balance the capacity (or *weight*) of each rack. Since Ceph needs only three racks for the replicas of each Placement Group (`Chapter 8`, *Ceph Architecture: Under the Hood*), modest variation in aggregate capacity will now be fully utilized. In the above layout, three racks of nominal 3 TB drives were supplemented by two expansion racks of 4 TB drives. Ceph did allocate more data to the larger drives, making the new servers fractionally busier than those in the original three racks, but by being able to choose only two of the other three racks for the other copies of that data Ceph was able to use all of the new space. If the expansion drives has been considerably larger than the existing, say 8 TB, it would have been prudent to swap some of them with smaller drives in the original racks in order to achieve a closer balance. With *grossly* imbalanced racks there remains a potential for the cluster filling up before the larger rack(s) do.

Server naming

This may seem trivial, but naming conventions for servers can be surprisingly controversial. Many Ceph deployments will use names like `ceph-osd-01` and `ceph-mon-03`. Others have organizational conventions of naming systems after their serial numbers or by location, encoding a datacenter room, row, rack, and RU into a name like `dh3a1r3ru42.example.com`. While location-based hostnames may seem awkward, their appeal grows after repeated painful mistakes resulting from role-based hostnames:

- Adhesive hostname labels can fall off or become illegible over time
- Worse yet, they can be picked up and stuck onto the *wrong* server
- Repurposed systems can all too easily retain role-based labels from previous lives
- Different departments sharing the same datacenter may happen to use very similar names

This author has personally suffered each of the above. At best they make finding a desired server difficult. At worst they result in the your—or someone else's—servers going down or being unracked unexpectedly. Your datacenter and platform folks may or may not afford you hostname flexibility, but if you do use role-based hostnames, I suggest that you plan for expansion. To wit: if you start with `ceph-osd-1`, `ceph-osd-2`, and `ceph-osd-3`, names might become awkward when you find yourself with dozens or hundreds of systems and potentially multiple clusters. Names like `ceph-osd-001.cluster1.example.com` and `ceph-cluster3-mon-042.example.com` thus accommodate future growth and convenient sorting behavior. In sites with multiple clusters it can be advantageous to follow the latter form, with a cluster designation in the short hostname. There can be parts of the overall ecosystem where the domain may not be visible, and this practice helps maintain clarity regarding which cluster names and data reference.

Architectural decisions

In this section we'll explore a number of choices to make regarding how your Ceph cluster's resources are deployed. Some of these may be adjusted after the fact with varying degrees of difficulty, but careful attention to your current and future needs here will save you considerable grief in the future.

Pool decisions

As we'll explore in `Chapter 8`, *Ceph Architecture: Under the Hood,* Ceph clusters provision one or more *pools* in which data is organized, for example, one for block storage and another for object storage. These pools may have different designs based on different use cases; they may even live on different hardware. Several important decisions must be made before provisioning each pool.

Replication

The keeping of redundant copies of data is fundamental to Ceph, and the manner in which this is done is a fundamental characteristic of each pool. One is not *prevented* from provisioning a pool with no redundancy, but it rarely if ever makes sense to do so. Ceph today provides two redundancy strategies for ensuring data durability and availability: *replication* and *erasure coding*.

Replication is familiar to anyone who has worked with drive mirroring aka RAID 1 or RAID 10: multiple copies of data are kept on each of multiple devices. Ceph has implemented replicated pools for years and offers an extremely mature and stable implementation. The loss of one or potentially more devices does not result in the loss or unavailability of user data. The price of replication is that the *usable* storage capacity of the cluster is a fraction of the *raw* capacity, for example, a cluster with 1000 GiB of individual drive space used for a pool with the default replication factor of 3 will be able to store 333 GiB (1000/3) of user data. Replication is easy to understand, straightforward to provision, and offers excellent data availability and durability. The cost however may be unpopular with your budget team or anyone accustomed to old-school mirroring which often maintains only two copies of data. Replication is suitable for any type of data pool on any version of Ceph.

Erasure Coding

Erasure Coding (EC) is a strategy by which one can realize a more favorable ratio of raw to usable storage capacity as well as potentially greater fault tolerance. The downsides are greater complexity, more computation, and potentially increased time to recover from failures. Depending on the EC parameters chosen, hardware, and workload, performance may be impacted as well.

Ceph has supported EC for RGW object storage pools for some time; new with the Kraken release and mature with the Luminous LTS release is support for RBD block storage pools as well, now that partial overwrites have been improved for significant write performance gains. As the latter is relatively new and production adoption in the community is tentative, conservative storage admins today may elect to continue provisioning replicated pools for RBD service, though the less strict latency demands of object storage service makes EC highly attractive for RGW bucket pools.

The space efficiency advantage and fault tolerance of an EC pool over a replicated pool depend on the k and m parameters chosen, but common strategies realize an overhead ratio of as low as 1.4:1 or 1.5:1, compared to the 3:1 ratio with typical Ceph replication. Thus the 1000 GiB raw space example cluster above could yield as much as 666 GiB of usable space—double that of replication on the same drives.

One consideration of EC is that to implement its magic one needs a cluster of at least moderate size: data is spread in smaller chunks but over a larger number of drives. EC pools also require careful datacenter planning if one wishes to ensure that the complete loss of a complete rack does not take out the entire pool; this is a significant factor when choosing an EC profile. We will discuss both replication and erasure coding in greater detail in `Chapter 8`, *Ceph Architecture: Under the Hood*.

Placement Group calculations

Choosing the correct number of PGs for each pool is one of the most important decisions when planning a Ceph cluster. A value that is too high or too low can severely affect performance. Too few PGs will result in uneven data distribution and excessive data movement during backfill/recovery. Too many PGs increase the overhead the cluster incurs when ensuring data availability, including memory usage by OSD daemons.

We can target the total number of placement groups for a pool using the following formula:

$$Total\ PGs = (Total\ OSDs\ *\ PGPerOSD) / Replication\ factor$$

Put another way the *ratio* can be calculated:

$$PGPerOSD = (Total\ PGs) / (Total\ OSDs / Replication\ factor)$$

Choosing the correct number of PGs for each pool is one of the most important decisions when planning a Ceph cluster. A value that is too high or too low can severely affect performance. Too few PGs will result in uneven data distribution and excessive migration during backfill / recovery. Too many PGs increase memory usage by OSD daemons and add to the overhead the cluster incurs when ensuring data availability.

We know the number of OSDs provisioned in a cluster; in many cases each pool uses all of them. It is important in clusters with complex topology to discount any OSDs that are not the part of our subject pool in the above calculation. The value of replication factor of the pool is denoted by the key called size; this defaults to and is usually left at three for a replicated pool.

In the above equations PGPerOSD is the PG:OSD ratio: the number of PGs to be allocated to each OSD housing the pool. When the OSD devices within a pool are homogenous this calculation is easy to make

Let's say we have 2 TB SSDs and wish to target 200 PGs per OSD: we substitute 200 for PGPerOSD in the above equations. Our pool uses the default replication factor (the size attribute) of 3 and comprises 50 OSDs. The calculated total number of PGs (pg_num) for our pool is:

$$(Total\ \ OSDs\ \ *\ \ PGPerOSD)/Replication\ factor => Total\ PGs$$
$$(50*200)\ /\ 3 => \textbf{3333}$$

Based on the above calculation, our decision would be to size this pool at 3333 PGs.

However, when Ceph distributes data across a pool's PGs it assigns bytes of data to PGs in powers of 2. This means if we do not set pg_num exactly to a power of 2 our distribution across PGs will be uneven. Each PG should ideally be handed an identically sized chunk of space. In the above example, though, 3333 is not a power of 2. Since Ceph allocates capacity to a number of 2 PGs as a set, the first 2048 PGs will have approximately 20 GB each allotted to them, the next 1024 PGs will also have around 20GB allotted for each, but allocations for the rest we quickly diverge. The remaining 261 PGs will each be assigned average of around 80 GB of the cluster's capacity. That's about 4 times more utilization on each of these stragglers than on most OSDs. It's bad enough that the devices that house them will see more than their share of the workload, but it's even more problematic that this will cause them to become full when other OSDs have room still to grow.

In order to avoid these problems it's best to select a power of 2 for each pool's pg_num. Common practice is to round up the calculated figure to the next power of two. In the above example, the next power of two higher than 3333 is 4096, so that's the ideal value to specify for this pool's pg_num.

$$ceil\_power\_of\_2(3333) -> \textbf{4096} \quad \textit{\#Value of pg\_num on the pool}$$

If our clusters comprise multiple drive capacities, types, or speeds his calculation can become tricky. If we pick the ratio based on the largest or fastest drive type, then slower drives will get more PGs than they can handle. Similarly at the other extreme if we choose the ratio based on the smallest or slowest drive type, then faster media would be underutilized. A better way to approach this situation is by choosing an average ratio ranging across all types of drives present to apply to our pool. It helps to avoid this problem entirely by sticking to a homogeneous cluster topology, at least for all OSDs within a single pool.

The overall *cluster's* ratio, calculated with the sum of all pools' pg_num values, is also a concern when we add new pools to a working cluster. Every new pool created will add its own set of PGs. Because they are all part of the same cluster we have to ensure that the aggregate collection of PGs doesn't overwhelm the OSDs, especially if as is common these pools share the same or overlapping sets of OSDs. If our PG to OSD ratio is already on the high side then the piling on of additional pools (and their requisite new PGs) may impact ongoing I/O on existing pools as well as workloads destined for the new pools. It is thus essential to plan cluster growth properly in advance. If we know that a particular cluster will require additional pools in the future, we should target a lower PG to OSD ratio for the initial pool(s) so that we can comfortably accommodate PGs created by the addition of future pools.

One author personally suffered a cluster where repeated addition of OpenStack Glance and Cinder pools resulted in a ratio of roughly 9000:1. When the datacenter hosting that cluster suffered complete power loss, the cluster became unrecoverable due to the outrageous amount memory that OSD processes attempted to allocate at startup. Everything had to be wiped and rebuilt from scratch. Fortunately that cluster was used for lab / dev work and not production data, but the object lesson (pun not intended, really!) was invaluable.

Conversely, when production Ceph clusters fill up as a victims of their own success, it is common to add additional OSD nodes and OSD drives to increase capacity. As existing PGs are redistributed across this added capacity, the PG to OSD ratio per pool and for the cluster as a whole will decrease. Thus it's important to consider potential future expansion when planning your pools. For this reason it can be beneficial to aim on the high side for each pool's PG to OSD ratio, so that expansion will not reduce the effective ratio below the advised minimum of 100:1. This phenomenon is somewhat at odds with that in the previous paragraph, when pools are added. Careful pre-planning is prudent, though as we'll see in Chapter 8, *Ceph Architecture: Under the Hood,* we can improve a too low ratio by incrementally adding PGs up to the next power of 2 but we can't remove them to fix a too-high ratio.

A valuable calculator for planning pg_num values for a cluster's collection of pools can be found at

http://ceph.com/pgcalc/.

As this book was about to be published the Luminous 12.2.2 release was announced. A notable change is that `ceph status` and other operations will now complain if the cluster's PG:OSD ratio exceeds 200:1. Releases from Hammer through Luminous 12.2.0 warn at the higher ratio threshold of 300:1. Earlier versions would silently let you paint yourself into a corner, as this author painfully reminisces above.

 Here's an excellent opportunity to visit the Ceph code base. To see the contribution that effects these changes, visit:

https://github.com/ceph/ceph/pull/17814

Resources including `http://ceph.com/pgcalc` previously suggested a target ratio of 200:1, often plus rounding up. As Ceph clusters grow larger, the consequences of higher PG:OSD ratios include significantly increased memory utilization by OSD processes and slower PG peering after cluster topology and state events. If you anticipate expanding your cluster's OSD count by a factor of 2 or more in the short to mid term, you may make an educated decision to still aim on the high side.

The Hammer through Kraken releases warn if the cluster's effective ratio is higher than the default or configured value. With Luminous certain cluster operations are now disallowed if the change would cause the effective ratio to exceed the limit:

- Splitting PG's by increasing `pg_num` (see `Chapter 8`, *Ceph Architecture: Under the Hood*)
- Changing a pool's replication factor (this can be traumatic)
- Adding new pools

The name of this setting has thus changed to reflect that it's no longer just a good idea; *it's the law*.

Like hundreds of other settings, this threshold can be adjusted. We recommend that you carefully do so if required to suppress the persistent `HEALTH_WARN` health state for legacy clusters that you can't bring into compliance. It would be all too easy to miss additional cluster events that would set `HEALTH_WARN` if the cluster is in that state all the time. If you *really* know what you're doing, say if you know you're going to treble the size of the cluster before long, you can still aim high and retrofit the threshold.

When a number of OSD drives (or entire OSD hosts) fail and are removed from the cluster, the reduced number of OSDs results in a corresponding increase in the effective PG:OSD ratio. This increased ratio may creep above the new hard threshold. Be aware of this potential so that in advance of cluster changes you can arrange for repairs to restore a compliant ratio.

As we'll explore below, we can increase the effective ratio by splitting PGs within a given pool to increase their population (and thus the denominator in the ratio calculation , but there are no takebacks to decrease it. A higher than optimal effective ratio can however be decreased by adding additional OSDs to the cluster, which distributes the existing PGs across a greater number of OSDs.

For Luminous 12.2.1 and later releases one can set the hard threshold:

```
[mon]
mon_max_pg_per_osd = 300
```

Earlier releases set a warning threshold:

```
[mon]
mon_pg_warn_max_per_osd = 300
```

OSD decisions

In this section we'll explore a number of decisions that affect how you'll deploy the many OSDs that house data within your Ceph clusters.

Back end: FileStore or BlueStore?

Prior to the very recent Luminous release of Ceph, the FileStore backend was the only one officially supported. With FileStore, OSD data is stored in a structured directory hierarchy within an XFS, EXT4, or even Btrfs filesystem. This leverages years of maturation in the codebases of those filesystems, and Ceph's developers were able to concentrate on other parts of the overall system. Over time, though, and as Ceph deployments became larger, busier, and more widespread the limitations of conventional filesystems—especially EXT4—have increasingly become a thorn in the sides of Ceph developers and admins.

The shiny new BlueStore back end is transparent to Ceph users and to much of Ceph itself. When deploying OSDs for example with the popular ceph-deploy utility, one simply adds the --bluestore switch to the command line. As we'll discuss in Chapter 6, *Operations and Maintenance*, and Chapter 8, *Ceph Architecture: Under the Hood*, BlueStore offers significant performance improvements over the mature FileStore back end. However, BlueStore is fairly new, and while officially supported in Luminous and later releases, many Ceph admins opt to let it mature and prove itself for some time before trusting it in production. Some are so conservative that they will wait for at least the Nautilus release before betting the [server] farm on it. While we all love *better*, *faster*, and *cheaper*, when a single cluster may serve thousands of virtual machines or other clients, *stable* has an undeniable appeal.

Some readers of this book will be running Jewel or even Hammer clusters for some time, so while the authors are giddy with excitement over BlueStore, even we are proceeding cautiously. FileStore is still supported with the Luminous and will be the foreseeable future. When planning from scratch cluster deployments, we suggest that you peruse articles, blogs, and the mailing lists mentioned in Chapter 2, *Ceph Components and Services* for up-to-the-minute experiences with BlueStore on specific dot releases of Luminous (or Mimic, or Nautilus).

 A wealth of data regarding the impetus and design of BlueStore may be found in this 2017 presentation from Sage Weil, the father and architect of Ceph. These slides are highly recommended for anyone managing or considering a BlueStore deployment.
http://events.linuxfoundation.org/sites/events/files/slides/20170323%20bluestore.pdf

We also highly encourage you to try it out on lab or PoC clusters before going production, or even on your production gear before **General Availability** (**GA**) release to users. You can always migrate from FileStore to BlueStore later without disrupting users, if you have any doubts regarding its safety. The Luminous release of Ceph also brings us new tools that make incremental rebuilding of OSDs (also known as *repaving*) easier than ever:

- `ceph osd crush swap-bucket <src> <dest>`
- `ceph osd destroy`

It is possible with Luminous or later to prepare a replacement OSD on an unused drive in advance of removing an existing one, or to partially remove an existing OSD for in-situ repaving. Either approach minimizes data movement and thus impact on users. Think of the former as a heart transplant, and the latter as open heart surgery.

OSD device strategy

With either back end, FileStore or BlueStore, it is strongly advised in production to deploy only one OSD per physical drive, be it HDD or SSD. Ceph's tools and code are designed with this strategy in mind; ignoring it may cost you exaggerated seek overhead, device wear, or operational issues including confounded CRUSH replication rules.

Similarly it is advised to deploy OSDs directly onto underlying physical devices, as opposed to hardware, embedded, or software RAID volumes. There was once interested in underlying RAID as a means to conserve RAM by limiting OSD count, or for specialized failure domains. However with modern hardware and the substantial refinements and improvements achieved by successive Ceph releases, the appeal of such strategies is very selective for specific, unusual use-cases. Also since Ceph ensures its own data replication, the redundancy offered by underlying RAID would be, well, redundant, and depending on topology write speeds may be severely limited. For most deployments management complexity and the potential for unexpected or suboptimal behavior strongly favors *one drive == one OSD*.

Journals

As touched upon in `Chapter 3`, *Hardware and Network Selection*, when using FileStore each OSD requires a *journal*. For the remainder of this section when discussing journals we assume that the FileStore back end is being used, as BlueStore does not employ journals as such. Ceph's FileStore employs journals for two reasons: performance and data integrity. The write performance of small random client requests is improved by combining them into fewer, more efficient sequential journal writes. Ceph returns writes to clients after a requisite number of copies are written to OSD journals, which often are faster than the OSD filesystem proper. If hardware fails before data is persisted to an OSD filesystem it can be recovered from the journal. It is is important to not confuse Ceph OSD journals with the internal journals that modern *logging* or *journaling* filesystems employ for related reasons.

When a client writes on a Ceph OSD, data is first written to the journal device, then later committed (or *flushed*) in a consolidated fashion to the permanent, main OSD filesystem. By default Ceph OSDs flush their journals every five seconds as a compromise between efficiency and consistent performance. If a system or daemon should fail, data may remain uncommitted in an OSD's journal, but when the OSD starts again it will process any lingering data in the journal and go about its merry way.

Each OSD's journal should be sized so that it doesn't fill up between flush intervals; to calculate this one would allow for at least double the expected speed of the journal device multiplied by the flush interval, which by default is five seconds. Many Ceph admins however opt for the convenience of an ample, one-size-fits-all size of 10 GiB.

In the previous chapter we discussed the selection of devices for journal duty. When deploying FileStore OSDs with journals, we have two options:

- Colocated (*colo*)
- Discrete

A colocated journal is provisioned as a dedicated partition at the logical end of each OSD device. Thus, with colo journals, the journal and main filesystem reside in two partitions on the same drive. This is efficient in terms of hardware: 10 GB is a trivial chunk to carve out of modern multi-TB drives. When OSDs are provisioned with colo journals on rotational HDDs, however, performance can suffer. Even with request coalescing each write to a given OSD is amplified into separate journal and filesystem writes, requiring additional head seeks. Seeks are relatively slow and thus the throughput (iops) of each OSD is decreased significantly. The aggregate throughput of the cluster as whole can consequently be significantly lowered.

Colo journals on HDD devices also result in a lot of long head seeks, as the drive's armature shuttles between the journal partition all the way at the end of the drive and the OSD filesystem that is spread across the balance of the device. This seek pattern may also decrease aggregate performance. SSD devices for OSD use, however, naturally do not seek and thus colocated journals are substantially less problematic on SSDs than they are on HDDs.

A discrete journal is one located on a different device than the OSD filesystem. This strategy, when properly implemented, results in significant performance gains as the write overhead (or amplification) is significantly reduced, especially on HDD devices. While separate HDD devices are sometimes used as journals, it is more common to use faster storage in order to increase performance. Since FileStore journals need only be a few GiB in size, modestly-sized journal devices suffice, which helps minimize cost. A single fast journal device may also serve multiple OSD devices, each configured to use a specified partition.

Provisioning of SSDs as journals for OSD absorb spikes in your workload. However, if journals are no faster than your backing store they will be a limiting factor on your cluster's write performance. With conventional SAS or SATA SSDs serving as journals for rotating HDD OSDs it is recommended to not exceed the ratio of 4 or at most 5 OSDs per journal drive. When using increasingly affordable and popular PCI-e NVMe SSD devices instead, one may reasonably partition journals for as many as 10 or 12 OSDs on a single device. Exceeding these ratios will result in performance bottlenecks, which are what fast journal devices are intended to avoid in the first place. Less obvious but just as important is the failure domain: the more OSDs a single journal device services, the more are lost if the devices fails. Thus the failure of a single journal device may take multiple OSDs out of service at the same time; the greater the OSD:journal device ratio, the greater the fraction of the overall cluster that is lost. Since we always configure production Ceph clusters to not store more than one copy of replicated data on each host, we won't lose any data when a journal device fails, but along with performance bottlenecks this is an additional reason to limit the ratio.

An additional benefit of fast PCI-e NVMe journals is that they free up drive bays that can be used for additional OSD devices. This increased OSD density helps offset the cost of faster, dedicated journal devices.

We've noted that Ceph OSDs built with the new BlueStore back end do not require journals. One might reason that additional cost savings can be had by not having to deploy journal devices, and this can be quite true. However, BlueStore does still benefit from provisioning certain data components on faster storage, especially when OSDs are deployed on relatively slow HDDs. Today's investment in fast FileStore journal devices for HDD OSDs is not wasted when migrating to BlueStore. When repaving OSDs as BlueStore devices the former journal devices can be readily re purposed for BlueStore's RocksDB and WAL data. When using SSD-based OSDs, this BlueStore accessory data can reasonably be colocated with the OSD data store. For even better performance they can employ faster yet NVMe or other technloogies for WAL and RocksDB. This approach is not unknown for traditional FileStore journals as well, though it is not inexpensive.Ceph clusters that are fortunate to exploit SSDs as primary OSD drives usually do not require discrete journal devices, though use cases that require every last bit of performance may justify NVMe journals. SSD clusters with NVMe journals are as uncommon as they are expensive, but they are not unknown.

Filesystem

We've noted that when using the FileStore back end for Ceph OSDs one has a choice of underlying filesystem. While EXT4, XFS, and Btrfs have been officially supported for some time, EXT4 suffers certain troublesome shortcomings, including its limited ability to store the XATTR metadata that Ceph requires. With the Luminous release, EXT4 as a filesystem choice for FileStore is strongly discouraged and in fact one must explicitly enable it if required, along with severe restrictions on Ceph OSD capabilities. Btrfs has both fans and detractors. Whatever one's feelings regarding it are, it is not widely used among Ceph deployments, and thus information within the community is limited.

This leaves XFS as the FileStore filesystem of choice. Ceph builds XFS filesystems for FileStore use with certain default parameters; adjust these only if you know exactly what you are doing. This author in the past inherited an architecture that had built thousands of OSD XFS filesystems with the added `-n size=65536` parameter. The intent was to minimize CPU utilization by filesystem code, though Ceph does not come remotely close to the use cases where this is in play. The downside was that the Linux kernel's code was not optimized for this non-default setting, resulting in memory allocation failures that caused OSD daemons to slow down and even crash.

The only fix was to wipe and redeploy every OSD with default XFS parameters, which would be massively expensive (though Luminous would have facilitated the process quite a bit). An ugly, embarrassing, and somewhat impactful hack of periodically dropping the kernel's cache to defragment memory was reluctantly placed as a workaround. The moral of the story is to stray from default XFS parameters at your own mortal peril.

A very few adventurous Ceph admins with unusual use-cases and no small amount of determination have experimented with FileStore on top of ZFS, though they're on their own with such a novel yet unsupported strategy.

Encryption

Ceph clusters usually service hundreds or thousands of clients, and the data for each is sliced and dice among as many as hundreds of OSD devices. This mixing and dissemination of data presents something of a barrier to would-be thieves who could gain physical access to your servers and even physically abscond with them. However, when data is truly sensitive, user or organizational requirements might dictate stronger protection in the form of encryption.

Storage drives are available that implement encryption of data at rest, which means the actual data stored persistently on them. **Self Encrypting Drive** (**SED**) is the most popular of these strategies, and a variety of drive models are available that implement it, albeit at increased cost over models. SED drives can be used transparently by Ceph, though the management of the keys required can be awkward and cumbersome.

A relatively new alternative is software-based encryption using dmcrypt. By simply adding the --dmcrypt switch to the ceph-deploy command line when creating OSDs, we can direct Ceph to create secure and encrypted partitions for both journal and OSD data. The encryption keys are stored in the MON database. A third, unencrypted partition is created to store an OSD bootstrap key in plaintext; this is required to authenticate each OSD to the MON store. Before an OSD with an encrypted data partition can be activated it must make a call to the MON store, providing the bootstrap key to authenticate itself to the MONs. If the authentication attempt is valid the OSD is permitted to download the encryption key required to in turn decrypt and access the journal and OSD partitions.

A new logical volume is created *in memory* to access the data in plaintext for each data and journal partition. All writes to these logical volumes are encrypted before being written to the OSD and journal drive(s), ensuring that persistent data is kept secure at all times. The encryption key pulled from the MON store is kept only in memory and is discarded once these mapped logical volumes are mounted and successfully opened for access. The combination of OSD local crypt partitions with encryption keys stored on the MONs make it very unlikely that an intruder would be able to decrypt sensitive data. Utilizing dmcrypt for OSDs does burn more CPU cycles, but with modern multi-core processors this is rarely a problem.

 More information on `dmcrypt` may be found at
https://en.wikipedia.org/wiki/Dm-crypt

Operating system decisions

There are a number of factors to consider when designing the operating system deployment of your Ceph clusters. Some, like the complement of packages to be installed can be tweaked later. Others, especially the size and layout of boot drive partitions and filesystems, would require substantial effort to adjust after the fact. It is best to carefully plan in advance when bootstrapping your systems.

Kernel and operating system

While some adventurous Ceph admins have worked to deploy Ceph on other operating systems such as Solaris or FreeBSD, Ceph is designed to be deployed on modern Linux systems. Determined implementers can build Ceph from source code, but most sites deploy pre-built packages. Ceph is available as `.deb` packages for Debian-derived distributions including Ubuntu, and as `.rpm` packages for Red Hat family distributions including RHEL and CentOS. SUSE also shows significant commitment to Ceph and offers packages as well.

While Ceph's backend servers run entirely in user space, there are often benefits from running as recent a Linux kernel as practical. The stock kernel in recent distributions including RHEL 7.4 and Ubuntu 16.04 suffices for many, though it is not altogether unusual for a site to cherry-pick or build a newer kernel to enjoy the latest drivers, bug fixes, and performance improvements.

Ceph packages

Some Linux distributions offer bundled Ceph packages for effortless installs, which cannot be beat for convenience. These however are not always ideally up to date. Most Ceph admins download pre-built, ready-to-eat install packages from the central repository at `https://download.ceph.com`, though it is also possible to build from source code, especially if one wishes to contribute to development or add local custom features or tweaks.

Some references and software tools will configure `download.ceph.com` directly as an `apt` or `yum` package repo. This appeals in that it requires minimal local effort and ensures that the latest dot release packages are always available. Problems of this approach include the potential for **Man In The Middle** (**MITM**) attacks if using HTTP URLs instead of HTTPS URLs, as well as a dependency on potentially slow or flaky internet connection. There are also times when the central servers are offline for various reasons, and it is also not uncommon for local security policy to prohibit production service systems from directly connecting to the external internet.

For these reasons it is advised to maintain a local repository of Ceph packages, mirrored from the upstream official site, ideally manually. Tools including createrepo, Pulp, and aptly facilitate the management of local, custom package repositories. One may also skate old-school by copying around `.rpm` or `.deb` files with scp, Ansible, or other tools.

Operating system deployment

Here we'll discuss a number of concerns when specifying the base operating system installation on your servers as well as platform-level options that facilitate the management of Ceph systems.

Firstly, mirror your boot drives. While a well-architected Ceph infrastructure can readily cope with the loss of an entire server if an unmirrored boot drive fails, it's much better to avoid this sort of large, sudden event. Boot drive mirroring can be done via HBA or in software using the Linux MD system. Many recent server product lines offer dual rear-panel or even internal drive bays for operating system installation. One reliable yet affordable strategy is a pair of 100-200 GB enterprise class SSDs that do not cannibalize the front panel drive bays you'll wish to fill with OSD and potentially journal drives. Any mirroring strategy of course is moot unless properly monitored so that a failing / failed mirror drive can be replaced before its partner fails.

Another concern when planning your operating system installation is the partitioning of the boot volume. With modern systems and memory capacities, traditional on-disk swap rarely makes sense any more, and is best not provisioned. Beyond that there are several strategies that vary by local taste and design goals.

Some admins prefer to provision all available space on the boot volume as a single root (/) filesystem. This has considerable appeal from the perspectives of simplicity and of efficient use—you'll never find the bulk of your free space in a different partition from where you need it.

Others prefer to split portions of the operating system filesystem tree across multiple partitions. This strategy helps fence off parts of the system from each other, limiting the potential for runaways to compromise the entire system. On an OSD server for example one might for example provision 50 GiB for the root filesystem, 200 GiB for /var/log, and the remainder for /home. On systems so laid out, incidental file storage by users is constrained and mistakes will not compromise the system's operation. Similarly, if something goes awry and rsyslogd experiences an elevated message volume, /var/log may fill up but other filesystems will be isolated, ensuring continued service. One may also wish to provision /tmp as a ramdisk, or as a dedicated partition, to ensure both that space is always available there when needed, and that a user inadvertently filling it up does not compromise other parts of the system.

On Ceph Monitor servers, /var/lib/ceph holds the ever-changing database files that house the variety of data that these daemons maintain. We really *really* do not want the heartburn of the ceph-mon daemon running out of space, so it may be highly desirable to partition off /var/lib/ceph to ensure that doesn't happen. During steady-state operation a Ceph MON only requires a handful of GiB of DB storage, a function to an extent of the size of the cluster. However during cluster expansion, component replacement, server maintenance, code upgrades, and other transient topology changes the MON DB may inflate for a time to tens of GiB. In order to ensure that such spikes in utilization do not fill the filesystem and thus cause the daemons massive grief, it is suggested to allot at least 100 GB for /var/lib/ceph on MON nodes. It is also very strongly urged that MON nodes provision SSD and not HDD storage. This author has suffered cluster-wide outages cascading from slow MON storage. The flexibility of partitioning means that one may even deploy separate drives for /var/log, /var/lib/ceph, and the operating system itself of varying sizes and speeds.

It is common to collect log files centrally, either through `syslog` mechanisms or tools like the **Elasticsearch, Logstash, and Kibana** (**ELK**) stack. There is significant value in centralized logging, but it it can also be valuable to retain logs local to each Ceph system. By default the `/etc/logrotate.d` components installed by Ceph retain logs for only seven days; I recommend increasing retention to at least 30 days. Even with compression, Ceph MON and OSD logs can be fairly large, especially when something goes wrong, so it is recommended to allocate at least several hundred MiB for `/var/log`.

Time synchronization

Ceph demands that back-end servers, especially the MONs, have closely synchronized clocks. Ceph warns if the MONs experience greater than 50ms of time skew among themselves, though with modern tools sub-millisecond accuracy is quite achievable. The venerable ntpd time daemon still works, though the newer and legacy-free chrony provides stronger syncing and better accuracy. One can sync against internal corporate time sources including GPS-source appliances or from public servers. It is strongly advised to provision multiple, diverse time sources; the daemons will pool them periodically and select the best to sync against. The more sources one configures, the more tolerant the system is of connectivity glitches and external sources coming and going.

Another note regarding time: configure all of your servers and shells to display time in UTC. While it can be somewhat awkward to mentally convert between UTC and your local timezone, it can be far more confusing if servers you have deployed across the country or around the world do not log timestamps that readily correlate with each other.

Much more about NTP (Network Time Protocol) configuration and servers may be found at `http://www.pool.ntp.org`

High quality time servers that serve thousands of clients may be sourced from companies including EndRun and Symmetricom. A novel, highly flexible appliance is also offered by NetBurner: `https://www.netburner.com/products/network-time-server/pk70-ex-ntp`

This small and inexpensive server can be placed almost anywhere the antenna can see the sky, including an office window. It can serve only a modest number of clients, but can be valuable to add source diversity to a configuration using unreliable public sources, or as a quality source for internal fanout servers.

There are lots of utilities and web sites to help convert among timezones, for example this author likes `https://www.worldtimebuddy.com`.

Packages

It is also suggested to work a rich set of utilities into your operating system installation. This can be accomplished via templates for provisioning tools like Ubuntu preseed and RHEL kickstart or by management systems like Puppet, Ansible, and Chef. Here's a list of packages that this author suggests; you may of course adjust to your own needs and preferences. The package names provided by your Linux distribution may vary, for example RHEL and CentOS provide emacs-nox vs the emacs24-nox that one selects on Ubuntu 14.04.

- Hardware management
    - lshw
    - lspci
    - lsscsi
    - pciutils
    - mcelog
    - ipmitool
    - HBA utils (perccli, storcli, hpssacli)
- System status and performance
    - atop
    - htop
    - iotop
    - dstat
    - iostat (sysstat)
- Editors (for example, emacs24-nox or mg or joe)
- Network utilities
    - subnetcalc also known as sipcalc
    - mtr
    - iperf
- Misc
    - jq
    - bc
    - facter
    - monkeytail also known as mtail

- `tmux`
- `fio`
- `chrony`
- `ntpdate`

Networking decisions

Recent releases of Ceph can work with either IPv4 or IPv6 addressing, but not both simultaneously. It is very common for the Ceph private aka replication network to be provisioned with non-routable IPs for example, RFC-1918 to conserve address space or increase privacy. While IPv6 is inarguably the best path into the future given the exhaustion of IPv4, many organizations have been slow to migrate. It is common to exploit the expansive `10.0.0.0` RFC-1918 network internally for systems that do not need to be reached from the Internet at large. This is one way that organizations have put off the difficult transition to IPv6. The choice for your deployment will likely be out of your hands, but it should be considered.

In `Chapter 3`, *Hardware and Network Selection*, we discussed networking strategies for Ceph clusters. When devising a bonding strategy you will need to work with your network team, but we'll offer some guidance. With any networking topology it is highly advised to configure Jumbo frames across the board for performance.

Ceph can use a single network for public (MONs and clients) and private (inter-OSD replication) traffic, though it is common to segregate these into separate physical or virtual networks. If a cluster (private) network is not defined, Ceph uses the public network for all traffic.

The authors' deployments currently enjoy dual 40 Mbit links for each network, though many installations will find that cost-effective bonded 10 Mbit links suffice. Emerging 25 Mbit strategies show considerable promise for both cost and flexibility as well. For production deployments with any scale at all 1 Mbit networks are likely to quickly become bottlenecks and are not recommended. If financial or infrastructure constraints limit your network architecture, if bandwidth must be unequal between the two it is usually better to devote more to the private replication network than to the public / client network. Since the replication network need not and indeed should not be routable or have external reachability, it may be less expensive to provision as uplinks and core switch/router ports need not be allocated.

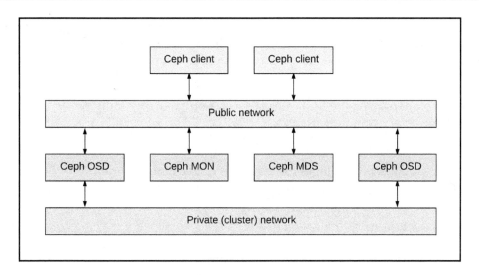

It is also recommended to provision dual switch and cabling paths so that each network enjoys both increased capacity and fault tolerance. For example, each Ceph OSD node may provision two dual port NICs, with the public and private bonds straddling each so that even total failure of one NIC does not result in an outage for the OSDs on the affected server. Naturally NIC ports bonded in this fashion are best cabled through dual parallel ToR switches or other redundant network infrastructure.

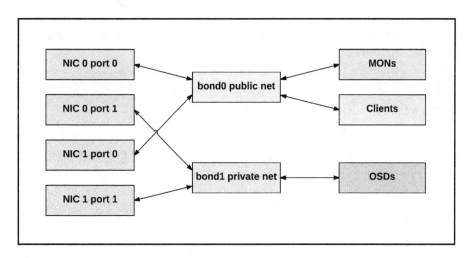

An active/active bonding strategy has advantages over an active/passive approach. Systems can exploit increased aggregate bandwidth and disruption is minimized if one link in the pair goes down. It is also advised to configure miimon link monitoring, say at 100 ms.

Ceph deployments used only for block storage services have no need for network load balancers. When deploying the RGW object service provisioning multiple servers behind a load balancer is a very common strategy:

- Workload is distributed among servers
- Individual server outages are transparent to clients
- Clients are insulated from the potentially dynamic set of RGW servers, which facilitates scaling and maintenance.
- Network security

There are multiple types of network load balancing

- Software for example, haproxy, nginx, Envoy
- Hardware appliances from companies like F5 and Cisco
- **Load Balancers as a Service** (**LBaaS**) available on cloud platforms including OpenStack and Digital Ocean

If you need network load balancers for capacity and fault tolerance, your choice will be informed by your use-case as well as practices within your organization. Software load balancing with haproxy is popular, flexible, and straightforward to configure, though as traffic grows the greater throughput capacity of hardware appliances may become attractive.

Summary

In this chapter we've explored a long list of factors and decisions to consider when planning your Ceph clusters. The lure of diving right in with purchase orders and deployments is strong, but we must stress the benefits of careful planning in advance so that you implement the right architecture for performance, reliability, scalability, and flexibility.

In the next chapter we'll deploy a real, working Ceph cluster in virtual machines. This sandbox will help you get a feel for the dynamics of a Ceph deployment and help practice a number of deployment and maintenance operations without committing to expensive and time-consuming physical server provisioning.

5
Deploying a Virtual Sandbox Cluster

In this chapter, we will explore the process of setting up a Ceph cluster in our sandbox environment. The following topics will be covered:

- Installing prerequisites for our sandbox environment
- Bootstrapping our Ceph Cluster
- Deploying our Ceph Cluster
- Scaling our Ceph Cluster

Sandbox environment will contain a set of virtual machines within which we will install and run our Ceph processes. In order to set up this environment we first need to install the necessary prerequisites on our system, including Vagrant, Git, Ansible, and VirtualBox. We will guide you through the installation of those prerequisites step-by-step before we bootstrap Ceph on your machine.

The virtual machines we will provision for running a Ceph cluster will be managed via HashiCorp's Vagrant (`https://www.vagrantup.com/`). Vagrant allows us to provision virtual instances and deploy custom configurations to those instances with minimal changes. It presents a provider interface that is pluggable and integrates with a wide-range of virtualization products. Recent versions have included support for Oracle VM VirtualBox, VMware, KVM, and even cloud providers including Amazon EC2 and DigitalOcean.

In this chapter, we will set up Vagrant with Oracle VirtualBox. VirtualBox is free software, available at `http://www.virtualbox.org`, that can be installed on Microsoft Windows, macOS X, and Linux. We must fulfill system requirements for VirtualBox so that it can run properly during our testing. Our virtual cluster's performance will be limited by the system resources (CPU, memory, disk) that the underlying physical host machine can provide. Our sandbox however will exhibit the full functional capabilities of a Ceph cluster matching the real-world deployments.

Installing prerequisites for our Sandbox environment

Before setting up our virtual instances and provisioning them with Ceph, we need to cover a few points. All the software we will be using is open source, with the release versions used in our testing specified later. The authors developed and tested this process on macOS X 10.12. It should also work on macOS X 10.9 or later and on Linux systems.

For Microsoft Windows, host machines should use an absolute path to invoke the VBoxManage command, which is usually found at `C:\Program Files\Oracle\ VirtualBox\VBoxManage.exe`.

The system requirements for VirtualBox depend upon the number and configuration of virtual machines running on top of it. Your VirtualBox host should offer an x86-type processor (Intel or AMD), a few gigabytes of memory (to run four to seven Ceph virtual machines), several gigabytes of drive space, and an internet connection. First, we must download VirtualBox from `http://www.virtualbox.org/`, open the archive file, then follow the installation procedure. The VirtualBox version we used when writing this chapter is shown below:

```
$ VBoxManage --version
5.1.18r114002
```

> Software behavior does change between versions and we can't predict how these instructions will interact with versions released after we write. We want you to experience a trouble-free Ceph deployment, which is why we suggest exact versions, even though they won't be the latest available as you read.
> This version of VirtualBox can be downloaded at `https://www. virtualbox.org/wiki/Download_Old_Builds_5_1`.

In order to use the VirtualBox provider, we now need to install Vagrant. Vagrant lets us create a custom configuration for all types of Ceph processes and allows us to specify and fine-tune the complete setup. This configuration is stored in a single file that simplifies the management of our virtual instances. We can specify options in this file including how many instances of each type we want to run, how many and which system resources should be allocated to them, which guest operating system should be installed on them, and even the OS kernel tuning parameters we want to set. Vagrant can be downloaded from `https://www.vagrantup.com/`and is available for macOS X, Linux and Windows. The latest version of Vagrant that we tested for the setup of our sandbox environment is as follows:

```
$ vagrant --version
Vagrant 1.9.3
```

> This version of Vagrant can be downloaded from
> `https://releases.hashicorp.com/vagrant/1.9.3/`

Vagrant and VirtualBox will be used for installing and starting virtual machines. Once we have those running we will need to install Ceph on them, and configure them properly to ensure Ceph processes start correctly, assume their designated responsibilities, and communicate with the rest of the processes in the cluster. We will use `ceph-ansible` (`https://github.com/ceph/ceph-ansible`) to bootstrap a complete Ceph cluster on our virtual machines. Ceph-ansible is a community-driven management system that automates Ceph deployments for both testing and production. We will use the very same mechanism designed for production deployments to install a Ceph cluster in our sandbox environment.

One prerequisite of ceph-ansible is installing Ansible itself on our host system. Ansible (`https://www.ansible.com/`) is an open-source configuration management system that is used to automate software provisioning and automate deployment. Ansible uses ssh to deploy resources from a control machine to client nodes. We write Ansible playbooks in the popular YAML format, which contains instructions for installing and configuring the desired resources. An inventory file is populated from which the control machine knows the set of nodes to be managed along with their characteristics. Experience with Ansible is not a requirement for setting up a Ceph cluster in a sandbox environment, though its popularity is growing and you may find it valuable to explore it later on your own. The Ansible version we used to set up our sandbox environment is as follows:

```
$ ansible --version
ansible 2.2.2.0
```

Follow the download and installation instructions found at `https://www.ansible.com`. You may need to first install `pip`. On Mac OS X you may also need to download Apple's Xcode from `https://developer.apple.com/xcode/` in order to install `gcc`.

> This version of Ansible may be installed with the command:
> `$ pip install ansible==2.2.2.0`
> If the `pip` install of Ansible gives you a `configure: error: C compiler cannot create executables` message.
> Ensure that you install Xcode from `https://developer.apple.com/xcode/downloads` then
> `$ sudo gcc`
> View and accept the license agreement:
> Run the `pip` command above again

And finally in order to ensure that we download and use the proper version of `ceph-ansible`, we will install git if you do not already have it installed.

```
$ git --version
git version 2.9.3 (Apple Git-75)
```

Git is one of the most commonly used revision control systems and is designed for distributed and non-linear workflows. It enables us to select a specific version of a remote code repository and can revert the state of all files within that repository to a specific point in time. Git is open source and available for download at `https://git-scm.com/`. There is no specific version requirement here for git, although downloading the latest is recommended.

Now that we have covered all the necessary dependencies, we will proceed to install `ceph-ansible` and setup a sandbox environment on your machine.

Bootstrapping our Ceph cluster

The first step is to download the latest copy of `ceph-ansible` on to your machine. It is important to note that all changes we will make to bootstrap a Ceph cluster will be made from within a dedicated directory so use `cd` to move to the appropriate location before downloading. The following command will download `ceph-ansible` within a new directory called `ceph-ansible` in your current directory:

```
$ git clone https://github.com/ceph/ceph-ansible.git ceph-ansible
```

If you want your directory name to be something other than `ceph-ansible` change the text of the last field in the above command. As all future changes and commands will be performed from within this directory we need to `cd` into it:

```
$ cd ceph-ansible
```

Now we are in the `ceph-ansible` directory. This directory holds the code for all Ansible playbooks that will be used to configure and install Ceph. The Ceph community is actively doing development on this repository so the very latest state may be unstable or incorporate incompatible changes and thus might not be ideal to work from. Fortunately git provides us with the ability to go back to a stable state at a time when we know the deployment mechanism worked as expected. We will use that ability here to revert:

```
$ git checkout v2.2.0
```

The v2.2.0 is called a git tag. We won't discuss git tags in detail since those are beyond the scope of this book, but basically the above command rolls back to version 2.2.0 of this repository. Using git tags we can move to any checkpoint that has been tagged by the repository maintainers.

Once we have the dependencies installed, we are ready to create the virtual machines that will run Ceph. The steps to build and get the virtual machines running should be performed from the `ceph-ansible` directory we created above.

The `ceph-ansible` repository contains various types of configuration files. They contain Ansible-specific configuration files and also vagrant-specific files. The repository also consists of samples that are conveniently present to aid cluster deployment. For this chapter, we will modify those sample files for setting our local sandbox environment, but they can also be modified in order to deploy a cluster in a production environment.

We will customize the following sample files for sandbox deployment:

- `vagrant_variables.yml.sample`: This file presents a sample of configuration options that ought to be supplied to `Vagrantfile`. The vagrant command uses the instructions from `Vagrantfile` to describe the types of virtual machine that need to be built and the actions to provision them.

- `site.yml.sample`: This represents a set of sample Ansible tasks as a part of main Ansible playbook. The vagrant provisioner that runs after you start all the virtual machines is tasked with the responsibility of running this playbook. This playbook is responsible for completing the final step of bringing the Ceph cluster up.

- `group_vars/all.yml.sample`: The all `.yml.sample` present within `group_vars/` directory contains an Ansible-specific configuration that applies to all virtual machine hostgroups. These variables will be consumed by the Ansible playbook when the vagrant provisioner runs it.

We will start with setting vagrant-specific configuration options first before we move on to customize the parameters for Ansible playbook.

Copy `vagrant_variables.yml.sample` to `vagrant_variables.yml` by running the following command:

```
$ cp vagrant_variables.yml.sample vagrant_variables.yml
```

Open `vagrant_variables.yml` in your favorite text editor and change the following variables to the values shown below:

```
mon_vms: 1 # A single monitor node is sufficient for now
osd_vms: 3
mds_vms: 0
rgw_vms: 0
nfs_vms: 0
rbd_mirror_vms: 0
client_vms: 1 # A client node to run CLI commands on the cluster
iscsi_gw_vms: 0
mgr_vms: 0
```

The changes indicate that we will create one virtual machine that will run Ceph monitor daemon, three that will run one or more OSD processes, and one for running clients. Throughout this chapter, we will revisit this file multiple times as this is how we control the number of VMs that comprise our running Ceph cluster. Once we are done with the initial Ceph cluster build we will use this file to scale the cluster up (or down) as appropriate.

Via `vagrant_variables.yml` we can also control the Linux distribution that will get installed on our Ceph virtual machines. The default is Ubuntu Xenial 16.04 as denoted by `ceph/ubuntu-xenial`.

The vagrant box provided in the sample `vagrant_variables.yml` file should be sufficient for, as here, installing a Ceph cluster, so for this exercise we will stick to its defaults.

The next step is to create a copy of Ansible's main playbook named `site.yml.sample` into `site.yml`:

```
$ cp site.yml.sample site.yml
```

We do not need to change the contents of this file for our exercise. The default parameters translate over to provisioning a Ceph cluster within the sandbox environment.

We then copy the sample hostgroup variables file to one with a proper name:

```
$ cp group_vars/all.yml.sample group_vars/all.yml
```

The hostgroup variables control the version of Ceph that will be installed on the nodes. We will need to change the configuration options in the newly created file to instruct Ansible where to find the Ceph packages we need to download. We presently recommend downloading Ceph packages in the way that the Ceph team recommends: by retrieving them from their official mirror at https://download.ceph.com/.

Open the newly created file named group_vars/all.yml in your favorite text editor and uncomment the following line:

```
#ceph_origin: 'upstream' # or 'distro' or 'local'
```

Since this is a YAML file, we uncomment this line by removing the # symbol in the first column. Our changed line should now look like:

```
ceph_origin: 'upstream' # or 'distro' or 'local'
```

This will assign the upstream value to the ceph_origin variable. The remainder of that line will be ignored since the # and any following characters will be treated as a comment.

The upstream value instructs the Ceph provisioner to download Ceph binaries and packages from an online source rather than looking for them locally. If you have downloaded Ceph packages separately or wish to use those provided by a Linux distribution and are aware of how Ansible works you can change this option to distro or local. Doing so however is an advanced topic beyond the scope of this chapter, and you'd be on your own.

Once we update the ceph_origin line, we also need to inform the provisioner where to find the packages we wish to use. We accomplish this by uncommenting the following lines in your group_vars/all.yml file below the line that says # COMMUNITY VERSION:

Here's how the unmodified section of this file looks out-of-the-box:

```
# STABLE
########

# COMMUNITY VERSION
#ceph_stable: false # use ceph stable branch
#ceph_mirror: http://download.ceph.com
```

```
#ceph_stable_key: https://download.ceph.com/keys/release.asc
#ceph_stable_release: kraken # ceph stable release
#ceph_stable_repo: "{{ ceph_mirror }}/debian-{{ ceph_stable_release }}"
```

Uncomment the five lines under COMMUNITY VERSION deleting the initial # character. We will also need to update the settings of ceph_stable to true and ceph_stable_release to jewel as we want to spin up a cluster using a stable version of the LTS Jewel release. As we write Luminous is still in development, but as you read this it will have reached general availability. You may experiment later with selecting Luminous here, but we suggest starting with a Jewel deployment. These lines in group_vars/all.yml should now look like this:

```
# STABLE
########
# COMMUNITY VERSION
ceph_stable: true # use ceph stable branch
ceph_mirror: http://download.ceph.com
ceph_stable_key: https://download.ceph.com/keys/release.asc
ceph_stable_release: jewel # ceph stable release
ceph_stable_repo: "{{ ceph_mirror }}/debian-{{
ceph_stable_release }}"
```

Save this file and exit your editor. Next we will proceed to create virtual machines and provision Ceph cluster up.

Deploying our Ceph cluster

So far we have downloaded and installed all the necessary dependencies and updated the necessary configuration files in order to prepare for Ceph deployment. In this section, we will make use of all of the work we did previously to finally deploy a Ceph cluster in the sandbox environment.

This proceeds in two phases:

The first phase will use Vagrant to create the virtual machines. Based on the modifications we did to the vagrant_variables.yml file at the end of this step we should see a total of five virtual machines created: 1 for Ceph monitor, 3 for Ceph OSDs, and 1 for the client.

```
$ vagrant up --no-provision --provider=virtualbox
```

This instructs vagrant to create the CPU, memory, and storage resources for each virtual machine and boot the machine up. It will use VirtualBox as a provider since we have it already installed on our machines. We are passing the `--no-provision` command-line flag to ensure that we do not provision each node with Ansible as soon as it comes up. The provisioning process needs all the nodes in the cluster to be active before running and hence we do that as a last step once we have all the VMs up and reachable from each other.

Vagrant may take quite a while to create and allocate resources to each virtual machine, depending on the resources available on your host. The Vagrant workflow creates virtual machines serially so we have to wait for each to complete booting.

If you see this message:

```
client0: /vagrant => /Users/aad/ceph-ansible
Vagrant was unable to mount VirtualBox shared folders.
This is usually because the filesystem vboxsf is not
available. This filesystem is made available via the
VirtualBox Guest additions and kernel module. Please
verify that these guest additions are properly installed
in the guest. This is not a bug in Vagrant and is usually
caused by a faulty Vagrant box. For context, the command
attempted was:
mount -t vboxsf -o uid=1000,gid=1000 vagrant /vagrant
```

Install the `vagrant-vbguest` plugin and try again:

```
bash-3.2$ sudo vagrant plugin install vagrant-vbguest
Password:
Installing the 'vagrant-vbguest' plugin. This can take a
few minutes...
Fetching: vagrant-share-1.1.9.gem (100%)
Fetching: micromachine-2.0.0.gem (100%)
Fetching: vagrant-vbguest-0.14.2.gem (100%)
Installed the plugin 'vagrant-vbguest (0.14.2)'!
When using a 64-bit OS image (such as Ubuntu Xenial
16.04) ensure that the host CPU supports hardware
virtualization, which VirtualBox requires for booting the
guest virtual machine properly. If it doesn't, you might
see the prompt stuck at "SSH-ing into a VM".
```

If hardware virtualization is disabled by default, you may need to enable it in BIOS. All modern CPUs support hardware virtualization natively. Intel calls it **VT-x** and AMD calls the BIOS option **AMD-V**.

If your processor is older (as old as, or older than, the Intel Celeron or AMD Opteron) you might need to choose a 32-bit OS image in order to successfully boot the necessary virtual machines.

When the `vagrant up` command finishes running we should have all the necessary virtual machines up-and-running. This can be verified by running a status check as below:

```
$ vagrant status
```

We should see 5 virtual machines created with the following names. Their order is not important:

```
mon0 running     (virtualbox)
osd0 running     (virtualbox)
osd1 running     (virtualbox)
osd2 running     (virtualbox)
client0 running (virtualbox)
```

After confirming we have all the virtual machines running we're ready for the second phase: install Ceph packages and bring up our cluster.

```
$ vagrant provision
```

This will run through the Ansible plays and create Ceph daemons respectively on each given machine. This will also take a while. Once this process completes we should have a Ceph cluster deployed and running on our hands.

We can verify that the cluster is installed and healthy by logging into the client host and running the ceph status command:

```
$ vagrant ssh client0
vagrant@ceph-client0:~$ sudo ceph status
    cluster 27af531f-31db-4eb9-a3e1-9e7592d2fec7
     health HEALTH_OK
     monmap e1: 1 mons at {ceph-mon0=192.168.42.10:6789/0}
            election epoch 4, quorum 0 ceph-mon0
     osdmap e33: 6 osds: 6 up, 6 in
            flags sortbitwise,require_jewel_osds
      pgmap v86: 64 pgs, 1 pools, 0 bytes data, 0 objects
            202 MB used, 65131 MB / 65333 MB avail
                  64 active+clean
```

In later chapters we'll explore in detail what this command is telling us; for now note that the health value is HEALTH_OK.

Scaling our Ceph cluster

Now that we have a working Ceph cluster at our disposal we can do all manner of cool things with it. We can add new OSD or mon nodes—or remove existing ones. We can add multiple clients and test performing simultaneous operations against the cluster. We can also add different types of daemons as separate VMs. In short, we can scale the cluster up or scale it down at will. In this section, we will show how easy it is to manipulate the cluster using variables in our configuration files.

Let's revisit the `vagrant_variables.yml` file that we previously edited to adjust the number of nodes before bootstrapping our cluster. We will tweak the numbers in this file to scale as we wish. Open this file in your favorite editor. Before making changes the variables reflecting your existing nodes should look like this:

```
mon_vms:  1
osd_vms:  3
mds_vms:  0
rgw_vms:  0
rbd_mirror_vms:  0
client_vms:  1
iscsi_gw_vms:  0
mgr_vms:  0
```

We know that one instance of a mon node is a single point of failure and thus that when that node does fail the cluster will be unmanageable and eventually will stop working altogether. In order to avoid loss of service, we should have at least 3 mon nodes in our cluster.

Why do we choose 3?

The odd number of mon nodes is necessary in order to break ties when electing a leader

- 5 mon nodes would be overkill for such a small proof-of-concept cluster
- Your host system's available resources may be limited
- As the number of mon nodes grows, the resources they consume grows non-linearly

In a real-world production, many smaller clusters provision 3 mons and the authors successfully run multi-petabyte clusters with 5 mon nodes.

Edit the number of mon nodes to 3 so that the changed variables are thus:

```
mon_vms: 3
osd_vms: 3
mds_vms: 0
rgw_vms: 0
nfs_vms: 0
rbd_mirror_vms: 0
client_vms: 1
iscsi_gw_vms: 0
mgr_vms: 0
```

Now that we have updated the `vagrant_variables.yml` file, we should run the `vagrant` command again to bring up the additional 2 VMs that will run the 2 new mon daemons:

```
$ vagrant up --no-provision --provider=virtualbox
```

When this command completes, we should have a total of 7 VM's running. We can confirm that this is the case:

```
$ vagrant status | grep running
client0                 running (virtualbox)
mon0                    running (virtualbox)
mon1                    running (virtualbox)
mon2                    running (virtualbox)
osd0                    running (virtualbox)
osd1                    running (virtualbox)
osd2                    running (virtualbox)
```

The 2 new mon nodes that we just spun up do not yet have Ceph provisioned on them and the cluster will not be aware of them until we configure and start the monitor daemons on them. Starting monitor daemons is as simple as provisioning those nodes. We will use the same command that we used earlier to provision the whole cluster to also provision these additional 2 nodes:

```
$ vagrant provision
```

Once the provisioner completes we should see the two newly created mon nodes in the cluster. We can confirm this by logging into the client and checking the latest *status* of the cluster:

```
vagrant@ceph-client0:~$ sudo ceph status
    cluster 27af531f-31db-4eb9-a3e1-9e7592d2fec7
     health HEALTH_OK
     monmap e3: 3 mons at {ceph-mon0=192.168.42.10:6789/0,ceph-
mon1=192.168.42.11:6789/0,ceph-mon2=192.168.42.12:6789/0}
            election epoch 10, quorum 0,1,2 ceph-mon0,ceph-
            mon1,ceph-mon2
     osdmap e33: 6 osds: 6 up, 6 in
            flags sortbitwise,require_jewel_osds
      pgmap v86: 64 pgs, 1 pools, 0 bytes data, 0 objects
            202 MB used, 65131 MB / 65333 MB avail
                   64 active+clean
```

Summary

In this chapter, we brought up a functioning Ceph cluster from scratch and incrementally scaled it without taking it down. We leveraged the popular open source tools Vagrant and VirtualBox to help model a real Ceph cluster. In the next chapter, we'll explore a number of operations we can perform to customize, populate, and manage Ceph clusters.

6
Operations and Maintenance

In this chapter, we explore the panoply of day-to-day tasks for maintaining your Ceph clusters. The topics covered include:

- Topology
- Configuration
- Common tasks
- Scrubs
- Logs
- Working with remote hands

We'll cover a lot of ground in this chapter. Be sure to take periodic breaks to refuel with garlic fries.

Topology

In this section, we'll describe commands to explore the logical layout of an example Ceph cluster. Before we go changing anything, we need to know exactly what we have first.

The 40,000 foot view

To visually see the overall topology of a Ceph cluster, run `ceph osd tree`. This will show us at once the hierarchy of CRUSH buckets, including the name of each bucket, the weight, whether it is marked up or down, a weight adjustment, and an advanced attribute of `primary affinity`. This cluster was provisioned initially with 3 racks each housing 4 hosts for a total of 12 OSD nodes. Each OSD node (also known as host, also known as server) in turn houses 24 OSD drives.

```
# ceph osd tree
ID    WEIGHT    TYPE NAME            UP/DOWN REWEIGHT PRIMARY-AFFINITY
 -1 974.89661 root default
-14 330.76886     rack r1
 -2  83.56099         host data001
  0   3.48199             osd.0       up  1.00000        1.00000
...
 23   3.48199             osd.23      up  1.00000        1.00000
 -3  80.08588         host data002
 24   3.48199             osd.24      up  1.00000        1.00000
 25   3.48199             osd.25      up  1.00000        1.00000
 26   3.48199             osd.26      up  1.00000        1.00000
 27   3.48199             osd.27      up  1.00000        1.00000
 28   3.48199             osd.28      up  1.00000        1.00000
 29   3.48199             osd.29      up  1.00000        1.00000
 30   3.48199             osd.30      up  1.00000        1.00000
 31   3.48199             osd.31      up  1.00000        1.00000
 32   3.48199             osd.32      up  1.00000        1.00000
 34   3.48199             osd.34      up  1.00000        1.00000
 35   3.48199             osd.35      up  1.00000        1.00000
 36   3.48199             osd.36      up  1.00000        1.00000
 37   3.48199             osd.37      up  1.00000        1.00000
 38   3.48199             osd.38      up  1.00000        1.00000
 39   3.48199             osd.39    down        0        1.00000
 40   3.48199             osd.40      up  1.00000        1.00000
 41   3.48199             osd.41      up  1.00000        1.00000
 42   3.48199             osd.42      up  1.00000        1.00000
 43   3.48199             osd.43      up  1.00000        1.00000
 44   3.48199             osd.44      up  1.00000        1.00000
 45   3.48199             osd.45      up  1.00000        1.00000
 46   3.48199             osd.46      up  1.00000        1.00000
 47   3.48199             osd.47      up  1.00000        1.00000
 -4  83.56099         host data003
 48   3.48199             osd.48      up  1.00000        1.00000
...
 -5  83.56099         host data004
 72   3.48199             osd.72      up  1.00000        1.00000
...
```

```
  95    3.48199              osd.95      up  1.00000           1.00000
 -15 330.76810       rack r2
  -6  83.56099           host data005
  96    3.48199              osd.96      up  1.00000           1.00000
  . . .
  -7  80.08557           host data006
 120    3.48199              osd.120     up  1.00000           1.00000
  . . .
  -8  83.56055           host data007
  33    3.48169              osd.33      up  1.00000           1.00000
 144    3.48169              osd.144     up  1.00000           1.00000
  . . .
 232    3.48169              osd.232     up  1.00000           1.00000
  -9  83.56099        host data008
 168    3.48199              osd.168     up  1.00000           1.00000
 -16 313.35965       rack r3
 -10  83.56099           host data009
 192    3.48199              osd.192     up  1.00000           1.00000
  . . .
 -11  69.63379           host data010
 133    3.48169              osd.133     up  1.00000           1.00000
  . . .
 -12  83.56099           host data011
 239    3.48199              osd.239     up  1.00000           1.00000
  . . .
 -13  76.60388           host data012
  . . .
 286    3.48199              osd.286     up  1.00000           1.00000
```

Let's go over what this tree is telling us. Note that a number of similar lines have been replaced with ellipses for brevity, a practice we will continue throughout this and following chapters.

After the column headers the first data line is:

```
-1 974.89661 root default
```

The first column is an ID number that Ceph uses internally, and with which we rarely need to concern ourselves. The second column under the WEIGHT heading is the *CRUSH weight*. By default, the CRUSH weight of any bucket corresponds to its raw capacity in TB; in this case we have a bit shy of a **petabyte (PB)** of raw space. We'll see that this weight is the sum of the weights of the buckets under the root in the tree.

Since this cluster utilizes the conventional replication factor of 3, roughly 324 TB of usable space is currently available in this cluster. The balance of the line is `root default`, which tells us that this CRUSH bucket is of the `root` type, and that it's name is `default`. Complex Ceph clusters can contain multiple roots, but most need only one. We'll explore these ideas in greater depth in `Chapter 8`, *Ceph Architecture: Under the Hood*.

The next line is as follows:

```
-14 330.76886      rack r1
```

It shows a bucket of type rack, with a weight of roughly 330 TB. Skipping ahead a bit we see two more rack buckets with weights 330 and 313 each. Their sum gets us to the roughly 974 TB capacity (weight) of the root bucket. When the rack weights are not equal, as in our example, usually either they contain different numbers of host buckets (or simply *hosts*), or more often their underlying hosts have unequal weights.

Next we see the following:

```
-2  83.56099          host data001
```

This indicates a bucket of type `host`, with the name `data001`. As with `root` and `rack` buckets, the weight reflects the raw capacity (before replication) of the underlying buckets in the hierarchy. Below `rack1` in our hierarchy we see hosts named `data001`, `data002`, `data003`, and `data004`. In our example, we see that host `data002` presents a somewhat lower weight than the other three racks. This may mean that a mixture of drive sizes has been deployed or that some drives were missed during initial deployment. In our example, though, the host only contains 23 OSD buckets (or simply OSDs) instead of the expected 24. This reflects a drive that has failed and been removed entirely, or one that was not deployed in the first place.

Under each `host` bucket we see a number of OSD entries.

```
24 3.48199 osd.24 up 1.00000 1.00000
```

In our example, these drives are SAS SSDs each nominally 3840 GB in size, which in `Chapter 2`, *Ceph Components and Services*, we describe as the *marketing* capacity. The discrepancy between that figure and the 3.48199 TB weight presented here is due to multiple factors:

- The marketing capacity is expressed in base 10 units; everything else uses base 2 units
- Each drive carves out 10 GB for journal use
- XFS filesystem overhead

Note also that one OSD under `data002` is marked down. This could be a question of the process having been killed or a hardware failure. The CRUSH weight is unchanged, but the weight adjustment is set to 0, which means that data previously allocated to this drive has been directed elsewhere. When we restart the OSD process successfully, the weight adjustment returns to one and data backfills to the drive.

Note also that while many Ceph commands will present OSDs and other items sorted, the IDs (or names) of OSDs on a given host or rack are a function of the cluster's history. When deployed sequentially the numbers will increment neatly, but over time as OSDs and hosts are added and removed discontinuities will accrue. In the above example, note that OSD 33 (also known as `osd.33`) currently lives on host `data007` instead of data002 as one might expect from the present pattern. This reflects the sequence of events:

- Drive failed on `data002` and was removed
- Drive failed on `data007` and was removed
- The replacement drive on `data007` was deployed as a new OSD

When deploying OSDs, Ceph generally picks the lowest unused number; in our case that was 33. It is futile to try to maintain any given OSD number arrangement; it will change over time as drives and host come and go, and the cluster is expanded.

A number of Ceph status commands accept an optional `-f json` or `-fjson -pretty` switch, which results in output in a form less readable by humans, but more readily parsed by code. The format of default format commands may change between releases, but the JSON output formats are mostly constant. For this reason management and monitoring scripts are encouraged to use the `-f json` output format to ensure continued proper operation when Ceph itself is upgraded.

```
# ceph osd tree -f json
{"nodes":[{"id":-1,"name":"default","type":"root","type_id":10,"children":[
-16,-15,-14]},{"id":-14,"name":"r1","type":"rack","type_id":3,"children":[-
5,-4,-3,-2]},{"id":-2,"name":"data001","type":"host","type_id":1,"children"
:
[23,22,21,20,19,18,17,16,15,14,13,12,11,10,9,8,7,6,5,4,3,2,1,0]},{"id":0,"n
ame":"osd.0","type":"osd","type_id":0,"crush_weight":3.481995,"depth":3,"ex
ists":1,"status":"up","reweight":1.000000,"primary_affinity":1.000000},{"id
":1,"name":"osd
.1","type":"osd","type_id":0,"crush_weight":3.481995,"depth":3,"exists":1,"
status":"up","reweight":1.000000,"primary_affinity":1.000000},{"id":2,"name
":"osd.2","type":"osd","type_id":0,"crush_weight":3.481995,"depth":3,"exist
s":1,"status":"
up","reweight":1.000000,"primary_affinity":1.000000},{"id":3,"name":"osd.3"
,"type":"osd","type_id":0,"crush_weight":3.481995,"depth":3,"exists":1,"sta
tus":"up","reweight":1.000000,"primary_affinity":1.000000},{"id":4,"name":"
```

```
osd.4","type":"
    ...
```

The `-f json-pretty` output format is something of a compromise: it includes structure to aid programmatic parsing, but also uses whitespace to allow humans to readily inspect visually.

```
# ceph osd tree -f json-pretty
{
    "nodes": [
        {
            "id": -1,
            "name": "default",
            "type": "root",
            "type_id": 10,
            "children": [
                -16,
                -15,
                -14
            ]
        },
        {
            "id": -14,
            "name": "1",
            "type": "rack",
            "type_id": 3,
            "children": [
                -5,
                -4,
                -3,
                -2
            ]
        },
        {
            "id": -2,
            "name": "data001",
            "type": "host",
            "type_id": 1,
            "children": [
                23,
                22,
                21,
                ...
```

One may for example extract a list of OSDs that have a non-default reweight adjustment value, using the `jq` utility that we mentioned in Chapter 4, *Planning Your Deployment*. This approach saves a lot of tedious and error-prone coding with `awk` or `perl`.

```
# ceph osd tree -f json | jq \
  '.nodes[]|select(.type=="osd")|select(.reweight != 1)|.id'
11
66
```

Some commands in Ceph that show a detailed status emit hundreds or thousands of lines of output. It is strongly suggested you to enable unlimited scroll back in your terminal application and to pipe such commands through a pager, for example, `less`.

 iTerm2 is a free package for macOS that offers a wealth of features not found in Apple's bundled Terminal.app. It can be downloaded from `https://www.iterm2.com/`.

Drilling down

Next we'll explore a number of commands that can help us collect specific information about the logical units within our topology.

OSD dump

The ceph osd dump command shows a wealth of lower-level information about our clusters. This includes a list of pools with their attributes and a list of OSDs each including reweight adjustment, up/in status, and more. This command is mostly used in unusual troubleshooting situations.

```
# ceph osd dump | head
epoch 33291
fsid 3369c9c6-bfaf-4114-9c31-ncc17014d0fe
created 2017-09-06 20:21:06.448220
modified 2017-09-17 21:38:44.530321
flags sortbitwise,require_jewel_osds
pool 1 'rbd' replicated size 3 min_size 2 crush_ruleset 0 object_hash
rjenkins pg_num 16384 pgp_num 16384 last_change 31616 flags
hashpspool,nodelete,nopgchange,nosizechange stripe_width 0
        removed_snaps [1~3]
max_osd 287
  osd.0 up   in   weight 1 up_from 31886 up_thru 33113 down_at 31884
last_clean_interval [4,31884) 10.8.45.15:6800/116320
```

```
10.24.49.15:6828/1116320 10.24.49.15:6829/1116320 10.8.45.15:6829/1116
    320 exists,up 34a68621-b8dc-4c3a-b47e-26acaacfc838
    osd.1 up   in  weight 1 up_from 8 up_thru 33108 down_at 0
last_clean_interval [0,0) 10.8.45.15:6802/117132 10.24.49.15:6802/117132
10.24.49.15:6803/117132 10.8.45.15:6803/117132 exists,up
f5a3a635-4058-4499-99af-1b340192e321
    . . .
```

OSD list

The ceph osd ls command simply returns a list of the OSD numbers currently deployed within the cluster.

```
# ceph osd ls | head -3
0
1
2
# ceph osd ls |wc
    280     280     1010
#
```

This information could be derived by processing the output of ceph osd tree, but this is a convenient way to drive all in a single command

OSD find

To locate the host on which a given OSD lives, the ceph osd find command is invaluable.

```
# ceph osd find 66 { "osd": 66, "ip": "10.8.45.17:6836\/130331",
"crush_location": { "host": "data003", "rack": "r1", "root": "default" } }
```

This is especially useful when monitoring detects that an OSD is down; the first step is typically to locate the host that houses it so that one may check it out, for example, by inspecting Ceph OSD and syslog files. In older Ceph releases, this command omitted the last newline, which was a bit awkward. As of the Ceph Jewel release this has been fixed.

CRUSH dump

This command presents much the same information as ceph osd tree, though in a different, JSON, format. Note a peek into the additional bucket types that Ceph predefines for large and complex deployments. As before many of the 2899 lines of output this command yielded on the author's reference cluster are cropped for brevity.

```
# ceph osd crush dump | more
{
    "devices": [
        {
            "id": 0,
            "name": "osd.0"
        },
        {
            "id": 1,
            "name": "osd.1"
        },
        ...
        {
            "id": 286,
            "name": "osd.286"
        }
    ],
    "types": [
        {
            "type_id": 0,
            "name": "osd"
        },
        {
            "type_id": 1,
            "name": "host"
        },
        {
            "type_id": 2,
            "name": "chassis"
        },
        {
            "type_id": 3,
            "name": "rack"
        },
        {
            "type_id": 4,
            "name": "row"
        },
        {
            "type_id": 5,
            "name": "pdu"
```

```
        },
        {
            "type_id": 6,
            "name": "pod"
        },
        {
            "type_id": 7,
            "name": "room"
        },
        {
            "type_id": 8,
            "name": "datacenter"
        },
        {
            "type_id": 9,
            "name": "region"
        },
        {
            "type_id": 10,
            "name": "root"
        }
    ],
    "buckets": [
        {
            "id": -1,
            "name": "default",
            "type_id": 10,
            "type_name": "root",
            "weight": 63890823,
            "alg": "straw",
            "hash": "rjenkins1",
            "items": [
                {
                    "id": -14,
                    "weight": 21677267,
                    "pos": 0
                },
                {
                    "id": -15,
                    "weight": 21677218,
                    "pos": 1
                },
                {
                    "id": -16,
                    "weight": 20536338,
                    "pos": 2
                }
            ]
```

```
        },
        {
            "id": -2,
            "name": "data001",
            "type_id": 1,
            "type_name": "host",
            "weight": 5476704,
            "alg": "straw",
            "hash": "rjenkins1",
            "items": [
                {
                    "id": 0,
                    "weight": 228196,
                    "pos": 0
                },
                {
                    "id": 1,
                    "weight": 228196,
                    "pos": 1
                },
                ...
```

Pools

Ceph allows us to create multiple pools of storage, with sizes and attributes specified according to the unique needs of each. For example, in an OpenStack deployment one will typically find a large Cinder pool, a medium to large Glance pool, and perhaps a number of pools for the RGW service. We'll cover more about pools in other chapters, but here we'll succinctly show you a number of commands for managing them.

To simply list the pools provisioned:

```
# rados lspools
rbd
# ceph osd lspools
1 rbd,
```

There are sometimes multiple ways to accomplish a given task within Ceph. Here's another, showing the larger constellation of pools provisioned for OpenStack and the RADOS GateWay service using the Ceph Firefly release. This same information can also be displayed with ceph osd pool ls detail.

```
# ceph osd dump | grep pool
    pool 3 'csi-a-cinder-volume-1' replicated size 3 min_size 2
crush_ruleset 0 object_hash rjenkins pg_num 16384 pgp_num 16384 last_change
```

```
261136 stripe_width 0
     pool 4 csi-a-glance-image-1' replicated size 3 min_size 2 crush_ruleset
0 object_hash rjenkins pg_num 16384 pgp_num 16384 last_change 261134
stripe_width 0
     pool 5 '.rgw' replicated size 3 min_size 2 crush_ruleset 0 object_hash
rjenkins pg_num 1024 pgp_num 1024 last_change 882 stripe_width 0
     pool 6 '.rgw.control' replicated size 3 min_size 2 crush_ruleset 0
object_hash rjenkins pg_num 1024 pgp_num 1024 last_change 884 stripe_width
0
     pool 7 '.rgw.gc' replicated size 3 min_size 2 crush_ruleset 0
object_hash rjenkins pg_num 1024 pgp_num 1024 last_change 886 stripe_width
0
     pool 8 '.log' replicated size 3 min_size 2 crush_ruleset 0 object_hash
rjenkins pg_num 1024 pgp_num 1024 last_change 888 stripe_width 0
     pool 9 '.intent-log' replicated size 3 min_size 2 crush_ruleset 0
object_hash rjenkins pg_num 1024 pgp_num 1024 last_change 890 stripe_width
0
     pool 10 '.usage' replicated size 3 min_size 2 crush_ruleset 0
object_hash rjenkins pg_num 1024 pgp_num 1024 last_change 892 stripe_width
0
     pool 11 '.users' replicated size 3 min_size 2 crush_ruleset 0
object_hash rjenkins pg_num 1024 pgp_num 1024 last_change 894 stripe_width
0
     pool 12 '.users.email' replicated size 3 min_size 2 crush_ruleset 0
object_hash rjenkins pg_num 1024 pgp_num 1024 last_change 896 stripe_width
0
     pool 13 '.users.swift' replicated size 3 min_size 2 crush_ruleset 0
object_hash rjenkins pg_num 1024 pgp_num 1024 last_change 898 stripe_width
0
  pool 14 '.users.uid' replicated size 3 min_size 2 crush_ruleset 0
object_hash rjenkins pg_num 1024 pgp_num 1024 last_change 165075
stripe_width 0
     pool 15 '.rgw.buckets' replicated size 3 min_size 2 crush_ruleset 0
object_hash rjenkins pg_num 16384 pgp_num 16384 last_change 902
stripe_width 0
     pool 17 'css-a-glance-image-1' replicated size 3 min_size 2
crush_ruleset 0 object_hash rjenkins pg_num 16384 pgp_num 16384 last_change
906 stripe_width 0
     pool 18 '.rgw.root' replicated size 3 min_size 2 crush_ruleset 0
object_hash rjenkins pg_num 8 pgp_num 8 last_change 908 stripe_width 0
     pool 19 '.rgw.buckets.index' replicated size 3 min_size 2 crush_ruleset
0 object_hash rjenkins pg_num 1024 pgp_num 1024 last_change 261117
stripe_width 0
     pool 20 '' replicated size 3 min_size 2 crush_ruleset 0 object_hash
rjenkins pg_num 8 pgp_num 8 last_change 7282 stripe_width 0
```

We see that each pool is configured to maintain three copies of data and to still service operations if only two are active. The CRUSH ruleset is specified; here all pools use the same ruleset as is fairly common for Ceph deployments. The three largest pools each contain 16,384 placement groups. We discussed some of these settings and their ramifications in `Chapter 4`, *Planning Your Deployment* and will delve into others in `Chapter 8`, *Ceph Architecture: Under the Hood*.

Yes, there's a pool with a null name, which is an artifact of an automation inventory misconfiguration. If this ever happens to you, use the following command to clean up:

```
# rados rmpool "" "" --yes-i-really-really-mean-it
successfully deleted pool
```

Ceph really really wants to be sure that we want to delete that pool, so it makes us enter the name twice and a strongly affirmative switch as well. With the Jewel and later releases there is another step yet we can take to really, really, REALLY make sure we don't accidentally delete a production pool (and with it our jobs).

```
# ceph osd pool set csi-a-cinder-volume-1 nodelete true
```

Monitors

We discuss Ceph Monitors (also known as MONs or mons) in other chapters in detail, but we'll describe them a bit here as well for context. Ceph MONs maintain and serves a wealth of information about cluster topology and status. In this way they are a clearinghouse of sorts, accepting connections and updates from other Ceph daemons including other MONs, OSDs, and MDS instances.

Ceph MONs operate as a cluster, exploiting the Paxos consensus algorithm to ensure reliable and consistent operation as a quorum. The vital information collected and distributed by MONs includes:

- The mon map, which includes names, addresses, state, epoch, and so on for all MONs in the cluster. The mon map is vital for quorum maintenance and client connections.
- The CRUSH map, which includes similar information for the collection of OSDs holding Ceph's payload data. `Chapter 8`, *Ceph Architecture: Under the Hood* details the rules contained in the CRUSH map and their management. The CRUSH map is also the source of the information displayed by `ceph osd tree` as shown earlier.

- The MDS map of CephFS MetaData Servers.
- The PG map of which OSDs house each PG.
- Cluster flags.
- Cluster health.
- Authentication keys and client capabilities.

The mon map and quorum status information can be displayed by the `ceph mon stat` and `ceph mon dump` commands.

```
# ceph mon stat
e2: 5 mons at
{mon001=10.8.45.10:6789/0,mon002=10.8.45.11:6789/0,mon003=10.8.45.143:6789/
0,mon004=10.8.46.10:6789/0,mon005=10.8.46.11:6789/0}, election epoch 24,
quorum 0,1,2,3,4 mon001,mon002,mon003,mon004,mon005
# ceph mon dump
dumped monmap epoch 2
epoch 2
fsid 3369c9c6-bfaf-4114-9c31-576afa64d0fe
last_changed 2017-09-06 20:21:09.396928
created 2017-09-06 20:20:42.336193
0: 10.8.45.10:6789/0 mon.mon001
1: 10.8.45.11:6789/0 mon.mon002
2: 10.8.45.143:6789/0 mon.mon003
3: 10.8.46.10:6789/0 mon.mon004
4: 10.8.46.11:6789/0 mon.mon05
```

The output of `ceph mon stat` may look familiar: the `ceph status` command we'll explore later in this chapter includes this very information.

CephFS

To check the status of Ceph's MDS, run `ceph mds stat` or `ceph mds dump`.

```
# ceph mds stat
e85: 1/1/1 up {0=ceph-mds001=up:active}
# ceph mds dump
dumped mdsmap epoch 85
epoch     85
flags     0
created 2017-10-20 11:11:11.1138
modified 2017-10-22 13:13:13.1701
tableserver     0
root      0
session_timeout 60
```

```
session_autoclose          300
max_file_size     1099511627776
last_failure      0
last_failure_osd_epoch    666
compat  compat={},rocompat={},incompat={1=base v0.20,2=client writeable
ranges,3=default file layouts on dirs,4=dir inode in separate object,5=mds
uses versioned encoding,6=dirfrag is stored in omap}
max_mds    1
in         0
up         {0=1138}
failed
stopped
data_pools        0
metadta_pool      1
inline_data       disabled
1138:  196.168.1.1:6800/2046 'ceph-mds001' mds.0 13 up; active seq 4252
```

Configuration

Ceph's behavior is highly configurable and tunable via settings, which allow us to control Ceph's behavior and performance. Chapter 7, *Monitoring Ceph*, and Chapter 11, *Performance and Stability Tuning*, will explore a number of these, but in this chapter we'll discuss methods of showing and changing these values.

Ceph daemons and clients at startup read /etc/ceph/ceph.conf to load configuration settings and other cluster information for the cluster named ceph. There are hundreds of values that can be set, but fortunately we mostly need to concern ourselves with only a much smaller subset.

Cluster naming and configuration

The startup configuration file defines values that Ceph components need to start up and find each other. Many Ceph admins think of the file as always being named /etc/ceph/ceph.conf, but other names are possible. The directory /etc/ceph is the default location, but the filename's base is actually the name of a given cluster, which itself defaults to Ceph. Many installations, especially those with a single cluster, leave this defaulted, but custom names are becoming increasingly popular.

Throughout this book we write in terms of the default cluster name ceph, but let's say we wish our cluster to be known as cephelmerman. Our configuration file will then be found at /etc/ceph/cephelmerman.conf. Most Ceph commands default to operating on a cluster named ceph, but now we would need to add the --cluster cephelmerman switch so that they find the proper cluster components. This quickly becomes cumbersome, but Ceph gives us a shortcut -- the contents of the CEPH_ARGS environment variable are appended to core commands. So in our example instead of typing the following:

```
# ceph status --cluster cephelmerman
# ceph -s --cluster cephelmerman
# ceph osd tree --cluster cephelmerman
```

We can instead issue (using the bash shell):

```
# export CEPH_ARGS="--cluster cephelmerman"
# ceph status
# ceph -s
# ceph osd tree
```

We do recommend using the default cluster name of ceph unless you have a compelling reason to vary it. As of the Jewel release, Ceph still suffers a few gotchas with non-default names, and the ceph-deploy utility we will explore later in this chapter does not yet honor CEPH_ARGS.

It is possible—though very uncommon—to run more than one Ceph logical cluster on the same set of hardware. At system startup Ceph will attempt to start daemons for any config file it files in /etc/ceph, that is, any file matching the pattern /etc/ceph/*.conf. Thus in this uncommon situation we might see something like:

```
# ls -1 /etc/ceph
ceph.conf
cephelmerman.conf
music.conf
rhythm.conf
```

This is important to remember even for default, single-cluster deployments, because it might seem convenient to stash backup copies when changes are made.

```
# ls -1 /etc/ceph
ceph.CR1138.conf
ceph.OLD.conf
ceph.conf
ceph.conf.old
ceph.old.conf
ceph.firefly.conf
```

In this example, when the system boots Ceph will most likely not behave as expected. For this reason if you elect to keep backup copies of `ceph.conf`, it is vital that their filenames not end in `.conf`.

The Ceph configuration file

Ceph's config files comprise multiple sections, one global and one for each core Ceph component daemon. A few entries are mandatory; many are optional. Each section begins with a bracketed name, a convention that is often called the `INI` format, after its widespread use in MS-DOS. Let's go through these sections with some examples of their contents. We'll start with the `ceph.conf` file from the sandbox cluster we explored in Chapter 5, *Deploying a Virtual Sandbox Cluster*.

```
# cat /etc/ceph/ceph.conf
[global]
fsid = 5591400a-6868-447f-be89-thx1138656b6
max open files = 131072
mon initial members = ceph-mon0
mon host = 192.168.42.10
public network = 192.168.42.0/24
cluster network = 192.168.43.0/24
[client.libvirt]
admin socket = /var/run/ceph/$cluster-$type.$id.$pid.$cctid.asok
log file = /var/log/ceph/qemu-guest-$pid.log
[osd]
osd mkfs type = xfs
osd mkfs options xfs = -f -i size=2048
osd mount options xfs = noatime,largeio,inode64,swalloc
osd journal size = 100
[client.restapi]
public addr = 192.168.42.10:5000
keyring = /var/lib/ceph/restapi/ceph-restapi/keyring
log file = /var/log/ceph/ceph-restapi.log
```

The `[global]` section contains settings that are common to all components of a Ceph deployment. Settings entered here will apply to all Ceph components unless overridden in a later, component-specific section.

We discuss `fsid` a bit in other chapters; briefly it is a unique identifier for a given cluster and must be present.

The `mon initial members` and `mon host` lines however are required; they enable Ceph Monitors to find each other. These lines also help Ceph OSD, RADOS Gateway, and other daemons find the cluster's MONs.

The `public network` definition is also required; it defines a network address range for Ceph's Monitor cluster. If `cluster network` is present it defines a dedicated IP network for Ceph's replication traffic. If no `cluster network` is defined, all traffic will share the `public network`.

The `[client.libvirt]` section includes settings appropriate for virtualization clients such as QEMU. Here the client is expected to be named `client.libvirt` and should possess the corresponding keyring to successfully authenticate to the cluster. Note that this section need not be present at all in `ceph.conf` files for MON, OSD, and RGW nodes, but it doesn't hurt to have it there. It may be convenient to include all sections in the `ceph.conf` file located on each Ceph node type; this can ease configuration management. In this example, we specify an `admin socket` to which one may connect to query the state of client library running within the hypervisor . We'll discuss admin sockets later in this chapter. The second line defines a `log file` to which the client should write events and other messages.

The `[osd]` section often garners the most attention from Ceph admins. In our example, `osd mkfs type` directs that FileStore OSDs should provision an XFS filesystem, vs EXT4, or btrfs.

The following `osd mkfs options xfs` line lists options to be specified on the command line when the OSD provisioning process invokes `mkfs.xfs`. The options in our example duplicate the defaults compiled into Ceph, but it can be useful to have them explicitly configured so that the parameters for new OSDs are very clear. One occasionally finds advice to add `-n size=65536` here, in an attempt to save CPU cycles. Don't do it. Ceph's use-case does not benefit from a non-default setting here, and this author has witnessed it precipitating untold grief. The defaults are best for almost everybody. Other options are possible if you *really* know what you are doing and understand that going back requires destroying and reprovisioning every OSD created by them.

Next we see the associated `osd mount options xfs` entry. Here again Ceph's defaults work well for most applications; change them only with careful study. Unlike `mkfs` options, mount options are only applied as each FileStore OSD is mounted at system startup, so changes here can be applied by stopping the OSD processes, unmounting their filesystems, and restarting. A somewhat more nuclear but entirely reasonable alternative is to temporarily set the `noout` flag and simply reboot the server.

The `osd mount options xfs` shown above is taken straight from our sandbox, which sets non-default values. The default option list as of Jewel is `rw,noatime,inode64`; please do not take the above excerpt as a recommendation.

Last in our example's `[osd]` section is `osd journal size`. Our sandbox does not serve a real workload so the value is unusually small so as to not strain desktop virtualization. The suggested value in production is `10240` which provisions a 10 GB partition when colocating FileStore journals. This value is recommended as a safe one-size-fits-all. You may never fill a 10 GB journal before it flushes, but the safety margin is an easy tradeoff against saving a few trivial GBs for the FileStore filesystem.

The last section in our example is `[client.restapi]`. This section is only required when using the REST API for interrogating and managing Ceph clusters externally.

When the RGW service is used, an additional section is required for it as well.

Sharp-eyed readers may notice that ceph configuration settings are sometimes written with spaces in their names, and sometimes with underscores. For example:
`osd journal size = 10240`
and
`osd_journal_size = 10240`
are both valid. We recommend sticking with the underscore form for ease of selection with mouse/pointer clicks and tools like grep. This can also simplify management within scripts and other places where space characters might need to be escaped or quoted.

Admin sockets

Each Ceph daemon (and client if so enabled) listens on an *admin socket* for requests to get or set information or to perform certain actions. We can see these sockets in `/var/run/ceph`; here are examples from both OSD and MON nodes.

```
osd-1701# ls /var/run/ceph
ceph-osd.0.asok     ceph-osd.10.asok    ceph-osd.11.asok
ceph-osd.12.asok    ceph-osd.13.asok    ceph-osd.14.asok
ceph-osd.15.asok    ceph-osd.16.asok    ceph-osd.17.asok
ceph-osd.18.asok    ceph-osd.19.asok    ceph-osd.1.asok
ceph-osd.20.asok    ceph-osd.21.asok    ceph-osd.22.asok
ceph-osd.23.asok    ceph-osd.2.asok     ceph-osd.3.asok
ceph-osd.4.asok     ceph-osd.5.asok     ceph-osd.69.asok
ceph-osd.7.asok     ceph-osd.8.asok     ceph-osd.9.asok
mon-05# ls /var/run/ceph
ceph-mon.mon05.asok
```

To interact with `osd.69` we first ssh into the `osd-1701` system. We can then ask `osd.69` machine admin socket what it can do for us.

```
# ceph daemon osd.69 help
{
"config diff": "dump diff of current config and default config",
"config get": "config get <field>: get the config value",
"config set": "config set <field> <val> [<val> ...]: set a config
variable",
"config show": "dump current config settings",
"dump_blacklist": "dump blacklisted clients and times",
"dump_blocked_ops": "show the blocked ops currently in flight",
"dump_historic_ops": "show slowest recent ops",
"dump_op_pq_state": "dump op priority queue state",
"dump_ops_in_flight": "show the ops currently in flight",
"dump_reservations": "show recovery reservations",
"dump_watchers": "show clients which have active watches, and on which
objects",
"flush_journal": "flush the journal to permanent store",
"get_command_descriptions": "list available commands",
"get_heap_property": "get malloc extension heap property",
"get_latest_osdmap": "force osd to update the latest map from the mon",
"getomap": "output entire object map",
"git_version": "get git sha1",
"help": "list available commands",
"injectdataerr": "inject data error to an object",
"injectmdataerr": "inject metadata error to an object",
"log dump": "dump recent log entries to log file",
"log flush": "flush log entries to log file",
"log reopen": "reopen log file",
"objecter_requests": "show in-progress osd requests",
"ops": "show the ops currently in flight",
"perf dump": "dump perfcounters value",
"perf reset": "perf reset <name>: perf reset all or one perfcounter name",
"perf schema": "dump perfcounters schema",
"rmomapkey": "remove omap key",
"set_heap_property": "update malloc extension heap property",
"set_recovery_delay": "Delay osd recovery by specified seconds",
"setomapheader": "set omap header",
"setomapval": "set omap key",
"status": "high-level status of OSD",
"truncobj": "truncate object to length","version": "get ceph version"
}
```

Holy options, Batman! For day-to-day operations we need not become immediately or intimately familiar with all of these commands; many of them are useful primarily for arcane troubleshooting and development tasks. The most frequently used commands are near the top of the list.

In this chapter, and in `Chapter 11`, *Performance and Stability Tuning*, we discuss a number of Ceph's configuration settings. The config commands presented by the admin socket allow us to extract the current settings from within a given OSD or MON. Just for a laugh, let's see how many of those there are, this time on a Ceph Jewel system:

```
# ceph daemon osd.1701 config show | wc -l
1116
```

Yikes! Over a thousand settings. How could we ever hope to understand and tune them all? As we'll explore more in the next section, for the most part we don't need to. Each Ceph release increasingly improves behavior and setting defaults; the vast majority of these settings are best left alone unless we have a compelling reason and really know what we're doing. Among the more frequently adjusted settings are ones that affect backfill and recovery.

```
# ceph daemon osd.1701 config show | egrep backfill\|recovery
  "osd_max_backfills": "3",
  "osd_min_recovery_priority": "0",
  "osd_backfill_full_ratio": "0.9",
  "osd_backfill_retry_interval": "10",
  "osd_allow_recovery_below_min_size": "true",
  "osd_recovery_threads": "1",
  "osd_backfill_scan_min": "64",
  "osd_backfill_scan_max": "512",
  "osd_recovery_thread_timeout": "30",
  "osd_recovery_thread_suicide_timeout": "300",
  "osd_recovery_sleep": "0",
  "osd_recovery_delay_start": "0",
  "osd_recovery_max_active": "3",
  "osd_recovery_max_single_start": "1",
  "osd_recovery_max_chunk": "8388608",
  "osd_recovery_max_omap_entries_per_chunk": "64000",
  "osd_recovery_forget_lost_objects": "false",
  "osd_scrub_during_recovery": "true",
  "osd_kill_backfill_at": "0",
  "osd_debug_skip_full_check_in_backfill_reservation": "false",
  "osd_debug_reject_backfill_probability": "0",
  "osd_recovery_op_priority": "3",
  "osd_recovery_op_warn_multiple": "16"
```

Yikes again! Twenty three settings just for recovery and backfill! Again, many of these are best left alone, but as we'll discuss below several of them are commonly adjusted. Best practice for knowing what to tweak and what to leave be is to err on the side of defaults unless research, professional advice, and/or thorough testing support changes.

 The `dump_historic_ops` and `dump_ops_in_flight` commands to the admin socket are also invaluable when troubleshooting complex issues. Interpretation of this information can require advanced knowledge of Ceph's innards and protocols.

Another method of extracting information from running Ceph daemons is the `ceph tell` command issued from a MON or admin node.

```
# ceph tell osd.* version
osd.0: {
    "version": "ceph version 10.2.6
(656b5b63ed7c43bd014bcafd81b001959d5f089f)"
}
osd.1: {
    "version": "ceph version 10.2.6
(656b5b63ed7c43bd014bcafd81b001959d5f089f)"
}
osd.2: {
    "version": "ceph version 10.2.6
(656b5b63ed7c43bd014bcafd81b001959d5f089f)"
}
...
```

This offers a more limited set of functionality compared to that provided through admin sockets, but the version command is very useful when ensuring that all components of a cluster are running the desired (and usually same) release versions.

Ceph's Luminous release adds additional and quite handy ways to survey cluster components.

- `ceph versions`
- `ceph {mon,mds,osd,mgr}`
  Summarize the running versions of each type of daemon
- `ceph {mon,mds,osd,mgr} metadata`
- `ceph {mon,mds,osd,mgr}count-metadata <property>`
  Gather other daemon metadata

- `ceph features`

  Reports features supported by both daemons and clients connected to the cluster. This is priceless when ensuring that planned Ceph upgrades and certain cluster map changes will not break existing clients.

Injection

Earlier in this chapter we discussed Ceph settings defined in the `ceph.conf` config file. When present as each Ceph daemon starts up, these settings override compiled-in defaults. To borrow a term from the network router world, `ceph.conf` is an example of *stored*, *startup* or *saved config*. As circumstances cause us to adjust or augment these explicit file-based settings we can effect them by rolling restarts of Ceph daemon processes or even server reboots.

While Ceph's resilient and fault-tolerant architecture affords us the flexibility to carefully apply configuration changes by service restarts, there is faster and less disruptive method: **injection**.

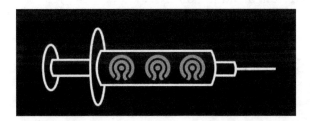

Ceph's injection mechanism is a handy and nearly immediate way to affect Ceph's *running config*, which is the set of values that each running daemon process holds within its memory address space. When we inject changes, we avoid the time and potential disruption that a sequential rolling restart of hundreds or thousands of Ceph daemons would entail.

Let's explore some real-world examples of the value of injection, and cover two important caveats as well.

One common use-case for injection is to adjust settings that affect the rate and distribution of backfill and recovery operations. Ceph initiates these as required to maintain data replication as OSDs come up and down or are added or removed from the cluster. It is natural to wish this process to complete as quickly as possible so that the cluster enjoys optimal resilience. Recovery operations however can contend with client I/O; during heavy recovery users may notice significant performance degradation or even failed operations.

When we anticipate heavy recovery traffic, say if we plan to remove an entire OSD node from service, we can use injection to temporarily throttle recovery to ensure that it does not overwhelm routine operations. First let's consider the following set of Ceph settings and their default values as of Ceph's Hammer release

osd_recovery_max_single_start (this setting may be undocumented for Hammer)	5
osd_max_backfills	10
osd_recovery_op_priority	10
osd_recovery_max_active	15

For many Hammer clusters, these default values are overly aggressive and can precipitate user impact and even dreaded *slow requests*. We can lower (or increase) them on a temporary or experimental basis to accommodate planned maintenance or to converge on an optimal balance between recovery speed and client impact. Each Ceph OSD daemon maintains its own running state, and we can inject new values into one or all of them with a single command issued from an admin or MON node.

```
# ceph tell osd.\* injectargs '--osd_max_backfills 1 --
osd_recovery_max_active 1 --osd_recovery_max_single_start 1 --
osd_recovery_op_priority 1'
osd.0: osd_max_backfills = '1' osd_recovery_max_active = '1' (unchangeable)
osd_recovery_max_single_start = '1' (unchangeable) osd_recovery_op_priority
= '1' (unchangeable)
osd.1: osd_max_backfills = '1' osd_recovery_max_active = '1' (unchangeable)
osd_recovery_max_single_start = '1' (unchangeable) osd_recovery_op_priority
= '1' (unchangeable)
    . . .
```

Note the (unchangeable) tags appended to the results for three out of our four variables. This is intended to alert us to values that we can inject, but which do not take effect immediately. Not all values change behavior when injected, some some may not be injected at all. In the above example these messages would lead us to believe that our efforts are in vain, and that we must change ceph.conf and restart all OSDs to effect the new values. As of Ceph's Jewel release, though, the code that issues these warnings does not always accurately determine the effectiveness of injection for certain values, including those above.

Experience tells us that these particular values do in fact take effect immediately. Until the code is improved, unfortunately one must either determine the truth via tests or by researching the experiences of others within the community. Other values known to this author to be effective when injected include

- `osd_scrub_max_interval`
- `osd_deep_scrub_interval`
- `mon_pg_warn_max_per_osd`

Alert readers may infer from the third setting above that one can also successfully inject values into not only OSDs but also Ceph MONs.

An important limitation of injection is that since it modifies only the running config and not the stored config, changes are lost when each Ceph daemon or server is restarted or reboots. Configuration via injection is invaluable for effecting immediate change with minimal disruption, especially when testing the efficacy of a given set of values. Injection helps us respond quickly to incidents within our clusters, and also to temporarily optimize behavior profiles during maintenance operations. Settings that we wish to persist permanently must be also be written to the stored config in `ceph.conf` or they will be lost in the future as servers are restarted.

> *Merci beaucoup* to Sébastien Han for his gracious permission to use the delightful syringe graphic above.
>
> Additional information regarding Ceph's myriad and subtle configuration settings may be found here `http://docs.ceph.com/docs/master/rados/configuration/ceph-conf`.
>
> Ceph's vast array of settings changes somewhat with each release; values for earlier versions are available under release-specific URL paths, for example, for Hammer consult `http://docs.ceph.com/docs/hammer/rados/configuration/osd-config-ref/`.
>
> The authoritative source for settings and their defaults is, of course, the source. For Luminous their definitions may be found here: `https://github.com/ceph/ceph/blob/luminous/src/common/options.cc`
>
> Older Ceph source releases define defaults in `config_opts.h`
> The community mailing lists described in `Chapter 1`, *Introducing Ceph Storage,* can be invaluable in discovering evolving best practices for settings.

Configuration management

Many Ceph admins exploit *configuration management* software to ensure correct and consistent application of packages and config files. Popular systems include Puppet, Chef, Ansible, and cfengine. Such systems are invaluable for ensuring that all systems remain consistent and up to date throughout their life cycle, especially when configuration settings are changed and hosts come and go.

Typical configuration management systems allow one to distribute an entire file to multiple managed systems. It is also usually possible to employ *templating*, a scheme by which a skeleton outline of a file is distributed to remote systems with embedded markup that allows variable interpolation, conditional inclusion of text, iterators, and even calculation of values for the destination file. This allows one to centrally and at scale manage files that may contain both invariant text and system-specific values.

Details of managing Ceph with each configuration management tool are beyond the scope of this book, but many resources are available online. Your natural choice may be a system already implemented by your organization.

One Ceph-specific management system that is rapidly maturing and gaining popularity is `ceph-ansible`, which as you might guess is built upon the popular Ansible configuration and orchestration tool. We employed `ceph-ansible` in the previous chapter for effortless provisioning of our sandbox cluster and suggest its use for those starting out with Ceph, or those fed up with doing everything by hand, iteratively.

`Ceph-ansible` may be found here:
`http://docs.ceph.com/ceph-ansible/master/`

Scrubs

Data corruption is rare but it does happen, a phenomenon described scientifically as *bit-rot*. Sometimes we write to a drive, and a surface or cell failure results in reads failing or returning something other than what we wrote. HBA misconfiguration, SAS expander flakes, firmware design flaws, drive electronics errors, and medium failures can also corrupt data. Surface errors affect between 1 in 10^{16} to as many as 1 in 10^{14} bits stored on HDDs. Drives can also become unseated due to human error or even a truck rumbling by. This author has also seen literal cosmic rays flip bits.

Ceph lives for strong data integrity, and has a mechanism to alert us of these situation: *scrubs*. Scrubs are somewhat analogous to `fsck` on a filesystem and the *patrol reads* or *surface scans* that many HBAs run. The idea is to check each replicated copy of data to ensure that they're mutually consistent. Since copies of data are distributed throughout the cluster this is done at **Placement Group** (**PG**) granularity. Each PG's objects reside together on the same set of OSDs so it is natural and efficient to scrub them together.

When a given PG is scrubbed, the primary OSD for that PG calculates a checksum of data and requests that the other OSDs in the PG's Acting Set do the same. The checksums are compared; if they agree, all is well. If they do not agree, Ceph flags the PG in question with the `inconsistent` state, and its complement of data becomes inaccessible.

See `Chapter 8`, *Ceph Architecture:Under the Hood*, for discussion of primary (lead) OSDs and Acting Sets.

Ceph scrubs, like dark glasses, come in two classes: *light* and *deep*.

Light scrubs are also known as *shallow* scrubs or simply *scrubs* and are, well, lightweight and by default are performed for every PG every day. They checksum and compare only object metadata (such as size, XATTR, and omap data) and completely quickly and without taking much in the way of resources. Filesystem errors and rare Ceph bugs can be caught by light scrubs.

Deep scrubs read and checksum all of the PG's objects payload data. Since each replica of a PG may hold multiple gigabytes of data, these require substantially more resources than light scrubs. Large reads from media take a much longer time to complete and contend with ongoing client operations, so deep scrubs are spread across a longer period of time, by default this is one week.

Many Ceph operators find that even weekly runs result in unacceptable impact and use the `osd_deep_scrub_interval` setting in `ceph.conf` to spread them out over a longer period. There are also options to align deep scrubs with off-hours or other times of lessened client workload. One may also prevent deep scrubs from slowing recovery (as Ceph scrambles to restore data replication) by configuring `osd_scrub_during_recovery` with a value of `false`. This applies at PG granularity, not across the entire cluster, and helps avoid the dreaded blocked requests that can result when scrub and recovery operations align to disrupt pesky user traffic.

Scrub settings can be dynamically adjusted throughout the cluster through the injection mechanism we explored earlier in this chapter, with the requisite caveat regarding permanence. Say as our awesome cluster has become a victim of its own success we find that deep scrubs are becoming too aggressive and we want to space them out over four weeks instead of cramming into just one, but don't want to serially restart hundreds of OSD daemons. We can stage the change in `ceph.conf` and also immediately update the running config (Note: the value is specified in seconds; 4 weeks x 7 days x 24 hours x 60 minutes x 60 seconds = 2419200) .

```
# ceph tell osd.* injectargs '--osd_deep_scrub_interval 2419200'
```

We can also exploit flags to turn scrubs off and on completely throughout the cluster, if say they are getting in the way of a deep dive into cluster protocol dynamics or if one wishes to test or refute an assertion that they are responsible for poor performance. Leaving deep scrubs disabled for a long period of time can result in a thundering herd phenomenon, especially in Ceph's Hammer and earlier releases, so it is wise to not forget to re-enable them.

A well-engineered cluster does just fine with scrubs running even during rolling reboots, so you are encouraged to resist the urge to disable them for the duration of maintenance. Ceph Jewel and later releases leverage the `osd_scrub_interval_randomize_ratio` to mitigate this effect by slewing scrub scheduling to distribute them evenly, which additionally helps prevent them from clumping up. Remember that light scrubs consume little in the way of resources, so it even more rarely makes sense to disable them.

```
# ceph osd set noscrub
set noscrub
# ceph osd set nodeep-scrub
set nodeep-scrub
...
# ceph osd unset noscrub
# ceph osd unset nodeep-scrub
```

Bit-flips affecting stored data can remain latent for some time until a user thinks to read the affected object and gets back an error -- or worse, something different from what she wrote. Ceph stores multiple replicas of data to ensure data durability and accessibility, but serves reads only from the lead OSD in each placement group's Acting Set. This means that errors in the other replicas may be unnoticed until overwritten or when peering results in a change in lead OSD designation. This is why we actively seek them out with deep scrubs, to find and address them before they can impair client operations.

Here's an example of HDD errors due to a drive firmware design flaw precipitating an inconsistent PG. The format of such errors varies depending on drive type, Linux distribution, and kernel version, but they're similar with respect to the data presented.

```
Dec 15 10:55:44 csx-ceph1-020 kernel: end_request: I/O error, dev
  sdh, sector 1996791104
Dec 15 10:55:44 csx-ceph1-020 kernel: end_request: I/O error, dev
  sdh, sector 3936989616
Dec 15 10:55:44 csx-ceph1-020 kernel: end_request: I/O error, dev
  sdh, sector 4001236872
Dec 15 13:00:18 csx-ceph1-020 kernel: XFS (sdh1): xfs_log_force:
  error 5 returned.
Dec 15 13:00:48 csx-ceph1-020 kernel: XFS (sdh1): xfs_log_force:
  error 5 returned.
  ...
```

Here we see the common pattern where drive errors result in large numbers of filesystem errors.

The server in the above example uses an HBA that we can manage with LSI's `storcli` utility, so let's see what we can discover about what happened.

```
[root@csx-ceph1-020 ~]# /opt/MegaRAID/storcli/storcli64 /c0 /eall
/s9 show all | grep Error
Media Error Count = 66
Other Error Count = 1
```

On these HBAs `Media Error Count` typically reflects surface (medium) errors and `Other Error Count` reflects something more systemic like drive electronics failure or accidental unseating.

Here's a log excerpt that shows Ceph's diligent deep scrubbing discovering the affected data replica.

```
2015-12-19 09:10:30.403351 osd.121 10.203.1.22:6815/3987 10429 :
[ERR] 20.376b shard 121: soid
a0c2f76b/rbd_data.5134a9222632125.0000000000000001/head//20
candidate had a read error
2015-12-19 09:10:33.224777 osd.121 10.203.1.22:6815/3987 10430 :
[ERR] 20.376b deep-scrub 0 missing, 1 inconsistent objects
2015-12-19 09:10:33.224834 osd.121 10.203.1.22:6815/3987 10431 :
[ERR] 20.376b deep-scrub 1 errors
```

This is then reflected in the output of `ceph health` or `ceph status`.

```
root@csx-a-ceph1-001:~# ceph status
  cluster ab84e9c8-e141-4f41-aa3f-bfe66707f388
    health HEALTH_ERR 1 pgs inconsistent; 1 scrub errors
    osdmap e46754: 416 osds: 416 up, 416 in
    pgmap v7734947: 59416 pgs: 59409 active+clean, 1
    active+clean+inconsistent, 6 active+clean+scrubbing+deep
root@csx-a-ceph1-001:~# ceph health detail
HEALTH_ERR 1 pgs inconsistent; 1 scrub errors
pg 20.376b is active+clean+inconsistent, acting [11,38,121]
1 scrub errors
```

The affected placement group has been flagged as inconsistent. Since this state impacts the availability of even a fraction of a percent of the cluster's data, the overall cluster health is set to HEALTH_ERR, which alerts us to a situation that must be addressed immediately.

Remediation of an inconsistent PG generally begins with identifying the ailing OSD; the log messages above direct us to `osd.121`. We use the procedure described later in this chapter to remove the OSD from service. Removal itself may clear the inconsistent state of the PG, or we may need to manually repair it.

```
root@csx-a-ceph1-001:~# ceph pg repair 20.376b
```

This directs Ceph to replace the faulty replicas of data by reading clean, authoritative copies from the OSDs in the balance of the Active Set.

Logs

Ceph performs extensive logging. In Chapter 4, *Planning your the Deployment*, we discussed the need to provision ample drive space to accommodate spikes in log volume and to allow healthy retention intervals. In Chapter 8, *Ceph Architecture: Under the Hood* we will explore the severity levels of Ceph's log messages.

Ceph can be configured to log directly through the central `syslog` or `rsyslog` service, but by default it writes to local files. These are managed by the stock Linux `logrotate` facility. Here's the default rotation stanza that the Ceph Jewel release installs.

```
# cat /etc/logrotate.d/ceph.logrotate
/var/log/ceph/*.log {
    rotate 7
    daily
    compress
    sharedscripts
```

```
     postrotate
         killall -q -1 ceph-mon ceph-mds ceph-osd ceph-fuse radosgw
             || true
     endscript
     missingok
     notifempty
     su root ceph
}
```

The default retention is 7 days, which this author at times finds to be too short. To increase to four weeks, replace the 7 with 30, but be careful that the filesystem where /var/log lives has adequate free space. As we note later in this chapter, Ceph logs can become quite large at times, and modestly-provisioned systems experience filled filesystems. To mitigate the risk of logjams (clogged logs?) it may be expedient to also add a maxsize directive to rotate and compress logs sooner than daily if their sizes surge. The tradeoff is that logged messages will not always be neatly partitioned into roughly 24 hour chunks, but zcat and zgrep will quickly become your best friends.

MON logs

Ceph MONs by default write logs to /var/log/ceph/ceph-mon.hostname.log. On each MON server there is also a global cluster log written by default to /var/log/ceph/ceph.log. The combined information in the latter can help correlate activity among the constellation of Ceph daemons one has deployed, so in this chapter we will focus on it. These default filenames are a function of the default cluster name, which as you may have deduced is ceph. Tricky, isn't it? One may configure a cluster to use a non-default name; we discuss that briefly below in the context of configuration file naming. Throughout this book we mostly write in terms of clusters with the default name. Mostly. It reduces clutter in text boxes that may already be awkwardly wrapped. Most Ceph admins roll with the default name and as of the Jewel LTS release support for custom names is still incomplete in certain utilities.

OSDs log into a file with a name that includes their ID number. The National Creature Consortium for example, might boldly run a Ceph cluster with a non-default name whose OSD log files are named for example /var/log/ceph/ncc-osd.1701.log. Let's peek at the entries one finds in each.

```
2017-09-15 00:16:55.398807 osd.83 10.8.45.18:6822/127973 788 :
cluster [INF] 0.26c5 deep-scrub starts
2017-09-15 00:16:56.800561 osd.177 10.8.45.148:6818/129314 572 :
cluster [INF] 0.691 deep-scrub ok
2017-09-15 00:17:02.032534 mon.0 10.8.45.10:6789/0 418279 : cluster
[INF] pgmap v372250: 16384 pgs: 2 active+clean+scrubbing, 3
```

```
active+clean+scrubbing+deep, 16379 active+clean; 77786 GB data, 228
TB used, 596 TB / 825 TB avail
2017-09-15 00:16:55.958743 osd.142 10.8.45.146:6844/137783 793 :
cluster [INF] 0.3833 scrub starts
2017-09-15 00:17:00.607877 osd.83 10.8.45.18:6822/127973 789 :
cluster [INF] 0.26c5 deep-scrub ok
2017-09-15 00:17:01.329174 osd.88 10.8.45.18:6832/132624 918 :
cluster [INF] 0.19bb scrub ok
```

Business as usual for a healthy Ceph cluster. We see OSDs reporting successful light and deep scrubs, and the lead MON summarized the pgmap and cluster utilization.

```
2017-09-15 19:23:52.733080 mon.0 10.8.45.10:6789/0 473491 : cluster [INF]
pgmap v419600: 16384 pgs: 1 active+clean+scrubbing, 16383 active+clean;
77786 GB data, 228 TB used, 596 TB / 825 TB avail
2017-09-15 19:23:52.749005 mon.0 10.8.45.10:6789/0 473493 : cluster [INF]
osdmap e19228: 238 osds: 237 up, 238 in
```

Here are entries from later the same day show a summary of the osdmap, with one OSD down.

```
2017-09-15 19:24:00.513677 osd.16 10.8.45.15:6832/131296 808 :
cluster [INF] 0.b0 starting backfill to osd.33 from (0'0,0'0) MAX
to 7447'3975
2017-09-15 19:24:32.733030 mon.0 10.8.45.10:6789/0 473556 : cluster
[INF] HEALTH_WARN; 331 pgs backfill_wait; 93 pgs backfilling; 132
pgs stuck unclean; recovery 1115024/60328695 objects misplaced (1.848%)
2017-09-15 19:24:32.889755 mon.0 10.8.45.10:6789/0 473557 : cluster
[INF] pgmap v419645: 16384 pgs: 331 active+remapped+wait_backfill,
93 active+remapped+backfilling, 15960 active+clean; 77786 GB data,
228 TB used, 599 TB / 828 TB avail; 1113183/60328695 objects
misplaced (1.845%); 15548 MB/s, 3887 objects/s recovering
2017-09-15 19:24:33.922688 mon.0 10.8.45.10:6789/0 473558 : cluster
[INF] osdmap e19237: 238 osds: 238 up, 238 in
2017-09-15 19:24:33.937792 mon.0 10.8.45.10:6789/0 473559 : cluster
[INF] pgmap v419647: 16384 pgs: 331 active+remapped+wait_backfill,
93 active+remapped+backfilling, 15960 active+clean; 77786 GB data,
228 TB used, 599 TB / 828 TB avail; 1112020/60328695 objects
misplaced (1.843%); 8404 MB/s, 2101 objects/s recovering
```

Here the `osdmap` shows that the down OSD has now come back up, and data has been remapped to utilize it. Note the pgmap entries. They show 93 separate PGs are actively backfilling, with 331 waiting their turn. In the Configuration section above we touched on Ceph's settings that limit how much backfill / recovery can run at any given time. This spreads out the impact in order to protect user operations.

```
2017-09-16 00:16:56.093643 mon.0 10.8.45.10:6789/0 511866 : cluster [INF]
pgmap v441064: 16384 pgs: 16384 active+clean; 44667 MB data, 1197 GB used,
963 TB / 964 TB avail; 4316 kB/s rd, 10278 kB/s wr, 5991 op/s
```

OSD logs

Next let's check out entries from osd.8's log. Since Ceph OSDs are more numerous than MONs and process a larger rate of transactions we find that they grow much more quickly. Be sure to allocate ample space for them. As above, this cluster is running Ceph's Jewel release.

```
2017-09-18 00:19:08.268212 7fe07b990700  1 leveldb: Compacting 4@0
+ 5@1 files
2017-09-18 00:19:08.327958 7fe07b990700  1 leveldb: Generated table
#14159: 55666 keys, 2129686 bytes
2017-09-18 00:19:08.382062 7fe07b990700  1 leveldb: Generated table
#14160: 52973 keys, 2129584 bytes
2017-09-18 00:19:08.434451 7fe07b990700  1 leveldb: Generated table
#14161: 54404 keys, 2129467 bytes
2017-09-18 00:19:08.488200 7fe07b990700  1 leveldb: Generated table
#14162: 54929 keys, 2129347 bytes
2017-09-18 00:19:08.553861 7fe07b990700  1 leveldb: Generated table
#14163: 53000 keys, 2129511 bytes
2017-09-18 00:19:08.570029 7fe07b990700  1 leveldb: Generated table
#14164: 14956 keys, 600195 bytes
2017-09-18 00:19:08.594003 7fe07b990700  1 leveldb: Generated table
#14165: 17061 keys, 710889 bytes
2017-09-18 00:19:08.594016 7fe07b990700  1 leveldb: Compacted 4@0 +
5@1 files => 11958679 bytes
2017-09-18 00:19:08.595153 7fe07b990700  1 leveldb: compacted to:
files[ 0 7 17 0 0 0 0 ]
2017-09-18 00:19:08.595317 7fe07b990700  1 leveldb: Delete type=2
#14154
```

This is normal housekeeping. The OSD maintains an internal metadata database that it periodically redds up.

```
2017-09-18 00:19:53.953129 7fe0b5c2f700  0 --
10.24.49.15:6816/123339 >> 10.24.49.147:6834/1012539
pipe(0x557b7551b400 sd=83 :6816 s=0 pgs=0 cs=0 l=0
c=0x557b76a0ea80).accept connect_seq 15 vs existing 15 state
standby
2017-09-18 00:19:53.953290 7fe0b5c2f700  0 --
10.24.49.15:6816/123339 >> 10.24.49.147:6834/1012539
pipe(0x557b7551b400 sd=83 :6816 s=0 pgs=0 cs=0 l=0
c=0x557b76a0ea80).accept connect_seq 16 vs existing 15 state
standby
2017-09-18 00:19:54.933317 7fe0b07db700  0 --
10.24.49.15:6816/123339 >> 10.24.50.15:6844/135559
pipe(0x557b7f57e000 sd=38 :6816 s=0 pgs=0 cs=0 l=0
c=0x557b7fb54700).accept connect_seq 57 vs existing 57 state
standby
2017-09-18 00:19:54.933774 7fe0b07db700  0 --
10.24.49.15:6816/123339 >> 10.24.50.15:6844/135559
pipe(0x557b7f57e000 sd=38 :6816 s=0 pgs=0 cs=0 l=0
c=0x557b7fb54700).accept connect_seq 58 vs existing 57 state
standby
```

The OSD has decided to relieve its boredom by accepting some connection requests.

```
2017-09-18 00:34:54.052375 7fe0b5c2f700  0 --
10.240.49.15:6816/123339 >> 10.240.49.147:6834/1012539
pipe(0x557b7551b400 sd=83 :6816 s=2 pgs=1045 cs=17 l=0
c=0x557b86d4e600).fault with nothing to send, going to standby
2017-09-18 00:34:55.031169 7fe0b07db700  0 --
10.240.49.15:6816/123339 >> 10.240.50.15:6844/135559
pipe(0x557b7f57e000 sd=38 :6816 s=2 pgs=3948 cs=59 l=0
c=0x557b76c85e00).fault with nothing to send, going to standby
```

The word `fault` in these messages is scary, but they're a normal part of the OSD request lifecycle.

```
2017-09-18 02:08:51.710567 7fe0e466f700  0 log_channel(cluster) log
[INF] : 1.35da deep-scrub starts
2017-09-18 02:08:52.040149 7fe0e466f700  0 log_channel(cluster) log
[INF] : 1.35da deep-scrub ok
```

Here a deep scrub started and completed successfully. We love it when that happens.

```
2017-09-18 02:27:44.036497 7fe0926fc700  0 --
10.240.49.15:6816/123339 >> 10.240.50.17:6834/1124935
pipe(0x557b95384800 sd=34 :6816 s=0 pgs=0 cs=0 l=0
c=0x557b80759200).accept connect_seq 4 vs existing 3 state standby
2017-09-18 02:39:53.195393 7fe118064700 -1 osd.8 33380
heartbeat_check: no reply from 0x557b91ccd390 osd.272 since back
2017-09-18 02:39:32.671169 front 2017-09-18 02:39:32.671169 (cutoff
2017-09-18 02:39:33.195374)
2017-09-18 02:39:54.195516 7fe118064700 -1 osd.8 33380
heartbeat_check: no reply from 0x557b91ccd390 osd.272 since back
2017-09-18 02:39:32.671169 front 2017-09-18 02:39:32.671169 (cutoff
2017-09-18 02:39:34.195502)
```

Ugh!!! The OSD with the ID number 272 has gone incommunicado. In `Chapter 8`, *Ceph Architecture: Under the Hood* we discuss how OSDs periodically check in with each other. These entries may indicate a network problem, exhaustion of the `nf_conntrack` table, or that `osd.272` machine's daemon process has given up the ghost. Go ahead and take a garlic fries break. You don't want to tackle this next block on an empty stomach. Ellipses indicate spots that have been edited for relative brevity.

```
-4> 2017-09-15 21:58:20.149473 7f158d64f700  0
    filestore(/var/lib/ceph/osd/ceph-231) write couldn't open
    meta/#-1:97b6cd72:::osdmap.25489:0#: (117) Structure needs
    cleaning
-3> 2017-09-15 21:58:20.149536 7f158d64f700  0
    filestore(/var/lib/ceph/osd/ceph-231)  error (117) Structure
    needs cleaning not handled on operation 0x55a18d942b88
    (17413.0.1, or op 1, counting from 0)
-2> 2017-09-15 21:58:20.149544 7f158d64f700  0
    filestore(/var/lib/ceph/osd/ceph-231) unexpected error code
-1> 2017-09-15 21:58:20.149545 7f158d64f700  0
    filestore(/var/lib/ceph/osd/ceph-231)  transaction dump:
    {
      "ops": [
        {
            "op_num": 0,
            "op_name": "write",
            "collection": "meta",
            "oid": "#-1:725cc562:::inc_osdmap.25489:0#",
            "length": 203,
            "offset": 0,
            "bufferlist length": 203
        },
        {
            "op_num": 1,
```

```
              "op_name": "write",
              "collection": "meta",
              "oid": "#-1:97b6cd72:::osdmap.25489:0#",
              "length": 404169,
              "offset": 0,
              "bufferlist length": 404169
        },
        {

              "op_num": 2,
              "op_name": "write",
              "collection": "meta",
              "oid": "#-1:7b3f43c4:::osd_superblock:0#",
              "length": 417,
              "offset": 0,
              "bufferlist length": 417
        }
    ]
}
    0> 2017-09-15 21:58:20.152050 7f158d64f700 -1
    os/filestore/FileStore.cc: In function 'void
    FileStore::_do_transaction(ObjectStore::Transaction&,
    uint64_t, int, ThreadPool::TPHandle*)' thread 7f158d64f700
    time 2017-09-15 21:58:20.149608
    os/filestore/FileStore.cc: 2920: FAILED assert(0 ==
    "unexpected error")
    ceph version 10.2.6
    (656b5b63ed7c43bd014bcafd81b001959d5f089f)
 1: (ceph::__ceph_assert_fail(char const*, char const*, int,
    char const*)+0x8b) [0x55a1826b007b]
 2: (FileStore::_do_transaction(ObjectStore::Transaction&,
    unsigned long, int, ThreadPool::TPHandle*)+0xefd)
    [0x55a1823a26ed]
 3: (FileStore::_do_transactions
                (std::vector<ObjectStore::Transaction,
     std::allocator<ObjectStore::Transaction> >&, unsigned long,
     ThreadPool::TPHandle*)+0x3b) [0x55a1823a842b]
 4:  (FileStore::_do_op(FileStore::OpSequencer*,
     ThreadPool::TPHandle&)+0x2b5) [0x55a1823a8715]
 5:  (ThreadPool::worker(ThreadPool::WorkThread*)+0xa6e)
     [0x55a1826a145e]
 6: (ThreadPool::WorkThread::entry()+0x10) [0x55a1826a2340]
 7: (()+0x8184) [0x7f159bbff184]
 8: (clone()+0x6d)  [0x7f1599d28ffd]  NOTE: a copy of the
    executable, or `objdump -rdS <executable>` is needed to
    interpret this. --- logging levels ---  0/ 5 none  0/ 0
    lockdep  0/ 0 context  0/ 0 crush  0/ 0 mds  0/ 1 optracker
...
log_file /var/log/ceph/ceph-osd.231.log
```

```
    --- end dump of recent events --- 2017-09-15 21:58:20.155893 7f158d64f700
-1 *** Caught signal (Aborted) **  in thread 7f158d64f700
thread_name:tp_fstore_op  ceph version 10.2.6
(656b5b63ed7c43bd014bcafd81b001959d5f089f)
    1: (()+0x8f3942) [0x55a1825bb942]
    2: (()+0x10330) [0x7f159bc07330]
    3: (gsignal()+0x37) [0x7f1599c61c37]
    4: (abort()+0x148) [0x7f1599c65028]
    5: (ceph::__ceph_assert_fail(char const*, char const*, int,
       char const*)+0x265) [0x55a1826b0255]
    6: (FileStore::_do_transaction(ObjectStore::Transaction&,
       unsigned long, int, ThreadPool::TPHandle*)+0xefd)
       [0x55a1823a26ed]
...
```

Yikes! This definitely does not serve Vaal. Here the Ceph OSD code has encountered an error it can't cope with. Backtraces and information about ops that were being processed are dumped for forensics. We've highlighted two lines out of the dozens above to discuss specifically.

The first highlighted line shows a failed code assertion. These often afford a quick stab at the general cause of the problem. In this case, the OSD formerly known as 231 has encountered a problem in FileStore code. These almost always reflect a problem with the underlying hardware, or at the very least an XFS filesystem that has gone astray for another reason.

```
os/filestore/FileStore.cc: 2920: FAILED assert(0 == "unexpected error")
```

In this specific case the kernel log shows I/O errors on the underlying SSD drive.

Skipping down to the second highlighted line we see

```
2017-09-15 21:58:20.155893 7f158d64f700 -1 *** Caught signal (Aborted) **
in thread 7f158d64f700 thread_name:tp_fstore_op
```

When grepping (or groping) through voluminous OSD logs to discern failure causes it can be handy to search for the word *signal* in order to quickly zero in on the region of interest. Note though that Ceph daemons also log signal messages when they are shut down normally, say for a server reboot.

Debug levels

The constellation of messages that Ceph OSDs can log is huge and changes with each release. Full interpretation of logs could easily itself fill a book, but we'll end this section with a brief note regarding the logging levels summary within the above excerpt.

```
--- logging levels ---
0/ 5 none
0/ 0 lockdep
0/ 0 context
```

Ceph's allows us to finely control the verbosity with which it logs events, status, and errors. Levels may be independently set for each subsystem to control verbosity. Moreover, each subsystem has separate verbosity levels for information kept in process memory and for messages sent to log files or the `syslog` service. Higher numbers increase verbosity. The output and memory levels can be set independently, or separately. For example, if our MONs are proving unruly, we might add lines like the below to `ceph.conf`.

```
[global]
debug ms = 1
[mon]
debug mon = 15/20
debug paxos = 20
debug auth = 20
```

Note how for the mon subsystem we have specified different levels for output and memory logs by separating the two values with a slash character. If only a single value is given, Ceph applies it to both.

Recall from earlier in this chapter that Ceph daemons only read configuration files at startup. This means that to effect the above changes, one would need to make them on each MON node and perform a rolling restart of all MON daemons. This is tedious and awkward; in times of crisis it can also be precarious to stir the pot by bouncing services.

This is a perfect example of how the admin socket and injection mechanisms described earlier in this chapter earn their keep.

Say yesterday `osd.666` and `osd.1701` were being squirrelly, so we elevated the logging levels of the `filestore` and `osd` modules. Today we find that the increased log flow has half-filled the OSD node's `/var/log` filesystem and need to back off on the verbosity. After logging into osd.666's node we check the settings that are currently active in the daemon's running config.

```
# ceph daemon osd.666 config show | grep debug
    "debug_none": "0\/5",
    "debug_lockdep": "0\/0",
    "debug_context": "0\/0",
    "debug_crush": "0\/0",
    "debug_mds": "1\/5",
...

    "debug_osd": "10\/10",
    "debug_optracker": "0\/0",
    "debug_objclass": "0\/0",
    "debug_filestore": "10\/10",
...
```

On Ceph's Jewel 10.2.6 release this matches no fewer than *98* individual settings, hence the ellipses for brevity. Now log into an admin or mon node and inject those puppies into submission.

```
# ceph tell osd.666 injectargs '--debug-filestore 0/0 --debug-osd
0/0'debug_filestore=0/0 debug_osd=0/0
```

Boom. Instant satisfaction. Since we can inject these values on the fly, we can set them low in `ceph.conf` and inject temporary increases on the fly, followed by decreases when we're through. In fact if the log file has grown so large that there isn't even space to compress it we can truncate and reopen it without having to restart the OSD daemon.

```
# rm /var/log/ceph/ceph-osd.666.log
# ceph daemon osd.666 log reopen
```

To quote my high school chemistry teacher, *Isn't this FUN!? NOW we're cooking with gas!*

Oh wait, we forgot about `osd.1701`. And maybe we also elevated `osd.1864` and ... we don't remember. It was late and we were groggy due to garlic fries deprivation. This morning after a waking up with a soy chai we remember that we can inject values into the running state of all OSDs with a single command.

```
# ceph tell osd.* injectargs '--debug-filestore 0/0 --debug-osd 0/0'
osd.0: debug_filestore=0/0 debug_osd=0/0
osd.1: debug_filestore=0/0 debug_osd=0/0
osd.2: debug_filestore=0/0 debug_osd=0/0
```
...

Better safe than sorry; we're best off being sure. Injecting values that may be identical to those already set is safe and idempotent, and sure beats nuking the site from orbit.

> Analysis of Ceph logs can involve lots of time and gnarly awk/sed pipelines. A singularly useful set of tools for identifying patterns in log files can be found here:
> `https://github.com/linuxkidd/ceph-log-parsers`
>
> By slicing and dicing Ceph log files and emitting CSV files ready for importing into a spreadsheet, these scripts help collate thousands of messages across hours or days so that we can discern patterns. They are especially useful for narrowing in on nodes or OSDs that are loci of chronic slow / blocked requests.

Common tasks

In this section we cover procedures for a number of common tasks that Ceph admins execute as needed. These include managing flags and services, dealing with component failures, cluster expansion, and balancing OSD utilization. We'll also touch on upgrades between Ceph releases.

Installation

In the previous chapter we built a full-fledged, operational Ceph cluster using virtualization and `ceph-ansible`. Here we will summarize the bootstrapping of Ceph on bare metal utilizing the same `ceph-ansible` tools but without Vagrant orchestrating. If you're using `for` loops, like Jack Butler you're doing it wrong.

First, clone the ceph-ansible GitHub repo onto a system or VM that will serve as your admin node.

```
$ git clone https://github.com/ceph/ceph-ansible/
```

Next install Ansible via your Linux distribution's package manager, `pip`, or download from `http://docs.ansible.com/ansible/latest/intro_installation.html` . The latest stable release is suggested.

Next populate Ansible's inventory file with hosts and host groups using `/etc/ansible/hosts` as a starting point. You'll end up with a file resembling this example:

```
[mons]
ceph-mon01
ceph-mon02
ceph-mon03

[osds]
ceph-osd001
ceph-osd002
ceph-osd003
ceph-osd004
ceph-osd005
ceph-osd006

[rgws]
ceph-rgw01

[clients]
ceph-client-01
```

Next follow your organization's usual process to populate SSH keys then use Ansible's handy `ping` module to verify that you can connect to each system without supplying a password.

```
$ ansible all -m ping
10.10.17.01 | success >> {
   "changed": false,
   "ping": "pong"
}
10.10.11.38 | success >> {
   "changed": false,
   "ping": "pong"
}
. . .
```

If you experience difficulty with the above test, check the permissions on your .ssh directory and examine `/etc/ansible/ansible.cfg`.

Next customize the `group_vars` and `site.yml` files, just like we did in the previous chapter.

```
$ cp group_vars/all.yml.sample group_vars/all.yml
$ cp group_vars/mons.yml.sample group_vars/mons.yml
$ cp group_vars/osds.yml.sample group_vars/osds.yml
$ cp site.yml.sample site.yml
```

As you might surmise, next we must edit the `group_vars/all.yml` file to reflect our local conditions.

First edit the entries for `public_nework` and `monitor_interface` as appropriate to your systems. Next consider where you wish to snag Ceph's installation package and configure the familiar `ceph_origin` line with distro, upstream, or local. When choosing the upstream package source you must designate how far upstream you wish to swim. The safe choice is `ceph_stable`, though `ceph_rhcs` is valid for RHEL deployments and the adventurous may skate with `ceph_dev`.

Our sandbox deployment did not touch on customization of OSD creation details, but for bare metal deployment you must edit `group_vars/osds.yml` and edit at the very least the `osd_scenario` line to select a strategy from among those presented: `journal_collocation`, `bluestore`, `osd_directory`, `raw_multi_journal`, `dmcrypt_journal_collocation`, `dmcrypt_dedicated_journal`. Note the spelling, collocation not colocation. It is worth reading through this entire file before proceeding. `Chapter 3`, *Hardware and Network Selection*, and `Chapter 4`, *Planning Your Deployment*, will help you with these decisions. Note that `osd_directory` has been problematic in some ways and may be removed in the future.

Also edit the `devices` and `raw_journal_devices` entries as appropriate for your deployment.

You're ready! Light the fuse by invoking

```
$ ansible-playbook site.yml
```

and enjoy the show as `ceph-ansible` does what in the bad old days we needed dozens of for loops and individual commands to accomplish. Remember earlier in this chapter when we advised unlimited scroll back history for your terminal application? And garlic fries? This is the time for both.

Ceph-deploy

Alternately, one may use the `ceph-deploy` tool to perform Ceph management tasks at a smaller granularity. If your Ceph infrastructure does not already have `ceph-deploy` enabled, below are succinct instructions on installation and configuration. We discuss the actions to be taken; you will need to apply them across your Ceph nodes via your usual server management practices.

First, create a dedicated user for `ceph-deploy` on all systems to be managed. Popular documentation creates the `ceph-server` user for this task, though you may choose a different name.

```
$ sudo useradd -d /home/ceph-server -m ceph
$ sudo passwd ceph-server
```

Installation of software packages, access to devices, and management of system services require root privileges. `Ceph-deploy` runs and connects to remote systems as our new dedicated user and escalates via `sudo` as it needs to, an approach that avoids having to enable password-less SSH trusts on your cluster nodes. We next enable password-less `sudo` for the unprivileged `ceph-server` user on all nodes to be managed.

```
$ echo "ceph-server ALL = (ALL) NOPASSWD: ALL" | sudo tee
    /etc/sudoers.d/ceph-server
$ sudo chmod 0440 /etc/sudoers.d/ceph-server
```

Next set up password-less SSH trust from your admin host to each of your Ceph production systems for the `ceph-server` user.

```
$ sudo -i -u ceph-server
ceph-server$ ssh-keygen
Generating public/private key pair.
Enter file in which to save the key (/home/ceph-server/.ssh/id_rsa):
Enter passphrase (empty for no passphrase):
Enter same passphrase again:
Your identification has been saved in /home/ceph-server/.ssh/id_rsa.
Your public key has been saved in /home/ceph-server/.ssh/id_rsa.pub.
```

Distribute the new key to each production node (or use your usual method).

```
$ ssh-copy-id ceph-server@some.node
# apt-get install -y ceph-deploy
```

Now install `ceph-deploy` itself on your admin node. Your Linux distribution may already provide this package, or you can download prebuilt packages from `https://download.ceph.com/`. Those so inclined can use the source at `https://github.com/ceph/ceph-deploy`.

```
# yum install -y ceph-deploy
```

That's all it takes! Remember that it is customary to sudo to the `ceph-server` user before running `ceph-deploy`, rather than running as the `root` user.

When invoking `ceph-deploy`, especially when creating OSDs, it's important to have an up-to-date copy of your `ceph.conf` configuration file in the `ceph-server` user's home directory. `ceph-deploy` will compare this to that present on the other side, and if differences are found may require the `--override-conf` flag to continue, which will overwrite `ceph.conf` on the remote system. This is handy when deploying the first OSD on a new node, if `ceph.conf` is not distributed via other means. Be sure that if you automate distribution of `ceph.conf` to your cluster nodes you must maintain the ceph-server user's copy as well.

Flags

Ceph has a number of *flags* that are usually applied across the cluster as a whole. These flags direct Ceph's behavior in a number of ways and when set are reported by `ceph status`.

The most commonly utilized flag is `noout`, which directs Ceph to not automatically mark out any OSDs that enter the down state. Since OSDs will not be marked out while the flag is set, the cluster will not start the backfill / recovery process to ensure optimal replication. This is most useful when performing maintenance, including simple reboots. By telling Ceph *Hold on, we'll be right back* we save the overhead and churn of automatically-triggered data movement.

Here's an example of rebooting an OSD node within a Jewel cluster. First we run `ceph -s` to check the overall status of the cluster. This is an excellent habit to get into before, during, and after even the simplest of maintenance; if something is amiss it is almost always best to restore full health before stirring the pot.

```
# ceph -s
    cluster 3369c9c6-bfaf-4114-9c31-576afa64d0fe
       health HEALTH_OK
       monmap e2: 5 mons at
{mon001=10.8.45.10:6789/0,mon002=10.8.45.11:6789/0,mon003=10.8.45.143:6789/
```

```
0,mon004=10.80.46.10:6789/0,mon005=10.80.46.11:6789/0}
            election epoch 24, quorum 0,1,2,3,4
mon001,mon002,mon003,mon004,mon005
      osdmap e33039: 280 osds: 280 up, 280 in
            flags sortbitwise,require_jewel_osds
      pgmap v725092: 16384 pgs, 1 pools, 0 bytes data, 1 objects
            58364 MB used, 974 TB / 974 TB avail
                16384 active+clean
```

Here we see that the cluster health is HEALTH_OK, and that all 280 OSDs are both up and in. Squeaky clean healthy cluster. Note that two flags are already set: sortbitwise and require_jewel_osds. The sortbitwise flag denotes an internal sorting change required for certain new features. The require_jewel_osds flag avoids compatibility problems by preventing pre-Jewel OSDs from joining the cluster. Both should always be set on clusters running Jewel or later releases, and you will not need to mess with either directly unless you're upgrading from an earlier release.

```
# ceph osd set noout
set noout
```

Now that we've ensured that the cluster is healthy going into our maintenance, we set the noout flag to forestall unwarranted recovery. Note that the cluster health immediately becomes HEALTH_WARN and that a line is added by ceph status showing the reason for the warning state. As we'll explore in Chapter 7, *Monitoring Ceph*, HEALTH_WARN usually denotes a cluster state that deserves attention but is likely not an emergency.

```
# ceph status
    cluster 3369c9c6-bfaf-4114-9c31-576afa64d0fe
        health HEALTH_WARN
                noout flag(s) set
        monmap e2: 5 mons at
{mon001=10.8.45.10:6789/0,mon002=10.8.45.11:6789/0,mon003=10.8.45.143:6789/
0,mon004=10.80.46.10:6789/0,mon005=10.80.46.11:6789/0}
            election epoch 24, quorum 0,1,2,3,4
mon001,mon002,mon003,mon004,mon005
      osdmap e33050: 280 osds: 280 up, 280 in
            flags noout,sortbitwise,require_jewel_osds
      pgmap v725101: 16384 pgs, 1 pools, 0 bytes data, 1 objects
            58364 MB used, 974 TB / 974 TB avail
                16384 active+clean
```

At this point we still have all OSDs up and in; we're good to proceed.

```
# ssh osd013 shutdown -r now
```

We've rebooted a specific OSD node, say to effect a new kernel or to straighten out a confused HBA. Ceph quickly marks the the OSDs on this system down; 20 currently are provisioned on this particular node. Note a new line in the status output below calling out these down OSDs with a corresponding adjustment to the number of up OSDs on the osdmap line. It's easy to gloss over disparities in the osdmap entry, especially when using fonts where values like 260 and 280 are visually similar, so we're pleased that Ceph explicitly alerts us to the situation.

This cluster has CRUSH rules that require copies of data to be in disjoint racks. With the default replicated pool size and min_size settings of three and two respectively all placement groups (PGs) whose acting sets include one of these OSDs are marked undersized and degraded. With only one replica out of service, Ceph continues serving data without missing a beat. This example cluster is idle, but in production when we do this there will be operations that come in while the host is down. These operations will manifest in the output of ceph status as additional lines listing PGs in the state backfill_wait. This indicates that Ceph has data that yearns to be written to the OSDs that are (temporarily) down.

If we had not set the noout flag, after a short grace period Ceph would have proceeded to map that new data (and the existing data allocated to the down OSDs) to other OSDs in the same failure domain. Since a multi-rack replicated pool usually specifies the failure domain as rack, that would mean that each of the surviving three hosts in the same rack as osd013 would receive a share. Then when the host (and its OSDs) comes back up, Ceph would map that data to its original locations, and lots of recovery would ensue to move it back. This double movement of data is superfluous so long as we get the OSDs back up within a reasonable amount of time.

```
# ceph status
    cluster 3369c9c6-bfaf-4114-9c31-576afa64d0fe
     health HEALTH_WARN
            3563 pgs degraded
            3261 pgs stuck unclean
            3563 pgs undersized
            20/280 in osds are down
            noout flag(s) set
     monmap e2: 5 mons at
{mon001=10.8.45.10:6789/0,mon002=10.8.45.11:6789/0,mon003=10.8.45.143:6789/
0,mon004=10.80.46.10:6789/0,mon005=10.80.46.11:6789/0}
            election epoch 24, quorum 0,1,2,3,4
mon001,mon002,mon003,mon004,mon005
     osdmap e33187: 280 osds: 260 up, 280 in; 3563 remapped pgs
            flags noout,sortbitwise,require_jewel_osds
      pgmap v725174: 16384 pgs, 1 pools, 0 bytes data, 1 objects
            70498 MB used, 974 TB / 974 TB avail
```

```
12821 active+clean
 3563 active+undersized+degraded
```

Note also that the tail end of this output tallies PGs that are in certain combinations of states. Here 3563 PGs are noted again as undersized but also active, since they are still available for client operations. The balance of the cluster's PGs are reported as active+clean. Sum the two numbers and we get 16384, as reported on the `pgmap` line.

We can exploit these PG state sums as a handy programmatic test for cluster health. During operations like rolling reboots it is prudent to ensure complete cluster health between iterations. One way to do that is to compare the total PG count with the active number. Since PGs can have other states at the same time as active, such as active+scrubbing and active+scrubbing+deep, we need to sum all such combinations. Here is a simple Ansible play that implements this check.

```
- name: wait until clean PG == total PG
  shell: "ceph -s | awk '/active\+clean/ { total += $1 }; END { print total
}'"
  register:    clean_PG
  until:       total_PG.stdout|int == clean_PG.stdout|int
  retries:     20
  delay:       20
  delegate_to: "{{ ceph_primary_mon }}"
  run_once:    true
```

There is room for improvement: we should use the more surgical ceph pg stat as input, and we should use the safer `-f json` or `-f json-pretty` output formats along with the `jq` utility to guard against inter-release changes. This is, as they say, left as an exercise for the reader.

While we were diverted to the above tip the OSD node we rebooted came back up and the cluster again became healthy. Note that the warning that 20 out of 280 OSDs are down is gone, reflected on the `osdmap` line as well. The health status however remains at HEALTH_WARN so long as we have a flag set that limits cluster behavior. This helps us remember to remove temporary flags when we no longer need their specific behavior modification.

```
# ceph status
  cluster 3369c9c6-bfaf-4114-9c31-576afa64d0fe
  health HEALTH_WARN
  noout flag(s) set
  monmap e2: 5 mons at
{mon001=10.8.45.10:6789/0,mon002=10.8.45.11:6789/0,mon003=10.8.45.143:6789/
0,mon004=10.80.46.10:6789/0,mon005=10.80.46.11:6789/0}
        election epoch 24, quorum 0,1,2,3,4
```

```
mon001,mon002,mon003,mon004,mon005
    osdmap e33239: 280 osds: 280 up, 280 in
          flags noout,sortbitwise,require_jewel_osds
    pgmap v725292: 16384 pgs, 1 pools, 0 bytes data, 1 objects
          58364 MB used, 974 TB / 974 TB avail
          16384 active+clean
```

We'll proceed to remove that flag. This double-negative command would irk your high school grammar teacher, but here it makes total sense in the context of a flag setting.

```
# ceph osd unset noout
unset noout
```

Now that we have no longer tied Ceph's hands the cluster's health status has returned to HEALTH_OK and our exercise is complete.

```
# ceph status
    cluster 3369c9c6-bfaf-4114-9c31-576afa64d0fe
    health HEALTH_OK
    monmap e2: 5 mons at
{mon001=10.8.45.10:6789/0,mon002=10.8.45.11:6789/0,mon003=10.8.45.143:6789/
0,mon004=10.80.46.10:6789/0,mon005=10.80.46.11:6789/0}
          election epoch 24, quorum 0,1,2,3,4
mon001,mon002,mon003,mon004,mon005
    osdmap e33259: 280 osds: 280 up, 280 in
          flags noout,sortbitwise,require_jewel_osds
    pgmap v725392: 16384 pgs, 1 pools, 0 bytes data, 1 objects
          58364 MB used, 974 TB / 974 TB avail
          16384 active+clean
```

With the Luminous release the plain format output of ceph status has changed quite a bit, showing the value of using the -f json output format for scripting tasks.

```
# ceph -s
 cluster:
 id: 2afa26cb-95e0-4830-94q4-5195beakba930c
 health: HEALTH_OK

   services:
     mon: 5 daemons, quorum mon01,mon02,mon03,mon04,mon05
     mgr: mon04(active), standbys: mon05
     osd: 282 osds: 282 up, 282 in

   data:
     pools: 1 pools, 16384 pgs
     objects: 6125k objects, 24502 GB
     usage: 73955 GB used, 912 TB / 985 TB avail
     pgs: 16384 active+clean
```

```
# ceph -s
  cluster:
    id: 2af1107b-9950-4800-94a4-51951701a02a930c
    health: HEALTH_WARN
            noout flag(s) set
            48 osds down
            2 hosts (48 osds) down
            Degraded data redundancy: 3130612/18817908 objects degraded
(16.636%), 8171 pgs unclean, 8172 pgs degraded, 4071 pgs undersized

  services:
    mon: 5 daemons, quorum mon01,mon02,mon03,mon04,mon05
    mgr: mon04(active), standbys: mon05
    osd: 282 osds: 234 up, 282 in
         flags noout

  data:
    pools: 1 pools, 16384 pgs
    objects: 6125k objects, 24502 GB
    usage: 73941 GB used, 912 TB / 985 TB avail
    pgs: 3130612/18817908 objects degraded (16.636%)
             8212 active+clean
             8172 active+undersized+degraded

  io:
    client: 8010 MB/s wr, 0 op/s rd, 4007 op/s wr

# ceph status
  cluster:
    id: 2afa26cb-95e0-4830-94q4-5195beakba930c
    health: HEALTH_WARN
            Degraded data redundancy: 289727/18817908 objects degraded
(1.540%), 414 pgs unclean, 414 pgs degraded

  services:
    mon: 5 daemons, quorum mon01,mon02,mon03,mon04,mon05
    mgr: mon04(active), standbys: mon05
    osd: 283 osds: 283 up, 283 in

  data:
    pools: 1 pools, 16384 pgs
    objects: 6125k objects, 24502 GB
    usage: 73996 GB used, 916 TB / 988 TB avail
    pgs: 289727/18817908 objects degraded (1.540%)
             15970 active+clean
             363 active+recovery_wait+degraded
             51 active+recovering+degraded
```

```
io:
    recovery: 1031 MB/s, 258 objects/s
```

Other flags include `noin`, `norecover`, `nobackfill`, and `norebalance`. Their effects are nuanced and use-cases are few. It is possible to shoot oneself in the foot, so it is suggested to research them and experiment in a busy but non-production cluster to gain full understanding of their dynamics before messing with them.

Later in this chapter we'll touch on the `noscrub` and `nodeepscrub` flags.

Service management

Each Ceph MON, OSD, RGW, MDS, and in recent releases Manager (`ceph-mgr`) daemon is structured as a Linux *service*. Starting and stopping these are at times necessary. The mechanics for doing so differ among Linux distributions, and even among releases of a given distribution.

Systemd: the wave (tsunami?) of the future

Let's first explore Ceph service management on `systemd`—based Linux releases. Loved, hated, but never ignored, `systemd` is becoming increasingly prevalent within major Linux distributions. These include the Red Hat family: RHEL 7 and later, CentOS 7 and later, and Fedora 15 and later. Debian adopted `systemd` with version 8 (Jessie), Ubuntu as of 16.04 (Xenial), and SUSE as of SLES 12.

Installation of Ceph packages leverages `udev` rules and the native service management system to start configured services at boot time. We may also list and manage them individually or on a host-wide basis.

`systemd` organizes services as *units*, which we manage as the root user with the `systemctl` command. To show all the Ceph units configured on a host we issue:

```
# systemctl status ceph.target
```

To stop all running Ceph daemons of any type on a node:

And to start them all back up:

```
# systemctl stop ceph.target
# systemctl start ceph.target
```

Sometimes we need to manage services more precisely, especially on converged (AIO) deployments. We can manage classes of individual Ceph component daemons by specifying their names:

```
# systemctl stop ceph-osd.target
# systemctl start ceph-osd.target
# systemctl stop ceph-mon.target
# systemctl start ceph-mon.target
# systemctl stop ceph-mds.target
# systemctl start ceph-mds.target
# systemctl stop ceph-radosgw.target
# systemctl start ceph-radosgw.target
```

As Ceph's OSDs are both the most numerous and most volatile components of any cluster, we often find ourselves needing to surgically manage individual OSDs without disturbing others on the same server. This applies to other daemons as well, so we can issue the above commands with a more narrow focus on an individual *instance*.

```
# systemctl stop ceph-osd@instance
# systemctl start ceph-osd@instance

# systemctl stop ceph-mds@instance
# systemctl start ceph-mds@instance
# systemctl stop ceph-mon@instance
# systemctl start ceph-mon@instance
# systemctl stop ceph-radosgw@instance
# systemctl start ceph-radosgw@instance
```

For OSDs the *instance* is simply the OSD's number; for other services we use the hostname.

```
# systemctl stop ceph-osd@11
# systemctl start ceph-osd@11
# systemctl stop ceph-mds@monhost-003
# systemctl start ceph-mds@monhost-003
# systemctl stop ceph-mon@monhost-002
# systemctl start ceph-mon@monhost-002
# systemctl stop ceph-radosgw@rgwhost-001
# systemctl start ceph-radosgw@rgwhost-001
```

If one wishes to be very sure, or is impatient, one may of course simply reboot the entire host to restart all services. Each reboot however takes considerably longer and holds a slight but nonzero risk of something going wrong, so it is advised to manage services surgically.

 An exhaustive dive into `systemd` is beyond the scope of this book, but an excellent resource for learning more is here:
`https://www.digitalocean.com/community/tutorials/systemd-essentials-working-with-services-units-and-the-journal`

Upstart

Ubuntu releases earlier than Xenial (such as Trusty) use the Upstart service management system, which is almost, but not entirely unlike `systemd`. Here we'll list analogous Upstart commands for each task explored above.

Showing all Upstart jobs and instances on a given system:

```
# initctl list | grep ceph
```

Stopping and starting all Ceph daemons on a host:

```
# stop ceph-all
# start ceph-all
```

To stop and start all instances of a particular Ceph component on a given host:

```
# stop ceph-osd-all
# start ceph-osd-all
# stop ceph-mon-all
# start ceph-mon-all
# stop ceph-mds-all
# start ceph-mds-all
```

To stop and start individual instances:

```
# stop ceph-osd id=11
# start ceph-osd id=11
# stop ceph-mon id=monhost-005
# start ceph-mon id=monhost-005
# stop ceph-mds id=mdshost-001
# stop ceph-mds id=mdshost-001
# stop ceph-radosgw id=rgwhost-003
# start ceph-radosgw id=rgwhost-003
```

sysvinit

Older releases of Ceph on older Linux releases, such as Firefly on CentOS 6, use traditional *sysvinit* service management with scripts located under /etc/init.d. Below are the analogous service management commands.

```
# /etc/init.d/ceph stop
# /etc/init.d/ceph start
# /etc/init.d/ceph stop mon
# /etc/init.d/ceph start mon
# /etc/init.d/ceph stop osd.69
# /etc/init.d/ceph start osd.69
```

On some systems you may also use the service command.

```
# service ceph start
# service ceph stop mon
# service ceph start osd.69
```

Component failures

Hardware failures are a fact of life. The larger your cluster grows, the more frequently you'll see failures. Fortunately Ceph goes to great lengths to ensure the durability and availability of your precious data.

With proper deployment and consideration of fault domains your Ceph cluster will cruise right through common hardware failures. It is however essential to integrate Ceph into your organization's monitoring framework so that you can address failed components before they pile up. Earlier in this chapter we introduced Ceph's logging strategies and showed some examples; in the next chapter we'll focus on monitoring. At the very least you will want to frequently consult your MON or admin node for cluster status, and alert on these conditions:

- One or more OSDs are down
- Cluster health is HEALTH_ERR
- Inconsistent PGs are reported

Hardware failures are by far the most common causes of these problems. Given the myriad choices of systems and components one may encounter as well as space constraints it would be impractical to cover the details of hardware diagnosis. Chances are that your organization already has mechanisms for checking for drive health, PSU status, HBA faults, memory errors, and dangerous environmental conditions. If your NICs are bonded, you should also ensure that both ports in each bond are up. Your Ceph servers are no less susceptible to these than others, and comprehensive monitoring can often alert you to problems before they become dire.

Probably the most common errors are OSD drive failures; these are the most heavily exercised drives in your deployment. Your servers' management controllers may offer drive error logging, but watching for Linux syslog messages may be more expedient and less hardware-specific. For example on Ubuntu 14.04 with a 3.19 kernel drive errors look like this:

```
2017-09-11T20:21:30 jank11 kernel: [965236] sd 0:0:9:0: [sdk]
FAILED Result: hostbyte=DID_OK driverbyte=DRIVER_SENSE
2017-09-11T20:21:30 jank11 kernel: [965236] sd 0:0:9:0: [sdk] Sense
Key : Medium Error [current] [descriptor]
2017-09-11T20:21:30 jank11 kernel: [965236] sd 0:0:9:0: [sdk] Add.
Sense: Unrecovered read error
2017-09-11T20:21:30 jank11 kernel: [965236] sd 0:0:9:0: [sdk] CDB:
2017-09-11T20:21:30 jank11 kernel: [965236] Read(16): 88 00 00 00
00 01 33 c9 bf 93 00 00 00 01 00 00
2017-09-11T20:21:30 jank11 kernel: [965236] blk_update_request:
critical medium error, dev sdk, sector 5163827091
2017-09-11T20:21:30 jank11 kernel: [965236] XFS (dm-18): metadata
I/O error: block 0x132895793 ("xfs_trans_read_buf_map") error 61
numblks 1
2017-09-11T20:21:30 jank11 kernel: [965236] XFS (dm-18): page
discard on page ffffea002c9b8340, inode 0x580008bc, offset 0.
```

In this case, the drive slot number is right there in the messages -- slot #9. It is common for drive errors to be followed by XFS errors when using FileStore. In most cases this type of error will not cause the associated OSD to crash, but it may continue in a degraded state.

When a hardware error is clearly identified, it's usually best to remove the affected OSD from the cluster, replace the drive, then redeploy. To remove an OSD from service, follow these steps:

- Positively identify the affected OSD, which may or may not show down in `ceph osd tree`.
- Use `ceph osd find` or `ceph osd tree` to find the host that serves that OSD.

- On the OSD host, stop the specific OSD's service instance as we described earlier in this chapter if it has not already crashed. Back on the admin node, ceph status will report the OSD going down.
- Unmount the OSD filesystem, for example,

```
# umount /var/lib/ceph/osd/ceph-1138 &
```

The backgrounding of this command is deliberate. Drive and filesystem errors may result in this hanging.

- Using `sgdisk` or other tools, wipe the partitions from the drive if possible. Again it is prudent to background this in case it blocks.
- Back on your admin node, `ceph status` may already show the cluster recovering from the OSD going down.
- Remove the OSD from the CRUSH map, from the cluster roster, and from the MONs' auth list. Mark it out first for good measure; there are race conditions that this can help avoid.

```
# ceph osd out 1138
# ceph osd crush remove osd.1138
# ceph osd rm osd.1138
# ceph auth del osd.1138
```

- You will now for sure see `ceph status` reporting recovery as the cluster heals, with the health status `HEALTH_WARN`. Once backfill / recovery completes status will return to `HEALTH_OK`.
- After replacing the drive, you can deploy a fresh OSD on it with ceph-deploy using the technique shown in the next section. For a single OSD deploy you most likely do not need to worry about the incremental weighting that we perform below when adding a large number of OSDs at once. If you don't see persistent `slow request`or users with torches and pitchforks most likely this goes unnoticed.

A proof of concept script to automate OSD removal, including additional housekeeping, may be retrieved from Digital Ocean's *Spaces* service:
`https://nyc3.digitaloceanspaces.com/learningceph2ed/remove_osd`

Expansion

In this section we'll cover strategies for growing capacity to meet your users' never-ending thirst for storage. In Chapter 5, *Deploying a Virtual Sandbox Cluster* we used ceph-ansible through Vagrant to add additional components to our cluster; in production on bare metal one can also use ceph-ansible directly to manage many aspects of cluster expansions. The addition of entire OSD hosts and logical racks to a running cluster is straightforward but must be planned carefully. Chapter 8, *Ceph Architecture: Under the Hood* of *Learning Ceph*, walks us through editing the CRUSH map to add logical racks and OSD nodes.

Below we'll summarize the process for adding a new OSD host to an existing Ceph cluster in a more manual, hands-on fashion. It is strongly encouraged that you practice this process with lab or pre-production. Another flexible strategy is to practice on virtualized systems, be they in-house or from a cloud provider such as Digital Ocean.

Visit https://github.com/cernceph/ceph-scripts. Here can be found a wealth of useful Ceph tools from the fine folks at CERN. Here we need to download tools/ceph-gentle-reweight onto our admin node. Around line 63 is a line that looks like the below; comment it out by adding a # at the beginning.

```
# latency = measure_latency(test_pool)
```

In a dedicated window run watch ceph -s to keep an eye on cluster status.

Now install Ceph packages on your new systems. This may be done witheph-ansible, with locally-appropriate invocations of yum, apt-get, or other package management tools. To install, say, the latest Jewel release of Ceph with the ceph-deploy utility, invoke

```
$ ceph-deploy install --release jewel mynewhostname
```

Add the new host(s) to our CRUSH topology. Our cluster for this example is spread across 12 existing hosts located in 4 sturdy metal racks named rack1-iommi, rack2-butler, rack3-ward, and rack4-dio. In order to maintain balance we're adding 1 host to the 3 in each existing rack. First we create host buckets.

```
$ ceph osd crush add-bucket newhost13 host
$ ceph osd crush add-bucket newhost14 host
$ ceph osd crush add-bucket newhost15 host
$ ceph osd crush add-bucket newhost16 host
```

For now, our new host buckets live outside of our cluster's default root bucket, so they are not allocated any data. This is deliberate so that we can set them up fully and bring them into service carefully and on our own terms.

Our `ceph -s` window shows us the OSD population.

```
osdmap e33981: 279 osds: 279 up, 279 in
flags sortbitwise,require_jewel_osds
```

Our new OSD drives may have been previously used for other purposes, and they may even come fresh from your system vendor with an unpredictable yet bizarre set of partitions on them. Our next step will be to survey drives on each remote system then wipe any such partitions from the drives so that they don't confuse our deployment tools. We can use ceph-deploy to show us the status of existing drives and to zap them clean.

```
$ ceph-deploy disk list newhost13 newhost14 newhost15 newhost16
[newhost13][DEBUG ]/dev/sda :
[newhost13][DEBUG ] /dev/sda1 other, linux_raid_member
[newhost13][DEBUG ] /dev/sda2 other, linux_raid_member
[newhost13][DEBUG ]/dev/sdb other, unknown
[newhost13][DEBUG ]/dev/sdc :
[newhost13][DEBUG ] /dev/sdc1 other, unknown
[newhost13][DEBUG ] /dev/sdc2 other, unknown
[...]
```

The `lsblk` utility is also handy for identifying the partitioning and mounts of each drive.

```
# lsblk
NAME    MAJ:MIN RM    SIZE RO TYPE  MOUNTPOINT
sda                   8:0    0 223.6G  0 disk
├─sda1                8:1    0   243M  0 part
│ └─md0               9:0    0 242.8M  0 raid1 /boot
└─sda2                8:2    0 223.3G  0 part
  └─md1               9:1    0 223.2G  0 raid1
    └─vg0-root (dm-0) 252:0  0 223.2G  0 lvm   /
  sdb                 8:16   0   3.5T  0 disk
├─sdb1                8:17   0   3.5T  0 part /var/lib/ceph/osd/ceph-0
└─sdb2                8:18   0    10G  0 part
sdc                   8:32   0   3.5T  0 disk
```

After verifying that the boot drives are the ones we think they are, zap the rest.

```
$ for i in {b..i} ; do ceph-deploy disk zap newhost13:$i ; ceph-
deploy disk zap newhost14:$i ; ceph-deploy disk zap newhost15:
$i; ceph-deploy disk zap newhost16:$i ; done
```

This will take a while but when finished we'll know that all of our drives are ready for deployment. When creating a new OSD, if `ceph-deploy` runs into any existing partitions, it will complain and fail.

Now we create an OSD on each of our new drives. These will automagically be placed inside the appropriate `host` buckets we created above. Since the new host buckets are still located outside of our CRUSH root, these OSDs will not yet receive any new data. If we would prefer to use dmcrypt encryption or the new BlueStore back end we could add `--dmcrypt` and `--bluestore` flags, but let's keep it simple for now.

```
$ ceph-deploy osd create newhost13:sd{b..i}
[ceph_deploy.cli][INFO  ] Invoked (1.5.37): /usr/bin/ceph-deploy osd
create newhost13:sdb
[ceph_deploy.cli][INFO  ] ceph-deploy options:
[ceph_deploy.cli][INFO  ]   username                 : None
[ceph_deploy.cli][INFO  ]   disk                     : [('newhost13',
'/dev/sdb', None)]
[ceph_deploy.cli][INFO  ]   dmcrypt                  : False
[ceph_deploy.cli][INFO  ]   verbose                  : False
[ceph_deploy.cli][INFO  ]   bluestore                : None
[ceph_deploy.cli][INFO  ]   overwrite_conf           : False
[ceph_deploy.cli][INFO  ]   subcommand               : create
[ceph_deploy.cli][INFO  ]   dmcrypt_key_dir          : /etc/ceph/dmcrypt-keys
[ceph_deploy.cli][INFO  ]   quiet                    : False
[ceph_deploy.cli][INFO  ]   cd_conf                  :
<ceph_deploy.conf.cephdeploy.Conf instance at 0x7feeb5599998>
[ceph_deploy.cli][INFO  ]   cluster                  : ceph
[ceph_deploy.cli][INFO  ]   fs_type                  : xfs
[ceph_deploy.cli][INFO  ]   func                     : <function osd at
0x7feeb5e641b8>
[ceph_deploy.cli][INFO  ]   ceph_conf                : None
[ceph_deploy.cli][INFO  ]   default_release          : False
[ceph_deploy.cli][INFO  ]   zap_disk                 : False
[ceph_deploy.osd][DEBUG ] Preparing cluster ceph disks
newhost13:/dev/sdb:
[newhost13][DEBUG ] connection detected need for sudo
[newhost13][DEBUG ] connected to host: newhost13
[newhost13][DEBUG ] detect platform information from remote host
[newhost13][DEBUG ] detect machine type
[newhost13][DEBUG ] find the location of an executable
[newhost13][INFO  ] Running command: sudo /sbin/initctl version
[newhost13][DEBUG ] find the location of an executable
[ceph_deploy.osd][INFO  ] Distro info: Ubuntu 14.04 trusty
[ceph_deploy.osd][DEBUG ] Deploying osd to newhost13
[newhost13][DEBUG ] write cluster configuration to
/etc/ceph/{cluster}.conf
[ceph_deploy.osd][DEBUG ] Preparing host newhost13 disk /dev/sdb
```

```
journal None activate True
[newhost13][DEBUG ] find the location of an executable
[newhost13][INFO  ] Running command: sudo /usr/sbin/ceph-disk -v
prepare --fs-type xfs -- /dev/sdb
[newhost13][WARNIN] command: Running command: /usr/bin/ceph-osd --show-
config-value=fsid
[newhost13][WARNIN] command: Running command: /usr/bin/ceph-osd --
check-allows-journal -i 0 --setuser ceph --setgroup ceph
[newhost13][WARNIN] command: Running command: /usr/bin/ceph-osd --
check-wants-journal -i 0 --setuser ceph --setgroup ceph
[newhost13][WARNIN] command: Running command: /usr/bin/ceph-osd --
check-needs-journal -i 0 --setuser ceph --setgroup ceph
[newhost13][WARNIN] get_dm_uuid: get_dm_uuid /dev/sdb uuid path is
/sys/dev/block/8:16/dm/uuid
[newhost13][WARNIN] set_type: Will colocate journal with data on
/dev/sdb
[newhost13][WARNIN] command: Running command: /usr/bin/ceph-osd --show-
config-value=osd_journal_size
[newhost13][WARNIN] get_dm_uuid: get_dm_uuid /dev/sdb uuid path is
/sys/dev/block/8:16/dm/uuid
[newhost13][WARNIN] get_dm_uuid: get_dm_uuid /dev/sdb uuid path is
/sys/dev/block/8:16/dm/uuid
[newhost13][WARNIN] get_dm_uuid: get_dm_uuid /dev/sdb uuid path is
/sys/dev/block/8:16/dm/uuid
[newhost13][WARNIN] command: Running command: /usr/bin/ceph-conf --
name=osd. --lookup osd_mkfs_options_xfs
[newhost13][WARNIN] command: Running command: /usr/bin/ceph-conf --
name=osd. --lookup osd_mount_options_xfs
[newhost13][WARNIN] get_dm_uuid: get_dm_uuid /dev/sdb uuid path is
/sys/dev/block/8:16/dm/uuid
[newhost13][WARNIN] get_dm_uuid: get_dm_uuid /dev/sdb uuid path is
/sys/dev/block/8:16/dm/uuid
[newhost13][WARNIN] ptype_tobe_for_name: name = journal
newhost13][WARNIN] get_dm_uuid: get_dm_uuid /dev/sdb uuid path is
/sys/dev/block/8:16/dm/uuid
[newhost13][WARNIN] create_partition: Creating journal partition num 2
size 10240 on /dev/sdb
newhost13][WARNIN] command_check_call: Running command: /sbin/sgdisk --
new=2:0:+10240M --change-name=2:ceph journal --partition-
guid=2:8733d257-5b21-4574-8537-95a040ae5929 --
typecode=2:45b0969e-9b03-4f30-b4c6-b4b80ceff106 --mbrtogpt -- /dev/sdb
[newhost13][DEBUG ] Creating new GPT entries.
[newhost13][DEBUG ] The operation has completed successfully.
[newhost13][WARNIN] update_partition: Calling partprobe on created
device /dev/sdb
[newhost13][WARNIN] command_check_call: Running command: /sbin/udevadm
settle --timeout=600
[newhost13][WARNIN] command: Running command: /usr/bin/flock -s
```

```
/dev/sdb /sbin/partprobe /dev/sdb
[newhost13][WARNIN] command_check_call: Running command: /sbin/udevadm
settle --timeout=600
[newhost13][WARNIN] get_dm_uuid: get_dm_uuid /dev/sdb uuid path is
/sys/dev/block/8:16/dm/uuid
newhost13][WARNIN] get_dm_uuid: get_dm_uuid /dev/sdb uuid path is
/sys/dev/block/8:16/dm/uuid
newhost13][WARNIN] get_dm_uuid: get_dm_uuid /dev/sdb2 uuid path is
/sys/dev/block/8:18/dm/uuid
[newhost13][WARNIN] prepare_device: Journal is GPT partition
/dev/disk/by-partuuid/8733d257-5b21-4574-8537-95a040ae5929
[newhost13][WARNIN] prepare_device: Journal is GPT partition
/dev/disk/by-partuuid/8733d257-5b21-4574-8537-95a040ae5929
[newhost13][WARNIN] get_dm_uuid: get_dm_uuid /dev/sdb uuid path is
/sys/dev/block/8:16/dm/uuid
[newhost13][WARNIN] set_data_partition: Creating osd partition on
/dev/sdb
[newhost13][WARNIN] get_dm_uuid: get_dm_uuid /dev/sdb uuid path is
/sys/dev/block/8:16/dm/uuid
[newhost13][WARNIN] ptype_tobe_for_name: name = data
[newhost13][WARNIN] get_dm_uuid: get_dm_uuid /dev/sdb uuid path is
/sys/dev/block/8:16/dm/uuid
[newhost13][WARNIN] create_partition: Creating data partition num 1
size 0 on /dev/sdb
[newhost13][WARNIN] command_check_call: Running comma_partition:
Calling partprobe on created device /dev/sdb
[newhost13][WARNIN] command_check_call: Running command: /sbin/udevadm
settle --timeout=600
[newhost13][WARNIN] command: Running command: /usr/bin/flock -s
/dev/sdb /sbin/partprobe /dev/sdb
[newhost13][WARNIN] command_check_call: Running command: /sbin/udevadm
settle --timeout=600
[newhost13][WARNIN] get_dm_uuid: get_dm_uuid /dev/sdb uuid path is
/sys/dev/block/8:16/dm/uuid
[newhost13][WARNIN] get_dm_uuid:size 8192
[newhost13][WARNIN] switching to logical sector size 512
[newhost13][DEBUG ] meta-data=/dev/sdb1 isize=2048
agcount=32,agsize=29220715 blks
[newhost13][DEBUG ]        =        sectsz=512 attr=2, projid32bit=0
[newhost13][DEBUG ] data =        bsize=4096 blocks=935062865,imaxpct=5
[newhost13][DEBUG ]        =        sunit=0time,
nodiratime,inode64,logbsize=256k,delaylog
[newhost13][WARNIN] command_check_call: Running command: /bin/mount
   -t xfs -o rw,noatime,nodiratime,inode64,logbsize=256k,delaylog --
   /dev/sdb1 /var/lib/ceph/tmp/mnt.LjUwTs
[newhost13][WARNIN] populate_data_path: Preparing osd data dir
   /var/lib/ceph/tmp/mnt.LjUwTs
[newhost13][WARNIN] command: Running command: /bin/chown -R
```

```
          ceph:ceph /var/lib/ceph/tmp/mnt.LjUwTs/ceph_fsid.44648.tmp
[newhost13][WARNIN7-95a040ae5929
[newhost13][WARNIN] command: Running command: /bin/chown -R
    ceph:ceph /var/lib/ceph/tmp/mnt.LjUwTs
[newhost13][WARNIN] unmount: Unmounting /var/lib/ceph/tmp/mnt.LjUwTs
[newhost13][WARNIN] command_check_call: Running command_check_call:
Running command: /sbin/udevadm settle --timeout=600
[newhost13][WARNIN] command_check_call: Running command:
    /sbin/udevadm trigger --action=add --sysname-match sdb1
[newhost13][INFO  ] checking OSD status...
[newhost13][DEBUG ] find the location of an executable
[newhost13][INFO  ] Running command: sudo /usr/bin/ceph osd stat --
    format=json
[newhost13][WARNIN] there is 1 OSD down
[newhost13][DEBUG ] Host newhost13 is now ready for osd use.
    . . .
$ ceph-deploy osd create newhost14:sd{b..i}
$ ceph-deploy osd create newhost15:sd{b..i}
$ ceph-deploy osd create newhost16:sd{b..i}
```

Wow, a lot went on there. You can see the value of using a tool like ceph-deploy to do the heavy lifting for you. We won't go over every line of output above, but in summary ceph-deploy ensures proper partitioning on the drive, creates an XFS filesystem, populates it with the wherewithal for OSD service, and invokes Ceph-specific udev rules that mount and start the OSD. The there is 1 OSD down message looks alarming, but it's harmless: OSDs can take a minute or two to fully boot and register themselves with the MONs

In our `ceph -s` window we see the new OSD added to the family, with the up, in, and osds numbers increment as the process progresses.

```
osdmap e33999: 97 osds: 97 up, 97 in
flags sortbitwise,require_jewel_osds
```

We can run ceph osd tree to see the new OSDs on our new host. With the addition of our nominal 3.84 TB drive, output is something like this.

```
    . . .
-18  3.48199          host
0    3.48199          osd.96       up  1.00000 1.00000
```

Once all our new OSDs are successfully provisioned, we still haven't moved data onto them. First we'll temporarily set their CRUSH weights to 0 to prevent a flood of data rushing in before we're ready. First be sure that you've captured the CRUSH weights displayed by `ceph osd tree`, as we'll need them later. On an admin or MON node as root execute this command with the ID of each of the new OSDs.

```
# ceph osd crush reweight osd.id 0
```

Now it's safe to move the new hosts with their flock of OSDs into their racks. Since the host and OSD weights are now 0, no new data will be allocated to them yet.

```
# ceph osd crush move newhost13 rack=rack1-iommi
# ceph osd crush move newhost14 rack=rack2-butler
# ceph osd crush move newhost15 rack=rack3-ward
# ceph osd crush move newhost16 rack=rack4-dio
```

Running `ceph osd tree` now will show the new hosts and OSDs under each rack.

Now we'll ever so gradually increase the CRUSH weights on our new OSDs so that Ceph will begin to add data. By going in small steps of a few PGs each, we avoid causing a bunch of churn and potential user impact from an avalanche of data flooding onto the new OSDs. Fill in the list of new OSD numbers shown by `ceph osd tree`, being very careful to get the numbers of all (and only) the new OSDs that are currently weighted to 0. For brevity we'll only list three here, but you should list all. Our new OSDs should return to weight 3.48199 but you must be careful to specify the proper number for yours. The -r flag indicates a trial run; when you are satisfied that the script's plan is sound, execute again without it.

```
# ceph-gentle-reweight -b 10 -d 0.01 -t 3.48199 -i 10 -r -o
osd.96,osd.97,osd.98
. . .
# ceph-gentle-reweight -b 10 -d 0.01 -t 3.48199 -i 10 -o
osd.96,osd.97,osd.98
```

While you watch this invaluable utility safely weight your OSDs up into full service, let's briefly discuss what's happening. This script checks the current CRUSH weights of the OSDs in question and keeps an eye on cluster health. When it's safe, each OSD's CRUSH weight is incremented by the -d absolute amount, and the script watches as the cluster rebalances. No additional steps will be taken until the number of PGs backfilling drops below 10, as specified by the -b argument. By setting this to a small but nonzero number we save a bit of time that would otherwise be spent waiting for the last bits of rebalancing to proceed. When backfilling is this light, it's OK to pile on more. The -t argument specifies the final CRUSH weight we want our OSDs to reach. In our case nearly 350 steps will be taken to get us there, a la the Tortoise and the Hare. Finally the -i argument asks the script to rest for an additional 10 seconds between steps, just for good measure.

You may of course adjust these settings to your local conditions, but these are a good starting point. Depending on how full your cluster is and especially the size of your new OSDs this may take a few hours to a few days. Consider running within a tmux session.

As it runs, and especially after it completes, you can invoke `ceph df; ceph osd tree` in a separate window to see the cluster's capacity and the OSD's CRUSH weights slowly but steadily increase. The capacity will also be reflected in your `ceph -s`window. When the script exits you may see a very very slightly different target weight than you had initially. Ceph has a way of truncating or rounding the last significant digit or two. This difference is insignificant and can be disregarded.

Now we've successfully expanded your cluster's capacity by 33% -- possibly more if the new OSD drives are larger than the originals. Your users did not even notice this was going on. Ceph FTW.

In `Chapter 8`, *Ceph Architecture: Under the Hood*, we employ Ceph's CLI tools to augment the CRUSH topology. A brief yet valuable summary of this process can be read at the below page. Consider reading Sébastien Han's superlative blog regularly for valuable insights into getting the most from your Ceph deployments:
https://www.sebastien-han.fr/blog/2014/01/13/ceph-managing-crush-with-the-cli/

Balancing

In the `Chapter 8`, *Ceph Architecture: Under the Hood*, section on OSD Variance we'll explore how a Ceph cluster's complement of OSD data stores can become non-uniformly utilized and the problem this can cause. In this section we'll explore what to do about it.

The larger a cluster's OSD count grows, the wider the variance can become, approximating a bell curve. The `ceph osd df` utility can be used to summarize the utilization of each OSD along with an indication of how much it varies from the overall average. Here's an example of a cluster's distribution before and after we take action. Here our least full OSD is 29% full, just 80% of the cluster's mean, and the most full is over 44% full, 124% of the cluster's mean.

```
# ceph status
    cluster ce2bcf60-efd0-1138-bxc5-936beak1s9a7
      health HEALTH_OK
      monmap e1: 5 mons at
{mon01=10.7.4.4:6789/0,mon02=10.7.4.5:6789/0,mon03=10.7.4.132:6789/0,mon04=
10.7.4.133:6789/0,mon05=10.7.5.4:6789/0}
            election epoch 10, quorum 0,1,2,3,4
mon01,mon02,mon03,mon04,mon05
```

```
       osdmap e14922: 285 osds: 285 up, 285 in
          flags sortbitwise,require_jewel_osds
        pgmap v18454754: 16384 pgs, 1 pools, 119 TB data, 32487 kobjects
              353 TB used, 638 TB / 992 TB avail
                  16364 active+clean
                     14 active+clean+scrubbing+deep
                      6 active+clean+scrubbing
     client io 814 MB/s rd, 537 MB/s wr, 18375 op/s rd, 7170 op/s wr
# ceph osd df | head -3
ID  WEIGHT  REWEIGHT SIZE   USE    AVAIL %USE VAR  PGS
  0 3.48199  1.00000 3565G 1250G 2314G 35.08 0.98 169
  1 3.48199  1.00000 3565G 1377G 2187G 38.64 1.08 186
# ceph osd df | sort -n -k 7 | head -6
ID  WEIGHT  REWEIGHT SIZE   USE    AVAIL %USE VAR  PGS
MIN/MAX VAR: 0.80/1.24  STDDEV: 2.90
                  TOTAL   992T  355T  636T 35.85
253 3.48199  1.00000 3565G 1028G 2536G 28.85 0.80 139
208 3.48199  1.00000 3565G 1046G 2518G 29.36 0.82 141
124 3.48199  1.00000 3565G 1051G 2514G 29.48 0.82 142
# ceph osd df | sort -n -k 7 |tail -3
176 3.48199  1.00000 3565G 1542G 2022G 43.27 1.21 208
241 3.48199  1.00000 3565G 1565G 1999G 43.92 1.22 211
283 3.48199  1.00000 3565G 1589G 1975G 44.58 1.24 214
```

This tabular data shows us what's going on in the cluster, but it can be helpful to visualize the distribution of data as well. Use a wide terminal window; you can see how the longer bars wrap in this rendering.

```
    # ceph osd df | egrep -v WEIGHT\|TOTAL\|MIN\|ID | awk '{print 1,
int($7)}' |  ./histogram.py -a -b 100 -m 0 -x 100 -p 1
    # NumSamples = 285; Min = 0.00; Max = 100.00
    # Mean = 35.385965; Variance = 8.587873; SD = 2.930507; Median
35.000000
    # each ▌ represents a count of 1
        0.0000 -    1.0000 [    0]:  (0.00%)
        1.0000 -    2.0000 [    0]:  (0.00%)
        2.0000 -    3.0000 [    0]:  (0.00%)
   ...
       26.0000 -   27.0000 [    0]:  (0.00%)
       27.0000 -   28.0000 [    1]: ▌ (0.35%)
       28.0000 -   29.0000 [    3]: ▌▌▌ (1.05%)
       29.0000 -   30.0000 [    6]: ▌▌▌▌▌▌ (2.11%)
       30.0000 -   31.0000 [   13]: ▌▌▌▌▌▌▌▌▌▌▌▌▌ (4.56%)
       31.0000 -   32.0000 [   29]:
▌▌▌▌▌▌▌▌▌▌▌▌▌▌▌▌▌▌▌▌▌▌▌▌▌▌▌▌▌ (10.18%)
       32.0000 -   33.0000 [   30]:
▌▌▌▌▌▌▌▌▌▌▌▌▌▌▌▌▌▌▌▌▌▌▌▌▌▌▌▌▌▌ (10.53%)
       33.0000 -   34.0000 [   25]:
```

```
■■■■■■■■■■■■■■■■■■■■■■■■■ (8.77%)
   34.0000 –      35.0000 [    37]:
■■■■■■■■■■■■■■■■■■■■■■■■■■■■■■■■■■■■■ (12.98%)
   35.0000 –      36.0000 [    46]:
■■■■■■■■■■■■■■■■■■■■■■■■■■■■■■■■■■■■■■■■■■■■■■■
                                                    (16.14%)
   36.0000 –      37.0000 [    32]:
■■■■■■■■■■■■■■■■■■■■■■■■■■■■■■■■ (11.23%)
   37.0000 –      38.0000 [    21]: ■■■■■■■■■■■■■■■■■■■■■
                                    (7.37%)
   38.0000 –      39.0000 [    22]: ■■■■■■■■■■■■■■■■■■■■■
                                    (7.72%)
   39.0000 –      40.0000 [     7]: ■■■■■■■ (2.46%)
   40.0000 –      41.0000 [     5]: ■■■■■ (1.75%)
   41.0000 –      42.0000 [     2]: ■■ (0.70%)
   42.0000 –      43.0000 [     5]: ■■■■■ (1.75%)
   43.0000 –      44.0000 [     1]: ■ (0.35%)
   44.0000 –      45.0000 [     0]:   (0.00%)
   45.0000 –      46.0000 [     0]:   (0.00%)
   46.0000 –      47.0000 [     0]:   (0.00%)
```

OSDs that are significantly underweight do not shoulder their share of the cluster's iops; OSDs that are overweight get more than their share and risk an outage when they fill prematurely.

We can squeeze this distribution into a narrower range by adjusting the reweight value of individual OSDs to cause them to receive more (or less) data. In the above example, we might attack the worst offender:

```
# ceph osd reweight 283 .98000
```

This will adjust osd.283's data allocation by a small amount; data will move off of it onto other OSDs. Runs of ceph status will show PGs in the remapped state while the cluster performs *recovery* to converge on the new data distribution. The reweight value must be between 0.0 and 1.0 so unfortunately we cannot assign a reweight greater than 1 to increase utilization of underfull OSDs. Thus we work down from the top; overfull OSD's are the real danger.

We chose to decrement the reweight value only slightly. The greater the change, the more data moves with more potential impact to the cluster. The wise course is slow and steady to avoid disruption and so that we don't overshoot and turn our overfull OSD into an underfull OSD.

We may continue this process iteratively, pushing down the worst offenders, allowing the cluster to rebalance, then pushing down the new worst offender. Rinse, lather, repeat. This becomes something of a Whack-a-Mole game, though, or like squeezing a balloon. A more effective and faster process is to reweight multiple OSDs at once.

This is where Ceph's `ceph osd reweight-by-utilization` tool comes in. This was introduced in the Hammer release, though documentation remains incomplete. One invokes with three arguments:

- A cutoff percentage (or *overload*) threshold; OSDs more full than this value are targeted for deweighting.
- The largest weight change permitted
- The maximal number of PG's to change

This process was initially a stab in the dark; it was difficult to predict how much data would move, and thus rightsizing parameters was a shot in the dark. Jewel introduced a `test-reweight-by-utilization` command to model sets of parameters with a dry run; this was also backported into later dot releases of Hammer.

Here are some example dry runs on the above cluster. We choose a conservative maximum weight change to take and a cap on the number of OSD's to tweak based on the total number in our cluster. It would be nice to add an option to specify this as a percentage versus an absolute number, but we don't have that today. We choose a conservative starting point for the cutoff percentage threshold based on the *overload* that `ceph osd df` shows for our most full OSD. Below we'll try increasingly aggressive thresholds; note that as we approach the mean value of 100% (roughly 35% full as per `ceph df`) the number of PGs affect grows. Once we find a set of parameters that results in a significant but tolerable degree of adjustment we fire it off for real.

```
# ceph osd test-reweight-by-utilization 120 0.01 30
no change
moved 7 / 49152 (0.0142415%)
avg 172.463
stddev 13.9391 -> 13.8722 (expected baseline 13.1095)
min osd.253 with 139 -> 139 pgs (0.805969 -> 0.805969 * mean)
max osd.283 with 214 -> 212 pgs (1.24084 -> 1.22925 * mean)
oload 120
max_change 0.01
max_change_osds 30
average 0.358507
overload 0.430208
osd.283 weight 1.000000 -> 0.990005
osd.241 weight 1.000000 -> 0.990005
osd.176 weight 1.000000 -> 0.990005
```

```
osd.144 weight 1.000000 -> 0.990005
osd.19 weight 1.000000 -> 0.990005
osd.158 weight 1.000000 -> 0.990005
```

The above parameters only move 7 PGs, that isn't much of a change. Let's dial down down the threshold value to grab more of the high end of the distribution's tail.

```
# ceph osd test-reweight-by-utilization 117 0.01 30
no change
moved 10 / 49152 (0.0203451%)
avg 172.463
stddev 13.9391 -> 13.8395 (expected baseline 13.1095)
min osd.253 with 139 -> 139 pgs (0.805969 -> 0.805969 * mean)
max osd.283 with 214 -> 212 pgs (1.24084 -> 1.22925 * mean)
oload 117
max_change 0.01
max_change_osds 30
average 0.358474
overload 0.419415
osd.283 weight 1.000000 -> 0.990005
osd.241 weight 1.000000 -> 0.990005
osd.176 weight 1.000000 -> 0.990005
osd.144 weight 1.000000 -> 0.990005
osd.19 weight 1.000000 -> 0.990005
osd.158 weight 1.000000 -> 0.990005
osd.128 weight 1.000000 -> 0.990005
osd.257 weight 1.000000 -> 0.990005
```

A bit better, but we can be more aggressive.

```
# ceph osd test-reweight-by-utilization 114 0.01 30
no change
moved 24 / 49152 (0.0488281%)
avg 172.463
stddev 13.9391 -> 13.7556 (expected baseline 13.1095)
min osd.253 with 139 -> 139 pgs (0.805969 -> 0.805969 * mean)
max osd.283 with 214 -> 212 pgs (1.24084 -> 1.22925 * mean)
oload 114
max_change 0.01
max_change_osds 30
average 0.358479
overload 0.408666
osd.283 weight 1.000000 -> 0.990005
osd.241 weight 1.000000 -> 0.990005
osd.176 weight 1.000000 -> 0.990005
osd.144 weight 1.000000 -> 0.990005
osd.19 weight 1.000000 -> 0.990005
osd.158 weight 1.000000 -> 0.990005
```

```
osd.128 weight 1.000000 -> 0.990005
osd.257 weight 1.000000 -> 0.990005
osd.171 weight 1.000000 -> 0.990005
osd.179 weight 1.000000 -> 0.990005
osd.149 weight 1.000000 -> 0.990005
osd.97 weight 1.000000 -> 0.990005
osd.37 weight 1.000000 -> 0.990005
osd.304 weight 1.000000 -> 0.990005
# ceph osd test-reweight-by-utilization 112 0.01 30
no change
moved 28 / 49152 (0.0569661%)
avg 172.463
stddev 13.9391 -> 13.7446 (expected baseline 13.1095)
min osd.253 with 139 -> 139 pgs (0.805969 -> 0.805969 * mean)
max osd.283 with 214 -> 212 pgs (1.24084 -> 1.22925 * mean)
oload 112
max_change 0.01
max_change_osds 30
average 0.358480
overload 0.401497
...
```

Better still, but on this all-SSD cluster we can afford to bite off more.

```
# ceph osd test-reweight-by-utilization 110 0.01 30
no change
moved 44 / 49152 (0.0895182%)
avg 172.463
stddev 13.9391 -> 13.6904 (expected baseline 13.1095)
min osd.253 with 139 -> 139 pgs (0.805969 -> 0.805969 * mean)
max osd.283 with 214 -> 212 pgs (1.24084 -> 1.22925 * mean)
oload 110
max_change 0.01
max_change_osds 30
average 0.358480
overload 0.394328
osd.283 weight 1.000000 -> 0.990005
osd.241 weight 1.000000 -> 0.990005
osd.176 weight 1.000000 -> 0.990005
...
```

You can see that as we enter the thicker part of the histogram each step adjusts increasingly more PGs. These parameters seem like a pretty good choice; prudent values for each cluster are be unique and must be determined by careful testing and simulation.

Let's go ahead and invoke the process with these parameters.

```
# ceph osd reweight-by-utilization 110 0.01 30
moved 44 / 49152 (0.0895182%)
avg 172.463
stddev 13.9391 -> 13.6904 (expected baseline 13.1095)
min osd.253 with 139 -> 139 pgs (0.805969 -> 0.805969 * mean)
max osd.283 with 214 -> 212 pgs (1.24084 -> 1.22925 * mean)
oload 110
max_change 0.01
max_change_osds 30
average 0.358437
overload 0.394280
osd.283 weight 1.000000 -> 0.990005
osd.241 weight 1.000000 -> 0.990005
osd.176 weight 1.000000 -> 0.990005
osd.144 weight 1.000000 -> 0.990005
osd.19 weight 1.000000 -> 0.990005
```

As the reweight values are changed the cluster shifts data to converge onto the new CRUSH mappings. This is equivalent to issuing 30 separate `ceph osd reweight` commands, or with Luminous a single `ceph osd reweightn` invocation acting on all at once.

The cluster now enters a period of backfill/recovery. In your trusty `watch ceph status` window you will see the number and percentage of degraded / misplaced objects increase as the PGs plan their adjustments. These values will then progressively decrease as PGs enter the backfilling state where they are actively moving data reflecting our changes to their Acting Sets.

```
    cluster cef00bar40-efd0-11e6-bcc5-936eieiob9a7
        health HEALTH_WARN
                44 pgs backfilling
                recovery 8/100169721 objects degraded (0.000%)
                recovery 157792/100169721 objects misplaced (0.158%)
        monmap e1: 5 mons at
{mon01=10.7.4.4:6789/0,mon02=10.7.4.5:6789/0,mon03=10.7.4.132:6789/0,mo
    n04=10.7.4.133:6789/0,mon05=10.7.5.4:6789/0}
                election epoch 10, quorum 0,1,2,3,4
        mon01,mon02,mon03,mon04,mon05
        osdmap e15516: 285 osds: 285 up, 285 in; 44 remapped pgs
                flags sortbitwise,require_jewel_osds
        pgmap v18489106: 16384 pgs, 1 pools, 120 TB data, 32578
        kobjects
                355 TB used, 636 TB / 992 TB avail
                8/100169721 objects degraded (0.000%)
                157792/100169721 objects misplaced (0.158%)
                    16313 active+clean
```

```
         44 active+remapped+backfilling
         18 active+clean+scrubbing+deep
          9 active+clean+scrubbing
recovery io 7568 MB/s, 2 keys/s, 2018 objects/s
  client io 1080 MB/s rd, 574 MB/s wr, 27120 op/s rd, 11987 op/s wr
```

When this process completes the cluster returns to HEALTH_OK and a histogram refresh shows that we have ever so gently squeezed down the most full OSDs.

```
# ceph osd df | sort -n -k 7 | tail -3
128 3.48199  0.99001 3565G 1541G 2023G 43.23 1.21 208
241 3.48199  0.99001 3565G 1565G 1999G 43.92 1.22 211
283 3.48199  0.99001 3565G 1574G 1990G 44.17 1.23 212
```

Above we see that the most full osd is now only 44.17% full and its variance from the mean has decreased to 123%. osd.283 now holds 15 GB less data than it did before.

```
    cluster cef00bar40-efd0-11e6-bcc5-936eieiob9a7
        health HEALTH_OK
        monmap e1: 5 mons at
{mon01=10.7.4.4:6789/0,mon02=10.7.4.5:6789/0,mon03=10.7.4.132:6789/0,mo
    n04=10.7.4.133:6789/0,mon05=10.76.50.4:6789/0}
            election epoch 10, quorum 0,1,2,3,4
mon01,mon02,mon03,mon04,mon05
        osdmap e15559: 285 osds: 285 up, 285 in
            flags sortbitwise,require_jewel_osds
        pgmap v18492138: 16384 pgs, 1 pools, 120 TB data, 32592 kobjects
            355 TB used, 636 TB / 992 TB avail
            16361 active+clean
               17 active+clean+scrubbing+deep
                6 active+clean+scrubbing
    client io 996 MB/s rd, 573 MB/s wr, 29542 op/s rd, 14264 op/s wr
    # ceph osd df | egrep -v WEIGHT\|TOTAL\|MIN\|ID | awk '{print 1,
int($7)}' | ./histogram.py -a -b 100 -m 0 -x 100 -p 1
    # NumSamples = 285; Min = 0.00; Max = 100.00
    # Mean = 35.392982; Variance = 8.182407; SD = 2.860491; Median
35.000000
    # each ▮ represents a count of 1
        0.0000 -     1.0000 [     0]:  (0.00%)
    ...
       26.0000 -    27.0000 [     0]:  (0.00%)
       27.0000 -    28.0000 [     1]: ▮ (0.35%)
       28.0000 -    29.0000 [     2]: ▮▮ (0.70%)
       29.0000 -    30.0000 [     6]: ▮▮▮▮▮▮ (2.11%)
       30.0000 -    31.0000 [    14]: ▮▮▮▮▮▮▮▮▮▮▮▮▮▮ (4.91%)
       31.0000 -    32.0000 [    26]: ▮▮▮▮▮▮▮▮▮▮▮▮▮▮▮▮▮▮▮▮▮▮▮▮▮▮ (9.12%)
       32.0000 -    33.0000 [    32]: ▮▮▮▮▮▮▮▮▮▮▮▮▮▮▮▮▮▮▮▮▮▮▮▮▮▮▮▮▮▮▮▮▮▮ (11.23%)
       33.0000 -    34.0000 [    26]: ▮▮▮▮▮▮▮▮▮▮▮▮▮▮▮▮▮▮▮▮▮▮▮▮▮▮ (9.12%)
```

```
       34.0000 -     35.0000 [    36]: ███████████████████████████████████████
(12.63%)
       35.0000 -     36.0000 [    45]: ████████████████████████████████████████████████
(15.79%)
       36.0000 -     37.0000 [    33]: ████████████████████████████████████ (11.58%)
       37.0000 -     38.0000 [    22]: ████████████████████████ (7.72%)
       38.0000 -     39.0000 [    25]: ████████████████████████████ (8.77%)
       39.0000 -.    40.0000 [     7]: ████████ (2.46%)
       40.0000 -     41.0000 [     3]: ███ (1.05%)
       41.0000 -     42.0000 [     2]: ██ (0.70%)
       42.0000 -     43.0000 [     4]: ████ (1.40%)
       43.0000 -     44.0000 [     1]: █ (0.35%)
       44.0000 -     45.0000 [     0]: (0.00%)
```

The post-reweight histgram reflects a modest improvement in variance and standard deviation. We actually made more of difference than the absolute values reported by ceph df indicate; in the time between out first look at distribution and our post-adjustment survey the cluster gained roughly 2TB of data, which pushes up the percentage fullness of all OSD's a bit as each accepts new data.

In production we would repeat this process with incrementally larger threshold and/or OSD count values to put the squeeze on the distribution curve, which will become flat on the high end and more narrow toward the low end. This ensures that our cluster can accept more data and be more fully utilized before most-full OSDs cross our warning and error thresholds described in the next chapter.

The histogram.py filter and other useful tools can be retrieved from: https://gitlab.cern.ch/ceph/ceph-scripts

Upgrades

Upgrading an existing, production Ceph cluster can be both straightforward and tricky. It is best to not leapfrog LTS releases when upgrading. For example, if you're still running Firefly, instead of upgrading directly to Luminous you should consider upgrading first to Hammer, then to Jewel, and only then to Luminous. This strategy considers that the constellation of old and new versions is as large as the resources to test all combinations are limited.

Each Ceph release is accompanied by release notes that detail the best process for upgrades. In some cases there are crucial gotchas that must be considered. For example, by default daemons in Jewel and later releases run as the ceph user, instead of root. When upgrading to Jewel from an earlier release one must carefully change the ownership of all files within each OSD's filesystem. Bear in mind as well that downgrading to an earlier major release of Ceph is generally not supported. Try out a new version in a test cluster before you commit it to production.

The logistics of upgrades include many variables, including your management tools, package management strategy, and the components one has deployed. In at least one case package names changed between releases, complicating their management. In general terms an upgrade follows this path:

- Upgrade the `ceph`, `ceph-common`, `librbd`, etc. packages with `yum`, `apt-get`, etc. This can be performed in parallel and without taking down servers, though you do not want to do this too far in advance. Validate the successful and full installation of all packages on every system.
- Sequentially restart the MONs, allowing each to boot and fully rejoin the quorum before proceeding to the next.
- Sequentially restart the OSDs. You may do them individually, or an entire host at a time. Don't forget the `noout` flag! Before proceeding to the next server and especially before crossing failure domains it is critical to ensure that all OSDs are up and in, that backfill/recovery has completed, and that all PGs are active+clean.
- Sequentially restart any RGW and MDS servers. Allow each to fully start and become active before proceeding.

That said, some major Ceph releases, or even dot releases within a major version, may require different ordering, say OSD nodes first then MONs. Read the release notes carefully.

Above we mentioned the need for pervasive file ownership permission changes on FileStore OSDs when one upgrades to Jewel. This adds up to considerable elapsed time even if one runs all OSDs on each host in parallel. There's a clever trick that allows us to perform this transition task incrementally. In `ceph.conf` one can configure
`setuser match path = /var/lib/ceph/$type/$cluster-$id`

This will direct daemons to run as the user who owns each individual data directory root. In this way one may then proceed at relative leisure to iterate across the OSD complement halting each individual OSD in sequence, `chown -R`, start the OSD anew, and remove the noout flag. Don't forget to bracket each set of OSDs with the `noout` flag!

Linux kernel or even whole operating system upgrades are often more straightforward than Ceph release upgrades. One can typically install updated packages in advance, effect any necessary configuration file changes, then sequentially reboot Ceph servers, again ensuring that they come back up fully and the cluster heals between each. Ordering is usually not important here, though it is not uncommon to follow the same MON=>OSD=>RGW=>MDS sequence as above.

> An excellent summary of many of the commands described in this chapter may be found here:
> `https://sabaini.at/pages/ceph-cheatsheet.html`
> The `ceph-ansible` project mentioned in this and other chapters offers convenient tools for Ceph release upgrades and other management tasks. See `http://ceph.com/geen-categorie/ceph-rolling-upgrades-with-ansible/` for details.

Working with remote hands

Practices for the actual physical management of servers and components varies by organization. In smaller settings especially Ceph admins may site near the datacenters in which production systems are housed, and be responsible for hardware installation and management. In other and larger organizations, especially those with multiple datacenters within a country or around the world, there may be a dedicated DC Ops team or contracted third party.

We often refer to anyone who performs physical server installation and maintenance tasks as *remote hands* or simply *hands*, referring to the fact that they are able to lay literal hands on the systems that a distant admin cannot.

Whichever arrangement floats your organization's boat, there are a number of practices that can optimize hardware management logistics. Some of us may work in busy, loud, shared office spaces, but datacenters are a whole new level of loud and cold. Careful co-ordination can save time and avoid mistakes when performing maintenance tasks, especially when replacing failed components. This topic may seem trivial and out of scope, but Ceph clusters comprise large numbers of twisty servers, all alike, and this author has seen this aspect of server management time and again fail horribly.

Here's a litany of best practices for working with datacenter hands.

- **Lose your voice**
  DCs house hundreds or thousands of spinning fans and cacophonous air handlers. They are *LOUD* and your hands folks should be wearing hearing protection. Fancy noise-cancelling headsets if available can vary in their effectiveness. But even in a silent room voice is a flawed way to communicate with DC hands. Like luggage at an airport, many names and digits do sound alike, and transcription errors are all too common. Was that serial number was 83423NCC1701 or A3423NEE1701? Should I yank drive twenty or twenty-one? The only way to win is not to play. Calls are fine for discussing logistics, but not for exchanging precise data.

- **Real-time digital communication**
  It's vital for admins and hands to be able able to communicate digitally. Ideal is a laptop or tablet with instant messaging or collaboration tools like Jabber, Slack, or Cisco Spark. In a pinch you can use a smartphone or even the chat pane of a Zoom, Cisco WebEx, Google Hangout conference. These media allow one to cut/paste information, avoiding transcription errors. Email is not the best medium here given propagation delays, but it can be useful when nothing else is available.

- **Network access**
  It's best for the DC hands to have network access, to the Internet at large or at least to your internal network. This allows them to retrieve firmware files and diagrams, and to send you photos and screen captures.

- **Just the right tool**
  Software and hardware: This author once worked with an excellent node engineer who was employed by a different and rather parsimonious business unit. They had him using hand tools for hundreds of fasteners every day. The gift of a $30 electric screwdriver was invaluable for efficiency and made me his new best friend.
  Simple hand tools also have a way of walking away even from a locked DC hall, and among the worst frustrations is discovering only after you take a system down that your system vendor uses T10 Torx screws but the tech has only a stripped Phillips driver.

- **Verify server identity**
  Adhesive stickers can be handy for visually locating a server, but they can just as easily be deadly. Don't rely on them. They can fade, fall off, be reattached to the wrong server, or be written incorrectly in the first place. Repurposed systems may not get a new and unique label. A different department's server in the next rack may have a name that varies from yours only by a hyphen. This author has been bit by all of these and has learned to not trust them. Modern systems often don't even have a space to attach a label given the desire to pack the front panel with as many connectors, indicator lights, and drive bays as possible.

  There are several better methods for ensuring that hands unplug and work on the proper server. Use them together when possible.
    - Indicator lights: tools like ipmitool, storcli, and hpssacli allow one to flash LED's for visual identification of desired servers
    - Serial numbers: Always refer to servers and drives by their serial numbers and never transcribe them. Cut/paste or extract digitally. The facter utility is great for this on a variety of hardware. Run facter hostname serialnumber productname and paste the results to your tech for multiple levels of identification. Utilities like hpssacli, dmidecode, facter, and storcli also help with component serials
    - Power: modern servers often have sophisticated BMCs or other ACPI power management systems. The last step of preparing a system for maintenance can be to run shutdown -P now; this will power down most server components, lights, and fans. The subject server is thus visually and audibly distinct.
    - Lockstep check-in
      Ensure that remote hands verify with you that your server is ready for them to tear into, that they have located the proper serial number, and that you're ready for them to reconnect power and network connections and boot it on up. Most importantly of all, make sure that they don't leave for the day until you both agree that the task is complete and the server is functional.

Summary

In this chapter, we covered a wide variety of operational and maintenance tasks that are part of a Ceph cluster's lifecycle. We explored cluster topology, a topic we'll continue in `Chapter 7`, *Monitoring Ceph*, as well as Ceph's logging system. We also delved into `ceph.conf` for startup configuration, injection for dynamic runtime configuration, and admin sockets for harvesting a wealth of status and configuration detail. Also touched upon was the value of a formal configuration management system such as `ceph-ansible`.

We also expanded on the topics of adding and replacing failed drives that were touched upon in the previous chapter and offered strategies for the oft-overlooked nuances of working effectively with remote hands.

It may seem odd that we have not devoted an entire chapter to the step by step initial deployment of production Ceph clusters. There are readily available automation tools and resources to help with this process. Duplicating their multivariate minutia here or cutting and pasting large swaths of ceph.com would leave less space to focus on the insights and wisdom the authors strive to share.

For initial cluster bootstrapping we recommend the excellent ceph-ansible project available here:

`https://github.com/ceph/ceph-ansible/wiki`

A useful blog post detailing one admin's experience using ceph-ansible to bootstrap a cluster can be read here:

`http://egonzalez.org/ceph-ansible-baremetal-deployment/`

Those wishing a more hands-on, under-the-hood bootstrap experience will enjoy the reference site:

`http://docs.ceph.com/docs/master/rados/deployment/`

In the next chapter, we will explore the monitoring of your Ceph clusters' well-being.

7
Monitoring Ceph

In this chapter, we will cover the following topics.

- Monitoring Ceph clusters
- Monitoring Ceph MONs
- Monitoring Ceph OSDs
- Monitoring Ceph PGs
- Monitoring Ceph MDS
- Open source dashboards and tools

Monitoring Ceph clusters

Monitoring is the process of gathering, aggregating, and processing important quantifiable information about a given system. It enables us to understand the health of the system and its components and provides information necessary to take steps to troubleshoot problems that arise. A well-monitored system will let us know when something is broken or is about to break. Deploying a Ceph cluster involves an orchestration dance among hundreds, thousands, or even tens of thousands of interconnected components including variety of kernels, processes, storage drives, controllers (HBAs), network cards (NICs), chassis, switches, PSUs,and so on. Each of these components can fail or degrade in its own unique way.

External monitoring of a complex system is itself a significant endeavor and is best worked right into the architecture and deployment model. When monitoring is an afterthought (*we'll get to it in phase 2*) it tends to be less effective and less pervasively implemented.

Ceph is in many ways a self-monitoring and self-healing system. It is however valuable to integrate with external monitoring and trending tools so that we can address hardware faults and ensure optimal performance and capacity. Identifying and fixing the root causes of hardware or non-Ceph process failures is beyond the scope of this chapter, so we will focus on the overall functionality and performance of Ceph clusters.

Third party components or services often provide their own monitoring interfaces. Production Ceph clusters typically serve a large set of clients. The types of those clients vary depending on whether a cluster is used for RBD images, CephFS volumes, as an Object Storage backend, or all of the above. Each deployment environment has different requirements for reliability that depend primarily on the use-case. Some Ceph clusters are used predominantly for internal clients and a **Service Level Agreement (SLA)** of less than 99% uptime suffices. Others serve users who are external actors/customers that pay for higher reliability and uptime guarantees. There are also clusters deployed with a mixed client population with separate tiers of SLAs. There are all sorts of use-cases for Ceph on varied types of client systems, too many to cover in this chapter so we will not dive into the details of client-side monitoring here.

When monitoring a Ceph system we will primary exploit native CLI tools that are provided by the ceph-common package. These tools are available as subcommands of the ceph utility and output reports on their standard output (stdout). These reports can offer a great deal of detail and usually provide ample information to help diagnose issues is and locate the where the problem lies. These tools provide invaluable information regarding the state of the cluster but do not always provide everything required for a thorough **root-cause analysis (RCA)**.

For this reason it is recommended to rely on other diagnostic utilities that your Linux distribution or hardware manufacturer provides. We touched upon some of these Ceph commands and external utilities in previous chapters. It is vital that in addition to the Ceph-specific monitoring that we monitor basic hardware state -- CPUs, memory modules, NICs, drive controllers, power supplies, and so on. We can do so either through the operating system with tools including mcelog, rsyslog, and ipmitool or directly leveraging a server's management controller (BMC) using network IPMI, Redfish, or SNMP traps. Some platforms offer rich proprietary tools as well, including the XML API to Cisco's UCS. Your existing infrastructure no doubt already exploits one or more of these hardware monitoring approaches, and your Ceph systems should slot right in.

Ceph cluster health

The health check is one of the most common and important commands that a Ceph system administrator will employ frequently to stay aware of any major issues. The output of the health check gives a quick 40,000 ft. view of whether the cluster is performing normally or if it is degraded. If a cluster is unhealthy, we can use the same command to get a detailed view of where the problem lies. Even though it might not always be able tell us what the exact problem is, we can use it in almost every case to narrow our scope and focus our investigation to a very specific area.

To check the health of the cluster, we will use the health subcommand of the ceph utility.

```
root@ceph-client0:~# ceph health
HEALTH_OK
```

When Ceph cluster is healthy the status will be HEALTH_OK. In all other cases, it will present a status of HEALTH_WARN or HEALTH_ERR followed by a short summary of the major problems the cluster is undergoing. There is talk of introducing additional states with future versions of Ceph, but as we write these are the only three.

It is useful to note that all Ceph commands emit output in a plain format that is easily readable by humans. There isn't always a human parsing the output, though: sometimes code may invoke commands for monitoring, to display in a dashboard, or to derive additional results based on analysis. In such cases we can use the --format switch to emit output in an appropriate format. This is especially useful for monitoring systems, as the plain, human-oriented formatting tends to change between releases, but the computer-oriented formats are largely invariant.

For instance if we desire the health output in JSON format we can invoke:

```
root@ceph-client0:~# ceph health --format json
```

```
{"health":{"health_services":[{"mons":[{"name":"ceph-
mon0","kb_total":306935960,"kb_used":2815616,"kb_avail":2
88505780,"avail_percent":93,"last_updated":"2017-09-17
19:07:59.682571","store_stats":{"bytes_total":98218171,"b
ytes_sst":0,"bytes_log":938237,"bytes_misc":97279934,"las
t_updated":"0.000000"},"health":"HEALTH_OK"}]}]},"timeche
cks":{"epoch":6,"round":0,"round_status":"finished"},"sum
mary":[],"overall_status":"HEALTH_OK","detail":[]}
```

The --format json switch emits output in JSON format. The details of plain and other formats may differ, so make sure to understand the output before sending to a parser.

Ceph currently avails us of following output formats:

- plain (default)
- xml
- xml-pretty (both parser and human friendly)
- json
- json-pretty (both parser and human friendly)

An unhealthy cluster, for example, can look as follows:

```
root@ceph-client0:~# ceph health
HEALTH_WARN 71 pgs degraded; 67 pgs stuck unclean; 71 pgs undersized;
recovery 57/573 objects degraded (9.948%); mds cluster is degraded; 1/6 in
osds are down
```

The first word in the output (HEALTH_WARN) indicates the current health of the cluster. As of Ceph's Jewel release, the health of a Ceph cluster can only be in 3 states:

1. HEALTH_OK: The cluster is healthy and client I/O is serviced as expected.
2. HEALTH_WARN: The cluster is degraded but there is a (possibly) minor problem. A host may have died or a rack may have lost power, but client I/O continues.
3. HEALTH_ERR: The cluster is unhealthy and there is major impact to some or all client I/O. This can be triggered by large scale degradation when multiple racks or hosts across multiple racks go down simultaneously.

Let's examine about the output of the above command in slightly more detail, splitting the output into distinct symptoms. Each symptom is separated by a semicolon (";").

- HEALTH_WARN: The cluster is degraded.
- 71 PGs degraded: A total of 71 PGs are affected, possibly because one or more of OSDs have gone down.
- 67 pgs stuck unclean: Out of a total of 71 affected PGs, 67 are in the unclean state. PGs that do not have their all the OSDs in their acting set completely up to date are marked unclean.
- 71 pgs undersized: There are 71 PGs which have fewer copies than configured as the replication size of the their pool.

- `Recovery 57/573 objects degraded (9.948%)`: The recovery process has begun and presently 53 RADOS objects are marked degraded and queued for recovery. The cluster holds a total of 573 RADOS objects, thus the fraction in the degraded state is 53 / 573 = 9.948%.
- `mds cluster is degraded`: The MDS cluster deployed for CephFS is degraded as well. This could be because one or more of MDS daemons are not started yet or not functioning as expected.
- `1/6 osds are down`: 1 OSD is down in our cluster out of a total of 6. The degradation of 67 PGs (across 53 objects) may have been a result of the OSD going down.

Every cluster is built and configured differently, with a different number of OSDs and unique pool settings. Thus all the above issues might not translate 1-to-1 to your setup; we provide them here as a reference example. However, if your cluster is showing HEALTH_WARN that does mean you might need to take a look even if the problem seems transient in nature.

There are other subcommands we can use to display the current state of a Ceph cluster, notably status (-s). The output of this command during the above degradation is shown in the following:

```
root@ceph-client0:~# ceph status
cluster e6d4e4ab-f59f-470d-bb76-511deebc8de3
health HEALTH_WARN
71 pgs degraded
67 pgs stuck unclean
71 pgs undersized
recovery 57/573 objects degraded (9.948%)
1/6 in osds are down
monmap e1: 1 mons at {ceph-mon0=192.168.42.10:6789/0}
election epoch 5, quorum 0 ceph-mon0
fsmap e10989: 1/1/1 up {0=ceph-mds0=up:active}
osdmap e4165: 6 osds: 5 up, 6 in; 71 remapped pgs
flags sortbitwise,require_jewel_osds
pgmap v10881: 128 pgs, 9 pools, 3656 bytes data, 191 objects
1570 MB used, 63763 MB / 65333 MB avail
57/573 objects degraded (9.948%)
71 active+undersized+degraded
57 active+clean
client io 15433 B/s rd, 14 op/s rd, 0 op/s wr
```

We will talk about the output of status command in detail further in this chapter.

Sometimes it is useful to pull detailed information about cluster health. We can pass in the detail flag to see a comprehensive report about degradation. This is especially useful when ceph status reports slow/blocked requests, as at a glance we can see if they are systemic or limited to a specific OSD:

```
root@ceph-client0:~# ceph health detail
HEALTH_WARN 71 pgs degraded; 67 pgs stuck unclean; 71 pgs undersized;
recovery 57/573 objects degraded (9.948%); 1/6 in osds are down
pg 0.f is stuck unclean for 358.447499, current
stateactive+undersized+degraded, last acting [3,2]
pg 8.7 is stuck unclean for 514634.143404, current state
active+undersized+degraded, last acting [2,3]
pg 8.6 is stuck unclean for 358.625153, current state
active+undersized+degraded, last acting [2,3]
pg 0.d is stuck unclean for 362.888847, current state
active+undersized+degraded, last acting [4,3]
pg 8.5 is stuck unclean for 358.446944, current state
active+undersized+degraded, last acting [3,2]
pg 0.a is stuck unclean for 362.888290, current state
active+undersized+degraded, last acting [4,3]
...
pg 0.38 is active+undersized+degraded, acting [0,4]
pg 0.37 is active+undersized+degraded, acting [3,2]
pg 0.34 is active+undersized+degraded, acting [4,3]pg 0.33 is
active+undersized+degraded, acting [4,0]
pg 7.4 is active+undersized+degraded, acting [0,4]
...
recovery 57/573 objects degraded (9.948%)
osd.1 is down since epoch 4160, last address 192.168.42.100:6800/11356
```

We have already discussed the summary at the top of this example output. We will now explore the balance of the output by breaking it down into the following segments.

- `pg X is stuck unclean for T, current state Y, last acting Z`

  This message is printed for each PG that is degraded (mainly in the stuck unclean state). The `X` indicates the ID of the PG, `T` shows the duration it has been degraded, the current state of the PG is `Y`, and `Z` denotes the acting set of OSDs that were last serving the I/O.

- `pg X is Y, acting Z`

  Building on what we learned about the above pattern, we can see that the ID (`pgid`) of the subject PG is `X`, the state is `Y`, and `Z` is the acting set of OSDs.

- `recovery A/B objects degraded (C%)`

  These messages tell us that A number of Ceph objects are being recovered, out of a total of B objects in the cluster. C's value is A divided by B, expressed as a percentage, and thus shows the fraction of data within the cluster that is not optimally replicated.

- `osd.X is down since epoch Y, last address Z`

  These entries list any Ceph OSDs that are marked with the down state. X is the numeric ID of the subject OSD. Y is the integer epoch of the cluster's OSD map. Z is the most recent IP address: the port pair from which the OSD last communicated to the MONs. There may also be a process ID appended to the `ip:port` pair separated by a slash character (/), which is 11,356 in the preceding example.

Watching cluster events

We can specify the `-w` switch in the ceph utility to watch the cluster for events in real time. We can watch for all types of messages including **debug (DBG)**, **info (INF)**, **warn (WRN)**, **error, (ERR)**, and **security (SEC)**. Output will be continually printed as events occur until we terminate the process.

```
root@ceph-client0:~# ceph -w
cluster e6d4e4ab-f59f-470d-bb76-511deebc8de3
health HEALTH_OK
monmap e1: 1 mons at {ceph-mon0=192.168.42.10:6789/0}
election epoch 5, quorum 0 ceph-mon0
fsmap e15527: 1/1/1 up {0=ceph-mds0=up:active}
osdmap e6264: 6 osds: 6 up, 6 in
flags sortbitwise,require_jewel_osds
pgmap v16377: 128 pgs, 9 pools, 3656 bytes data, 191 objects
2102 MB used, 63231 MB / 65333 MB avail
128 active+clean
2017-09-16 23:39:10.225183 mon.0 [INF] pgmap v16377: 128 pgs: 128
active+clean; 3656 bytes data, 2102 MB used, 63231 MB / 65333 MB avail
2017-09-16 23:40:28.009152 mon.0 [INF] osd.1 marked itself down
2017-09-16 23:40:28.087948 mon.0 [INF] osdmap e6265: 6 osds: 5 up, 6 in
2017-09-16 23:40:28.101414 mon.0 [INF] pgmap v16378: 128 pgs: 128
active+clean; 3656 bytes data, 2102 MB used, 63231 MB / 65333 MB avail
2017-09-16 23:40:29.111695 mon.0 [INF] osdmap e6266: 6 osds: 5 up, 6 in
2017-09-16 23:40:32.152057 mon.0 [INF] pgmap v16381: 128 pgs: 71
active+undersized+degraded, 67 active+clean; 3656 bytes data, 2100 MB used,
63233 MB / 65333 MB avail; 57/573 objects degraded (9.948%) ...
```

The severity for events will be familiar to those who have worked with syslog. The DBG severity is at the lowest level and ERR is at the highest. If we specify the DBG level (and implicitly all higher levels) while watching events, we will track everything happening on the cluster. By default the event level is INF, which is one level higher than DBG, and thus we see everything in the event stream with the exception of debug entries.

The following are the levels we can add to constrain event reporting:

- `--watch-debug`: Watch all events, including debug events. This is the most verbose level.
- `--watch-info`: Watch info and all events at higher levels. Debug events won't be visible.
- `--watch-sec`: Watch security and higher level events.
- `--watch-warn`: Watch warning events and the ones at a higher level.
- `--watch-error`: Watch only error events. No other events will be visible.

You may recognize the preamble of the output of ceph -w as identical to that of the ceph status command.

Utilizing your cluster

Your awesome Ceph clusters will find themselves increasingly full of user data. It will be necessary to track and anticipate utilization over time to plan future cluster expansion. It's important to plan ahead: acquiring and provisioning new servers can take months. Your users will be doubly unhappy if the cluster runs out of space before you can expand. Ceph provides tools that show the overall cluster utilization as well as the distribution per Ceph pool. We will use the df subcommand of the ceph utility to display the current stats.

```
root@ceph-client0:~# ceph df
GLOBAL:
SIZE AVAIL RAW USED %RAW USED
65333M 63376M 1957M 3.00
POOLS:
NAME ID USED %USED MAX AVAIL OBJECTS
rbd 0 0 0 21113M 0
cephfs_data 1 0 0 21113M 0
cephfs_metadata 2 2068 0 21113M 20
.rgw.root 3 1588 0 21113M 4
default.rgw.control 4 0 0 21113M 8
default.rgw.data.root 5 0 0 21113M 0
default.rgw.gc 6 0 0 21113M 32
default.rgw.log 7 0 0 21113M 127
```

```
default.rgw.users.uid 8 0 0 21113M 0
```

The `df` subcommand presents utilization stats in two sections, global and per-pool. A single Ceph cluster may have multiple pools for RBD, RGW, and CephFS services, each with their own level of utilization.

The columns in `GLOBAL` section present the following:

- `SIZE`: The total usable capacity in bytes of the Ceph cluster, accounting for replication.
- `AVAIL`: The amount of total capacity that is yet to be utilized, that is available for user data. This value is equal to total capacity of the pool subtracted from `Raw Used`.
- `RAW USED`: The total number of bytes that have already been allocated on the cluster.
- `%RAW USED`: This value is denoted by the percentage of utilized space on the cluster. This value is calculated by *(Raw Used / Size) * 100*.

The columns in the `POOLS` section present the following:

- `NAME`: The name of the pool.
- `ID`: The unique integer identifier of the pool. The ID of the pool prefixes the placement group pgids of all PGs belonging to that pool. This ensures that the `pgid` of a PG is unique across the entire cluster.
- `Used`: Size in amount of bytes allocated within the pool.
- `%Used`: Total percentage utilized to be allocated capacity within the pool.
- `Max Avail`: The capacity available to be allocated within the pool. Note that this value is a function of the replication size of the pool, a topic we'll cover in more detail in the next chapter. We can see from the preceding example that for each of our example's pools Max Avail is 21 GB. Each of our pools is configured with a replication size of three and thus their total raw unused is equal to 63 GB raw (which is the capacity of the cluster). Also note that this value is shared across all pools and is calculated relative to the total capacity of the cluster. This distinction can be tricky: PGs themselves belong strictly to a given pool, but when multiple pools share the same OSDs their PGs all contend for the same available drive space.
- `objects`: The count of Ceph objects within each pool.

The holistic view is quite useful, especially while forecasting growth for the entire cluster and planning for expansion. At times we may also want to check how evenly the data is internally distributed within the cluster and how much each OSD holds. Ceph releases starting with Hammer provide the invaluable osd df subcommand to display the internal distribution, allowing us to see if any one or more OSDs are taking on more capacity, and thus workload, than they should. This is similar to the Linux `df` command used for traditional filesystem statistics.

```
root@ceph-client0:~# ceph osd df
ID WEIGHT REWEIGHT SIZE USE AVAIL %USE VAR PGS
0 0.01039 1.00000 10888M 325M 10563M 2.99 1.00 57
3 0.01039 1.00000 10888M 323M 10565M 2.97 0.99 71
1 0.01039 1.00000 10888M 332M 10556M 3.05 1.02 71
5 0.01039 1.00000 10888M 325M 10563M 2.99 1.00 57
2 0.01039 1.00000 10888M 326M 10562M 3.00 1.00 71
4 0.01039 1.00000 10888M 326M 10562M 3.00 1.00 57
TOTAL 65333M 1959M 63374M 3.00
MIN/MAX VAR: 0.99/1.02 STDDEV: 0.03
```

We can see that the OSDs are barely utilized (at approximately 1% each) and to nearly equal degrees. Let's discuss the columns shown in the output below:

- `ID`: The unique OSD identifier.
- `WEIGHT`: The CRUSH weight of the OSD. This should be equal to the size of your disk expressed usually in tebibytes (2^{30}).
- `REWEIGHT`: An adjustment factor that is applied to the CRUSH weight of an OSD to determine the final weight of the OSD. This defaults to 1.0, which makes no adjustment. Occasionally the placement of PGs in your cluster might not distribute data in a balanced manner and some OSDs might end up with more or less than their share. Applying an adjustment to the CRUSH weight helps rebalance this data by moving the objects from incongruously heavier OSDs to lighter OSDs. Refer to the OSD variance section below for more details on this problem. This `REWEIGHT` is often used instead of changing the CRUSH weight, so that the CRUSH weight remains an accurate indicator of the size of the underlying storage drive.
- `SIZE`: The size of your disk in bytes.
- `USE`: The capacity of your disk that is already utilized for data.
- `AVAIL`: The unused capacity of your disk in bytes.
- `%USE`: The percentage of disk that is used.

- VAR: Variance of data distribution relative to the overall mean. The CRUSH algorithm that Ceph uses for data placement attempts to achieve equal distribution by allocating PGs to OSDs in a pseudo-random manner. Not all OSDs get exactly the same number of PGs, and thus depending on how those PGs are utilized, the variance can change. OSDs mapped to PGs that have undergone more allocations relative to others will show a higher variance.
- PGs: The count of PGs located on a given OSD.

The last row summarizes the variance among OSDs. Values of minimum and maximum variance as well as the standard deviation are printed.

OSD variance and fillage

The variance in OSD utilization is crucial in determining whether one or more OSDs need to be reweighted to even out workload. A reasonably uniform distribution of PGs, and thus of data, among OSDs is also important so that outliers allocated significantly more than their share do not become full. In this section we'll explore this phenomenon and how to watch for it. In Chapter 6, *Operations and Maintenance*, we described a strategy for mitigating uneven distribution; here we explore why it happens and how adjust thresholds to meet your local needs.

The variance for some OSDs can increase when objects are not allocated in a balanced manner across all PGs. The CRUSH algorithm is designed to treat every PG as equal and thus distributes based on PG count and OSD weight, but usually this does not match real world demands. Client-side workloads are not aware of PGs or their distribution in the cluster; they only know about S3 objects or RBD image blocks. Thus, depending on the name of the underlying RADOS objects that comprise the higher level S3 objects or RBD image blocks, these objects may get mapped to a small set of PGs that are colocated a small set of OSDs. If this occurs, the OSDs in which those PGs are housed will show a higher variance and hence are likely to reach capacity sooner than others. Thus we need to watch out for the OSDs that show higher utilization variance. Similarly, we also need to watch out for OSDs that show significantly lower variance for a long period of time. This means that these OSDs are not pulling their weight and should be examined to determine why. OSDs that have variance equal or close to 1.0 can be considered to be in their optimal state.

CRUSH weights reflect disk capacity, while the OSD reweight mentioned in the previous chapter acts as an override (or fudge factor) to ensure balanced PG distribution. Ceph has configurable limits that allow us to control the amount of space being utilized within an OSD and take actions when those limits are reached. The two main configuration options are `mon_osd_nearfull_ratio` and `mon_osd_full_ratio`. The nearfull ratio acts as a warning; OSDs that exceed this threshold result in the overall Ceph cluster status changing to `HEALTH_WARN` from `HEALTH_OK`. The full ratio provides a hard threshold above which client I/O cannot complete on the disk until the usage drops below the threshold. These values default to 85% and 95% respectively, of the total disk capacity.

It is vital to note that unlike most Ceph settings, the compiled-in defaults and any changes in `ceph.conf` provide initial values. Once a cluster goes through multiple OSD map updates, however, the nearfull and full ratio from the PG map override the initial values. In order to ensure that the thresholds we set are always respected for all drives within the cluster, we should ensure that the values that we configure for the nearfull and full ratio match those in the PG map. We can set the PG map values as below:

```
root@ceph-client0:~# ceph pg set_nearfull_ratio 0.85
root@ceph-client0:~# ceph pg set_full_ratio 0.95
```

These commands may be used to raise the thresholds in an emergency, in order to restore cluster operation until the situation can be addressed properly, but be warned that these thresholds are there for a reason and it is vital for the continued well-being of your cluster to promptly address very full OSDs.

Cluster status

Cluster status checks are among the most frequent tasks of any Ceph administrator; indeed like driving a manual transmission car they quickly become reflexive. These dovetail with the health check we discussed above. The overall status of the cluster can be checked by using the ceph status subcommand or the `-s` switch.

```
root@ceph-client0:~# ceph status
cluster e6d4e4ab-f59f-470d-bb76-511deebc8de3
health HEALTH_OK
monmap e1: 1 mons at {ceph-mon0=192.168.42.10:6789/0}
election epoch 5, quorum 0 ceph-mon0
fsmap e15527: 1/1/1 up {0=ceph-mds0=up:active}
osdmap e6279: 6 osds: 6 up, 6 in
flags sortbitwise,require_jewel_osds
pgmap v16658: 128 pgs, 9 pools, 3656 bytes data, 191 objects
1962 MB used, 63371 MB / 65333 MB avail
128 active+clean
```

The output of the ceph status is split into two columns. The first column on the left side displays each key and its value is displayed to the right. The keys are always single words but the values can occupy multiple lines.

- `cluster`: The unique identifier for a given cluster, also known as `fsid`.
- `health`: The present state of cluster health.
- `monmap`: This value summarizes the output of the cluster MON map. It shows the epoch version of the MON map, a list of Ceph MONs with their IP addresses and ports the, election epoch version, and quorum members with their IDs.
- `fsmap`: Displays the values from MDS map (in older versions of Ceph this was keyed with `mdsmap`). This includes the latest epoch version, total MDSs that are up, and their sync status.
- `osdmap`: This represents the cluster OSD map including the most recent epoch version, total number of provisioned OSDs, and the number of OSDs that are marked up and in. When OSDs go down, the up count reduces, but it stays the same until they are removed from the OSD map. The flags entry shows any cluster flags applied to the OSD map.
- `pgmap`: This contains the epoch version of the cluster's PG map, total counts of PGs and pools, bytes allocated for data, and the total count of objects within the cluster. The next line shows the amount of data the cluster holds and the balance available out of the total cluster capacity. The last line shows the count of PGs that are in active and clean states. If cluster has degraded PGs, there will be additional lines summarizing the numbers of PGs in each state.

If the cluster has ongoing recovery or client I/O, that will be displayed as two more lines at the end.

We typically use the status command to observe PG state transitions when we are performing changes within the cluster like reweighting OSDs during a maintenance or adding new OSDs or hosts. In such scenarios it best to open a dedicated window that continually updates this crucial status information instead of us repeatedly issuing this command manually. We can leverage the Linux watch command to periodically update the display of changes in cluster state. By default, watch will run the command every 2 seconds, displaying a timestamp at the upper right. This timestamp itself is valuable. If we notice that the value is not updating as expected, it's likely that our cluster's Monitor nodes are experiencing problems.

```
$ watch ceph status
```

Cluster authentication

Ceph provides Kerberos-type authentication for all clients and daemons of the cluster using the cephx protocol. Each entity that communicates with other cluster components needs to communicate using their respective keys. Any MON can authenticate a client based on the key it provides, then send it a session key to use when talking to other processes within the cluster, such as OSDs. Once the session expires the clients need to authenticate to the cluster again before they can resume talking to OSDs. The list of keys that authorized clients can use are retrieved by the auth list subcommand.

```
root@ceph-client0:~# ceph auth list
installed auth entries:
client.admin
key: AQBSdLVZN8DNDBAAIwIhHp/np5uUk9Rftzb5kg==
caps: [mds] allow *
caps: [mon] allow *
caps: [osd] allow *
client.bootstrap-mds
key: AQBSdLVZIC0yMhAAmRka3/+OpszwNPNSXuY5nQ==
caps: [mon] allow profile bootstrap-mds
client.bootstrap-osd
key: AQBSdLVZ99T2FxAAIj54OM3qAVxeLz+ECF3CyA==
caps: [mon] allow profile bootstrap-osd
client.bootstrap-rgw
key: AQBSdLVZPUiDIhAAAPCNfNceDU3eGSvrwYNQUg==
caps: [mon] allow profile bootstrap-rgw
client.restapi
key: AQBUdLVZFVdQLhAA/PxeXrWDHP9c8dtY3Mu2sA==
caps: [mon] allow *
caps: [osd] allow *
client.rgw.ceph-rgw0
key: AQB1drVZ8OmfBhAAw8Uxu3tKJ2uz5OvdR8nu/A==
caps: [mon] allow rw
caps: [osd] allow rwx
```

Monitoring Ceph MONs

A proper Ceph cluster comprises three or more Monitor daemons, ideally situated on distinct physical servers. As discussed in Chapter 4, *Planning your Deployment*, multiple MONs are recommended to ensure fault tolerance and maintainability. If a cluster's MONs cannot form a quorum, which happens if not enough of the provisioned MONs are up, then new clients won't be able to connect to the system. Worse yet, existing clients will no longer be able to perform operations once their sessions expire. It is paramount for cluster health to have a majority of MONs up and able to fulfill their quorum duties.

MON status

We can retrieve basic information about all MONs in the cluster by running the ceph utility's mon stat subcommand. If our clusters contains MONs that are down or unavailable and thus have been temporarily kicked out of quorum, this command will alert us to the situation so that we can address it.

```
root@ceph-client0:~# ceph mon stat
e1: 1 mons at {ceph-mon0=192.168.42.10:6789/0}, election epoch 5, quorum 0
ceph-mon0
```

Inf we need detailed information about the state of the entire cluster MON map, we can use the mon dump subcommand.

```
root@ceph-client0:~# ceph mon dump
dumped monmap epoch 1
epoch 1
fsid e6d4e4ab-f59f-470d-bb76-511deebc8de3
last_changed 2017-09-10 20:20:16.458985
created 2017-09-10 20:20:16.458985
0: 192.168.42.10:6789/0 mon.ceph-mon0
```

Most of this information is also present in the Ceph health status summary, but it is sometimes useful to detect issues when we are adding new MONs to an existing cluster if they are not making themselves a part of the quorum. Examining the MON map dumps on the new MONs and comparing them with those of the existing MONs might help point a finger towards the problem.

MON quorum status

The concept of *quorum* is fundamental to all consensus algorithms that are designed to access information in a fault-tolerant distributed system. The minimum number of votes necessary to achieve consensus among a set of nodes is called a quorum. In Ceph's case, MONs are exploited to persist operations that result in a change of the cluster state. They need to agree to the global order of operations and register them synchronously. Hence, an active quorum of MON nodes is important in order to make progress. To keep a cluster operational, the quorum (or majority) of MON nodes needs to be available at all times. Mathematically, it means we need (n/2)+1 MON nodes available at all times, where n is the total number of MONs provisioned. For example, if we have 5 MONs, we need at least (5/2)+1 = 3 MONs available at all times. Ceph considers all MONs equal when testing for a majority, and thus any three working MONs in the above example will qualify to be within the quorum.

We can obtain the cluster quorum status by using the `quorum_status` subcommand of our trusty Swiss Army Knife—like the Ceph utility.

```
root@ceph-client0:~# ceph quorum_status
{
"election_epoch": 6,
"quorum": [
0
],
"quorum_names": [
"ceph-mon0"
],
"quorum_leader_name": "ceph-mon0",
"monmap": {
"epoch": 1,
"fsid": "e6d4e4ab-f59f-470d-bb76-511deebc8de3",
"modified": "2017-09-10 20:20:16.458985",
"created": "2017-09-10 20:20:16.458985",
"mons": [
{
"rank": 0,
"name": "ceph-mon0",
"addr": "192.168.42.10:6789/0"
}
]
}
}
```

The output is displayed in JSON format. Let's discuss the fields below:

- `election_epoch`: A counter that indications the number of re-elections that have been proposed and completed to date.
- `quorum`: A list of the *ranks* of MON nodes. Each active MON is associated with a unique rank value within the cluster. The value is an integer and starts at zero.
- `quorum_names`: The unique identifier of each MON process.
- `quorum_leader_name`: The identifier of a MON that is elected to be the leader of the ensemble. When a client first talks to the cluster, it acquires all the necessary information and cluster maps from the current or acting leader node.
- `monmap`: The dump of the cluster's MON map.

A MON leader acts as an arbiter to ensure that writes are applied to all nodes and in the proper order. In Ceph versions up to and including Jewel the leader of MON nodes was selected based on the advertised IP address. The MON node with the lowest IP address (*lowest* is calculated by transforming the IP address from a quad-dotted notation to a 32-bit integer value) was picked as the leader. If it was unavailable, then the one with the next highest IP address was selected, and so on. Once the unavailable, MON came back up, assuming that it still had the lowest IP address of all MONs, it would be re-elected the leader.

Ceph's Luminous release adds a new configuration setting called `mon priority` that lets us adjust priorities of MONs regardless of the values of their IP addresses. This helps us apply custom ordering to all MONs that we want to act as temporary leaders when the previous leader dies. It also allows us to change the existing leader dynamically and in a controlled manner. We might for example switch the leader a day before performing firmware upgrades or a disk/chassis replacement, so that the former lead server going down does not trigger an election at a time when we need to concentrate on other priorities.

Monitoring Ceph OSDs

OSDs are the workhorses within a Ceph cluster; they are responsible for performing all the work to store and manage client data. Monitoring OSDs is crucial, though complex, because they are typically present in large numbers. This task is relatively trivial but even more critical in very small clusters with only 5 to 10 OSDs, especially if high availability and durability guarantees are required. We will take a look at the Ceph commands available for monitoring OSDs.

OSD tree lookup

If we need a quick view into the state and availability of all OSDs, we will use the OSD tree subcommand. This command is usually the second-most used (or abused) after the Ceph status command.

```
root@ceph-client0:~# ceph osd tree
ID WEIGHT TYPE NAME UP/DOWN REWEIGHT PRIMARY-AFFINITY
-1 0.06235 root default
-2 0.02078 host ceph-osd1
0 0.01039 osd.0 up 1.00000 1.00000
```

```
 3  0.01039 osd.3 up 1.00000 1.00000
-3  0.02078 host ceph-osd0
 1  0.01039 osd.1 up 1.00000 1.00000
 5  0.01039 osd.5 up 1.00000 1.00000
-4  0.02078 host ceph-osd2
 2  0.01039 osd.2 up 1.00000 1.00000
 4  0.01039 osd.4 up 1.00000 1.00000
```

Let's dive into the columns of the preceding output and their particulars a little more in the follwing:

- `ID`: The unique identifier of each bucket. All buckets that are not leaf nodes or devices always have negative values and all devices or OSDs have positive values. The IDs for OSDs are prefixed by osd to form their names. These values are pulled directly from the CRUSH map.
- `WEIGHT`: This value shows the weight of a bucket in tebibytes (i.e. 2^30). The weight of each bucket is a critical input to the CRUSH placement algorithm, and thus for balanced placement of data across the cluster.
- `TYPE`: This field shows the bucket type. Valid default types include: device, host, chassis, rack, row, pdu, pod, room, datacenter, region, and root. We can create custom types if desired, but it is recommended to employ the predefined types in most cases. This helps Ceph's CRUSH map accurately mimic your physical topology. The root bucket, as its name implies, is at the root of the hierarchical map of buckets, and all the rulesets (replicated or erasure coded) for a pool will be applied to a given root.
- `NAME`: The name of each bucket. In the above example, we have one root bucket named default, three host buckets named `ceph-osd1`, `ceph-osd2`, and `ceph-osd3`, and six device or OSD buckets.
- `UP/DOWN`: This column displays the state of the OSD devices. Up means the OSD is actively communicating with other OSDs in the cluster and readily accepting the client I/O. Down indicates that the OSD is unavailable. It may be running slowly or its process is dead and thus unable to communicate with the cluster. This OSD should be looked at and fixed.
- `REWEIGHT`: If we have applied an override weight to an existing OSD, that will show up here. The floating point values for overrides lie between zero and one.

- PRIMARY AFFINITY: This value controls the probability of an OSD being elected as a primary. Changing this value to zero will ensure that the corresponding OSD is never elected primary for any PGs that are stored on it. This is sometimes useful when you are deploying a hybrid SSD-HDD cluster and want all your primary OSDs to be on SSD nodes to maximize performance, especially for reads. Tread carefully when changing those values because they do add limitations to how well Ceph can handle failures when the primaries go down.

It might be easy in a small cluster to determine by inspection which OSD belongs to which host. Within a large cluster comprising hundreds or thousands of OSDs located in tens of servers, it is distinctly harder to quickly isolate a problem to a specific host when an OSD fails and thus is marked down. Ceph provides us with the osd find subcommand that makes it really easy to identify which host a broken OSD belongs to.

```
root@ceph-client0:~# ceph osd find 1
{
"osd": 1,
"ip": "192.168.42.100:6802\/4104",
"crush_location": {
"host": "ceph-osd0",
"root": "default"
}
}
```

The command takes the numeric OSD ID in as an input and prints a list of important fields as JSON output.

- osd: The numeric ID of an OSD.
- ip: The IP address, port of the OSD host and PID of the OSD process running on that host.
- crush_location: This prints the hostname and also the root which the OSD is part of.

OSD statistics

The counts of provisioned, up, and down OSDs is available via the osd stat subcommand as shown in the following:

```
root@ceph-client0:~# ceph osd stat
osdmap e7785: 6 osds: 6 up, 6 in
flags sortbitwise,require_jewel_osds
```

Note that the above information is exactly same as the information present in the Ceph health status we described earlier in this chapter. The output of Ceph status is useful when watching problems visually, but if you want to isolate only the basic OSD stats, `osd stat` may be convenient.

OSD CRUSH map

The CRUSH map holds a variety information necessary for Ceph to distribute and place objects. Sometimes it is useful to find out if this distribution isn't working properly because of a wrong value in the CRUSH map. The CRUSH map can be downloaded as a file in binary format that we decompile locally for viewing. It is also possible to dump the CRUSH map and rules directly from the command line, which is expedient for a quick check.

We can use osd crush dump to display the entire CRUSH map.

```
root@ceph-client0:~# ceph osd crush dump
{
"devices": [
{
"id": 0,
"name": "osd.0"
},
...
"rules": [
{
"rule_id": 0,
"rule_name": "replicated_ruleset",
"ruleset": 0,
...
"tunables": {
"choose_local_tries": 0,
"choose_local_fallback_tries": 0,
"choose_total_tries": 50,
"chooseleaf_descend_once": 1,
...
```

This might not always be useful depending on the information sought. A better way to dump individual rules is by using the osd crush rule dump subcommand.

We first list the CRUSH rules currently defined within our cluster:

```
root@ceph-client0:~# ceph osd crush rule ls
[
"replicated_ruleset"
]
```

Here we only have one rule, and it is named `replicated_ruleset`. Let's see what it does.

```
root@ceph-client0:~# ceph osd crush rule dump replicated_ruleset
{
"rule_id": 0,
"rule_name": "replicated_ruleset",
"ruleset": 0,
"type": 1,
"min_size": 1,
"max_size": 10,
"steps": [
{
"op": "take",
"item": -1,
"item_name": "default"
},
{
"op": "chooseleaf_firstn",
"num": 0,
"type": "host"
},
{
"op": "emit"
}
]
}
```

This rule is applied to replicated pools and distributes one copy of all objects to separate hosts. For more details of how CRUSH rulesets work please refer to `Chapter 8`, *Ceph Architecture: Under The Hood*, in the *Customizing Crush* section.

Monitoring Ceph placement groups

Ceph objects are mapped to distinct and unique **placement groups** (**PGs**) that are stored by OSDs. The health of the cluster depends on the state and health of the placement groups, both individually and collectively. If a placement group is degraded then the health of the cluster is impacted, even though the rest of the PGs may be healthy and do not experience issues with client I/O. The cluster status will be `HEALTH_OK` only when all placement groups are in active and clean states. An unhealthy cluster manifests PGs that may be either in the active or clean state but not both—and possibly neither. The active state is required to serve client I/O, while clean indicates that the PG is not only serving I/O but also meeting other necessary requirements including replication.

PG states

We can divide PG states into three categories: Critical, Warning, and Info. PG states in the *Critical* category indicate severe damage to the cluster and immediate action should be taken to resolve their issues. For example, if we are running out of space on an OSD, we will see the backfill-toofull state being applied. If a PG has lost all OSDs assigned to hold its replicas, then it will be marked as inactive and the client I/O grinds to a halt. PGs in the *Warning* category indicate that something is wrong with the cluster that needs to be fixed, but there most likely is not major impact to client I/O that would lead to its complete stoppage. PGs in the *Info* category do not indicate an issue with the cluster, but rather convey routine information regarding the state of PGs.

Category	PG States
Critical	inactive, backfill-toofull
Warning	down, degraded, inconsistent, repair, recovering, backfill, backfill-wait, incomplete, stale, remapped, undersized
Info	peering, scrubbing, scrubbing+deep, active, clean

The state of placement groups can be monitored via the Ceph health status check described in the sections above. To display the just summary information about our collection of PGs and extract specific stats, we can use the ceph utility's `pg stat` subcommand.

```
root@ceph-client0:~# ceph pg stat
v40524: 128 pgs: 128 active+clean; 3656 bytes data, 1736 MB used, 63597 MB
/ 65333 MB avail
```

There may be a desire, at times, to view the state and the history of all PGs in your cluster. It is possible to dump a complete state information of all PGs including the total count of objects, the total bytes they hold, the up and acting sets, the primaries of both those sets of OSDs, and the timestamps of the most recent shallow and deep scrubs. This extensive information can be overwhelming for humans, so it is recommend to filter it through a parser or script that transforms it to supply answers to the questions that humans pose. We can extract this data by using the ceph subcommand `pg dump`.

```
root@ceph-client0:~# ceph pg dump
dumped all in format plain
version 40582
stamp 2017-09-18 00:39:21.452578
last_osdmap_epoch 15487
last_pg_scan 15487
full_ratio 0.95
nearfull_ratio 0.85
```

```
pg_stat objects mip degr misp unf bytes log disklog state state_stamp v
reported up up_primary acting acting_primary last_scrub scrub_stamp
last_deep_scrub deep_scrub_stamp
0.39 0 0 0 0 0 0 0 0 active+clean 2017-09-17 17:52:23.574152 0'0 15424:130
[5,3,4] 5 [5,3,4] 5 0'0 2017-09-17 17:52:23.574107 0'0 2017-09-16
16:32:04.037088
0.38 0 0 0 0 0 0 0 0 active+clean 2017-09-17 22:29:40.588864 0'0 15439:183
[1,0,4] 1 [1,0,4] 1 0'0 2017-09-17 22:29:40.588828 0'0 2017-09-17
22:29:40.588828
0.37 0 0 0 0 0 0 0 0 active+clean 2017-09-17 17:52:41.700284 0'0 15425:178
[1,3,2] 1 [1,3,2] 1 0'0 2017-09-17 17:52:41.700258 0'0 2017-09-10
20:20:17.163705
. . .
```

Sometimes we might want to know the details of just a specific PG. This can be achieved by issuing ceph pg <pgid> query. The pgid string is the PG identifier of the placement group we wish to query. For instance:

```
root@ceph-client0:~# ceph pg 0.39 query
{
"state": "active+clean",
"snap_trimq": "[]",
"epoch": 15502,
"up": [
5,
3,
4
],
"acting": [
5,
3,
4
],
"actingbackfill": [
"3",
"4",
"5"
],
"info": {
"pgid": "0.39",
"last_update": "0'0",
"last_complete": "0'0",
. . .
```

Querying PGs is useful for troubleshooting potential issues with them. Sometimes PGs can degrade due to issues with the scrubbing process that can case blocks for extreme amounts of time. In such cases, querying the PG can provide enlightening information about why the scrub is blocked and on which OSD. If we deem it to be a bug with Ceph as opposed to a hardware fault, we can easily restart the OSD to resolve the issue.

Ceph also allows us to list all PGs that are marked unclean, inactive, degraded, undersized, or stale. The subcommand we use for this operation is `dump_stuck`.

```
root@ceph-client0:~# ceph pg dump_stuck undersized
pg_stat state up up_primary acting acting_primary
0.f active+undersized+degraded [3,2] 3 [3,2] 3
8.7 active+undersized+degraded [2,3] 2 [2,3] 2
8.6 active+undersized+degraded [2,3] 2 [2,3] 2
...
```

Please see the *Placement group states* subsection in `Chapter 8`, *Ceph Architecture: Under The Hood* for additional info on PG states.

Monitoring Ceph MDS

Ceph MDS servers manage CephFS filesystems. A Ceph MDS server can be in various states including up, down, active, and inactive. An MDS server should always be up and active when it is in a correct and functioning state.

There are two main commands we can use to monitor an operational MDS cluster. We use `mds stat` to get a quick insight into the present state of MDSs. You might recognize this output format as the same one presented by the Ceph status `fsmap` key.

```
root@ceph-client0:~# ceph mds stat
e38611: 1/1/1 up {0=ceph-mds0=up:active}
```

If we would like detailed output of the MDS map of a given cluster, we can use the `mds dump` subcommand. Like all other subcommands containing dump, it prints the entire MDS map, which contains detailed information about active MDS daemons as well as other stats.

```
root@ceph-client0:~# ceph mds dump
dumped fsmap epoch 38611
fs_name cephfs
epoch 38611
flags 0
created 2017-09-10 20:20:28.275607
modified 2017-09-10 20:20:28.275607
tableserver 0
```

```
root 0
session_timeout 60
session_autoclose 300
max_file_size 1099511627776
last_failure 0
last_failure_osd_epoch 15221
compat compat={},rocompat={},incompat={1=base v0.20,2=client writeable
ranges,3=default file layouts on dirs,4=dir inode in separate object,5=mds
uses versioned encoding,6=dirfrag is stored in omap,8=file layout v2}
max_mds 1
in 0
up {0=38784}
failed
damaged
stopped
data_pools 1
metadata_pool 2
inline_data disabled
38784: 192.168.42.70:6800/1630589528 'ceph-mds0' mds.0.38608 up:active seq
5
```

Open source dashboards and tools

Ceph storage administrators can perform most cluster monitoring and management with the CLI commands provided by Ceph. Ceph also provides a rich admin API that can be used to monitor and visualize the entire Ceph cluster. There are several open source projects that make use of Ceph's REST admin API and present a GUI dashboard for a visual overview of your entire cluster. Some tools focus on monitoring; others have more expansive scopes and include orchestration and lifecycle management features as well.

Kraken

Kraken is an open source Ceph dashboard written in Python. Initial development was by Don Talton, who was later joined by David Moreau Simard. Don has over twenty years of experience with prominent companies and runs Merrymack, an IT consulting company.

The development of Kraken came about because, at the time, Ceph's Calamari tool was only available to commercial customers of Inktank. Don believed that it was desirable to have a good open source dashboard for monitoring Ceph clusters and components from a single window. This would enable better management and the adoption of Ceph proper. Don utilized Ceph's RESTful API to extract necessary cluster data for monitoring and reporting.

While Kraken has not received updates in two years as we write, you may still find it useful. You can find Kraken's GitHub page at `https://github.com/krakendash/krakendash`. Kraken is fully open source with BSD licensing.

Kraken leverages several other open source projects; details can be found at the above GitHub page. The first edition of *Learning Ceph* included detailed instructions for installation. As Kraken may be abandonware at this point, it is left to interested readers to visit GitHub, where these instructions may be found.

 Since the first edition of this book was released, a Ceph version also named Kraken was released. The above section, to be clear, refers to the dashboard tool, and not the Ceph release.

Ceph-dash

The ceph-dash project is another free open source dashboard/monitoring dashboard, developed by Christian Eichelmann, at 1&1 Internet AG in Germany as a senior software developer. As Don did with Kraken, Christian began this project at a time when there were very few open source dashboards available for Ceph. Moreover, the other available dashboards had complex architectures and did not work well with large clusters. Also like Kraken, as we write this second edition of *Learning Ceph*, Ceph-dash may now be stagnant, though it has seen commits within the preceding year. We carry forward this section in condensed form, as it may still be useful or interesting to Ceph admins.

The home of ceph-dash may be found at `https://github.com/Crapworks/ceph-dash`.

Decapod

Another interesting Ceph management tool is Decapod from Mirantis. Decapod builds on the popular Ansible-based ceph-ansible management framework. One can read all about it here:

`https://www.mirantis.com/blog/introducing-decapod-easier-way-manage-ceph/`

Rook

Rook is a young but promising open source tool for distributed storage management in cloud-native environments. As with some of the other tools we describe here, Rook does more than just monitoring; it is a full-blown orchestration tool. You can read all about it on Rook's GitHub page, maintained by an active contributing community.

```
https://github.com/rook/rook
```

Calamari

Calamari is a management platform for Ceph, an attractive dashboard to monitor and manage your Ceph cluster. It was initially developed by Inktank as proprietary software that shipped with Inktank's Ceph Enterprise product. After Inktank was acquired by Red Hat, Calamari was open sourced and has received additional development. The Calamari back end leverages Python, SaltStack, ZeroRPC, Graphite, Django, and gevent. The Calamari backend has been open sourced with the LGPL2+ license; you can find the repository and ample information at `https://github.com/ceph/calamari`.

Excellent Calamari documentation is available at `http://calamari.readthedocs.org`.

Ceph-mgr

New with the Luminous release is the core `ceph-mgr` daemon, which offers a promising dashboard plugin that is bound to receive considerable attention from the community.

Enabling this dashboard is straightforward:

Edit `ceph.conf` on each node that runs the `ceph-mgr` daemon; these are usually the MONs. Add the following section:

```
[mgr]
mgr_modules = dashboard
```

Next configure IP addressing on each `ceph-mgr` server:

```
# ceph config-key put mgr/dashboard/server_addr ::
```

The value `::` enables the dashboard on port `7000` of each system.

Next restart the `ceph-mgr` daemon. On systemd-centric distributions this is done with:

```
$ systemctl restart ceph-mgr@
```

You should now be able to browse to the dashboard on the active ceph-mgr server's 7000/tcp port.

Prometheus and Grafana

The last two tools we'll discuss in this chapter are excellent general purpose monitoring and trending solutions. Prometheus is a flexible monitoring and time-series tool for alerting and trending all manner of system data. While standalone operation is possible, linkage with the Grafana visualization dashboard provides a visually appealing and user-friendly experience. Prometheus enables flexible and powerful analysis of data from a variety of sources. Ceph integration is done through the sophisticated Ceph Exporter data collector.

You can discover each of these tools at their respective links:

Grafana: `https://github.com/grafana/grafana`

Prometheus: `https://prometheus.io/`

Ceph Exporter: `https://github.com/digitalocean/ceph_exporter`

Summary

In this chapter, we covered Ceph's monitoring needs and utilities. This included overall cluster states as well as individual Ceph components including MONs, OSDs, and MDS. We also investigated placement groups. The states of placement groups can change dynamically and they require close monitoring. Most of the changes that happen in a Ceph cluster are visibly surfaced from changes to placement groups. This chapter also covered several open source GUI monitoring dashboard projects. Some of these are managed and developed outside of Ceph proper, but they are also open source, so you can contribute to and benefit from these projects freely. We also covered an overview of Calamari and the new ceph-mgr dashboard. In the next chapter we will dive deeply into the guts of Ceph, exploring in detail all things CRUSH, replication and erasure coding, and additional detail surrounding Ceph's placement groups and data flow.

8

Ceph Architecture: Under the Hood

In this chapter, we will cover the internals of Ceph. The components we will explore include the following:

- Ceph objects
- Placement groups
- The CRUSH algorithm and customization
- Ceph pools
- Ceph data management

Objects

Data produced by a Ceph client is stored in **objects**. In fact, even most of the associated metadata that Ceph stores for client-generated payload data is also stored either as separate Ceph Objects or within existing objects alongside payload data. Each object is identified by a unique name. Once a name is assigned to a newly created object, no other objects can be created with that exact name in the same namespace within a cluster.

Objects in Ceph are called **Reliable, Autonomic, Distributed Object Store (RADOS)** objects, and operations on them can be performed by using the `rados` command line tool. It facilitates a balanced distribution of data and workloads across a heterogeneous cluster that can grow or shrink in capacity dynamically. It provides all its client applications (including RBD and RGW) the illusion of a single logical object store with safe semantics and strong consistency guarantees.

It's important to remember the distinction between the RADOS objects that Ceph manages behind the scenes versus the user-visible objects accessed through the RGW service.

RADOS objects are similar in some ways to the concept of a file; they both act as an abstraction for storing data, but they are inherently quite different in terms of functionality. File-based storage is limited by the structures and semantics enforced by an underlying filesystem. Blocks within a filesystem are typically fixed in size. The addition of custom metadata information to a traditional file might be significantly restricted or not possible at all. In Ceph, each object stores data and is capable of storing rich metadata along with it. Each object can be of arbitrary size and its internal characteristics are independent of other objects in the cluster. An object's metadata allows users to manage and access the unstructured content or data within.

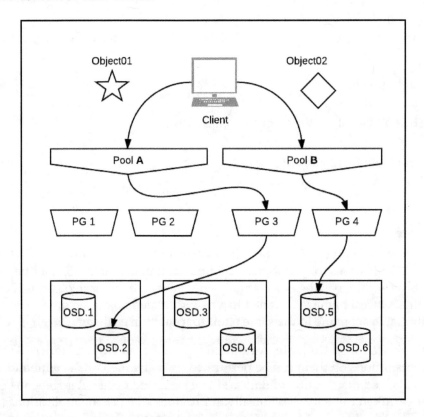

Ceph does not impose a conceptual hierarchy of objects like a filesystem does for files and directories. All objects within a namespace are at the same level. Avoiding hierarchical namespaces helps Ceph scale out across thousands of machines and tens of thousands of devices. Ceph stores Objects in **Object-based Storage Devices** (**OSDs**). These objects are grouped together and mapped to OSDs by using the CRUSH algorithm. Objects are logically collected into larger sets known as placement groups, which provide a way to manage their distribution so that data is stored in a reliable, highly-available, and fault-tolerant manner. We will examine these concepts in much more detail later in this chapter.

Accessing objects

Data within Ceph is stored in indivisible units called Objects. All Objects are allocated within a user-specified namespace called a *pool*. A Ceph pool is a logical partition of all Objects within its storage space. Objects can be replicated within a pool, but cannot be replicated across multiple pools automatically. Users will need to manually copy an object to another pool if that type of replication is needed, but this is not the part of a typical workflow. We will look into pools more holistically later in this chapter.

When a new Ceph cluster is deployed, it needs pools to store data. Default pools may be created depending on the release of Ceph and type of service that is deployed. Deploying an MDS for CephFS will automatically create two pools named `cephfs_data` and `cephfs_metadata`. Similarly, deploying a new RGW service will create necessary data, metadata, and user pools to serve S3 or Swift API operations. In Ceph releases prior to Luminous (including the Jewel cluster we created in `Chapter 5`, *Deploying a Virtual Sandbox Cluster*) a pool named `rbd` is always created by default. It is also possible to create new custom pools manually and to rename or delete existing pools.

In order to understand how objects are created and accessed, we will start by first creating a Ceph pool. For this hands-on exercise, we will use the cluster that we created in `Chapter 5`, *Deploying a Virtual Sandbox Cluster*. If you do not have a working Ceph cluster at your disposal to run the commands in this exercise, it is strongly recommended you go through `Chapter 5`, *Deploying a Virtual Sandbox Cluster* first to have a cluster running in your sandbox.

Log in to our client virtual machine in order to perform our operations on the cluster:

```
$ vagrant ssh client0
vagrant@ceph-client0:~$sudo -i
root@ceph-client0:~#
```

Verify that the cluster is in a healthy state:

```
root@ceph-client0:~# ceph health
HEALTH_OK
```

Everything looks good! Let's start creating objects. Before creating an object, let's first create a new Ceph pool. We will use this pool to store our new objects.

```
root@ceph-client0:~# ceph osd pool create my_pool 64
pool 'my_pool' created
```

The preceding command will create a pool named my_pool in our cluster. We can name our pool anything we like. The command-line parameter after the pool name is a number called pg_num. This value is used to specify the number of **PGs** to be created within our new pool. We will cover PGs in detail in this chapter in the next section, but for now we'll note that each pool contains a dedicated set of PGs.

You can list all pools that your cluster owns by running ceph osd pool ls:

```
root@ceph-client0:~# ceph osd pool ls
rbd
my_pool
```

You can also get a detailed view of all the attributes of a pool by adding the detail parameter at the end of the preceding command:

```
root@ceph-client0:~# ceph osd pool ls detail
pool 2 'my_pool' replicated size 3 min_size 2 crush_ruleset 0
object_hashrjenkinspg_num 64 pgp_num 64 last_change 12409 flags
hashpspoolstripe_width 0
```

The output is presented as key-value pairs but without any special delimiter around each, which does make reading the values a bit tricky. We can see that the pool that we just created has an ID of 2. It's a replicated pool with a default replication factor of X, a minimum replication factor to serve I/O of 2, and it is part of the CRUSH ruleset with ID of 0. Don't worry if the preceding output looks cryptic at this stage, the keys and their use will become much more clear as we proceed through this chapter.

Now that we have a pool ready to store objects, let's go store some objects:

```
root@ceph-client0:~# echo "somedata" > data.txt
root@ceph-client0:~# rados -p my_pool put my_data data.txt
```

The `rados` command will store the data from our dummy file named `data.txt` into the Ceph pool named `my_pool` that we select using the `-p` flag. The syntax for creating a new object in Ceph is `rados -p <pool-name> put <object-name><file-path>`. We can also pipe data to `radosput` from `stdin` if necessary, but uploading it from a file is a standard practice.

Congratulations! You have just created a brand new pool and saved your first shiny new object in it. If we list all objects in our pool, we should be able to find ours in the list. We are also able to display other attributes of our object, including when it was last modified and its current size:

```
root@ceph-client0:~# rados -p my_pool ls
my_data
root@ceph-client0:~# rados -p my_pool stat my_data
my_pool/my_datamtime 2017-08-30 01:49:27.000000, size 9
```

It should be clear, that the `rados ls` subcommand lists all objects in the given pool. The `stat` subcommand shows certain key properties of the object, including when it was last modified (`mtime`) and its actual size in bytes (`size`).

We have introduced many new terms in the preceding exercise and we will attempt to cover most of them in the remainder of this chapter.

Placement groups

In the previous section, we described what objects in Ceph are and how we can access them. Ceph distributes objects pseudo-randomly to storage devices based on predefined data assignment policies. The assignment policy uses a novel placement algorithm called CRUSH to choose a probabilistically balanced distribution of objects throughout the cluster. This ensures that devices are presented with a nearly uniform storage and workload distribution for most use-cases. When a cluster is expanded by adding new storage or old/failed devices are removed, it is necessary to restore balance by migrating data to restore the configured replication policies. Since this data movement is kept a minimum, augmenting an existing cluster is significantly less cumbersome compared to the use of other, less-sophisticated placement algorithms. CRUSH will be explored in detail in the next section.

When Ceph receives requests to store data, it needs to determine the set designated objects the requests should be sent to as well as their locations. Each object is mapped to a logical collection of Objects that we call PGs. A single object can only be mapped to one PG at a time. This mapping between an object and its PG stays constant until we change the number of PGs within a pool. A matching PG is computed using the CRUSH hashing algorithm. The external inputs to the hashing function are pool ID and object name. Using the pool ID, it extracts the pool's profile, which indicates the pool's replication or erasure coding policy and thus how many copies or stripes of an Object the pool should store. The pool ID and object name combination also helps to determine the **Placement Group ID** (**pgid**).

Here's the formula used to calculate an Object's Placement Group:

$$pgid = func\left(hash(o) \,\&\, m, r\right)$$

The `pgid` is a function of object name (**o**), the bitmask for current keyspace (**m**), and the replication factor (**r**). We first compute the hash of an object using its name o and perform a bitwise binary AND operation with the bitmask **m**. The bitmask is internally derived from the number of PGs we have configured our pool to have. This limits the range (output) of the hash function to fall within the set of PGs that presently exist. The variable **r** is the replication factor of the pool and is used to determine the number of OSDs that the PG should map to, since Ceph will generally store copies of data in disjoint OSDs.

Devices or OSDs are selected based on the count or stripes that a policy requires a replicated- or erasure- coded Object to have and are associated to a given `pgid`, and thus a unique PG. It is the responsibility of the PG to guarantee that objects are reliably accessed and stored. Assuming we set the replication factor of a pool to 3 (specified by the key named *size*), every PG within the pool must ensure that an object, in its healthy state, is replicated exactly three times across multiple distinct devices or OSDs. PGs are designed to enforce strong consistency among all copies of an object.

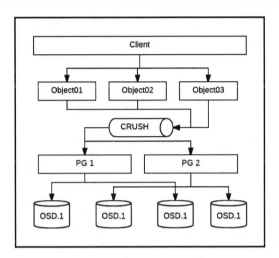

An important characteristic of a PG is that the mapping between its `pgid`, which is a unique identifier for a PG, and object name is not stored persistently on clients, nor on OSDs or MONs. In fact, this mapping is not explicitly stored *anywhere*. It is dynamically and independently computed at the origin every time an object-based data or control request is sent from a client Ceph. Empowering clients to independently compute object placement on the fly eliminates the need for allocating a large centralized metadata index containing an entry for every Object ever created. By avoiding this potential single point of failure, Ceph can quickly scale across large number of clients and Objects in highly dynamic environments.

Objects within every pool are collected into PGs and these PGs are assigned to multiple OSDs according to the pool strategy and policy. Each PG stores thousands to millions of Objects and each OSD stores tens to hundreds of PGs. The limits are dictated more strongly at the OSD level by partition size, the throughput and latency limits of the underlying device, and the sizes of the Objects. It is typical for a traditional magnetic spinning disk to store anywhere between 50 to 100 PGs, whereas for OSDs running on AHCI-controlled **solid state disks** (**SSDs**) it is not uncommon for the PG count to be in between 100 and 500. The count can be even larger for PCIe-based SSD or NVMe devices. A greater number of PGs on a drive results in higher I/O to the device. Every drive type and model has unique characteristics and you should benchmark your setup before picking an optimal ratio of PG per OSD. Configuring more than one pool in your cluster can complicate this calculation, but as long as the total number of PGs per OSD (at the cluster level) stay within the recommended limits, the cluster's behavior and performance should not be impacted.

That said, Ceph has a default but configurable PG to OSD threshold. With Luminous and later releases operations that would result in this threshold being crossed will be refused. We explored the specifics and ramifications of this ratio in Chapter 4, *Planning your Deployment.*

Setting PGs on pools

In Chapter 4, *Planning your Deployment,* we discussed the importance of an appropriate number of placement groups per pool.

Every Ceph pool needs pg_num PGs set and created before we can write data to it. Ceph avails us of two settings for the PG count. One controls the number of PGs present in the pool, while the second controls the number of PGs actually used to hold Objects in the pool. These are pg_num and pgp_num respectively.

Let's discuss pg_num and pgp_num in more detail. The pg prefix of pg_num means simply placement groups while the pgp prefix of pgp_num stands for PGs for placement. When we increase the value of pg_num, some or all of the existing PGs are broken into multiple PGs, a process we call *splitting*. A smaller, incremental increase in pg_num will result in fewer existing PGs being split into multiple new PGs. If we exactly double a pool's current pg_num value—remember that we strongly favor powers of 2—all existing PGs are split. Splitting is a very expensive process on XFS or EXT4-based FileStore OSDs as it requires Ceph to create additional directories on every OSD device for every PG then simultaneously update the **directory entries** (**dentries**) of both existing and new PGs throughout the entire cluster.

This can result in a lag in the busy OSDs while processing normal user traffic, thus resulting in slow requests. In most cases, we thus increment pg_num in small steps spaced out over time so as to diffuse the impact on the cluster and thus user operations. Say we have a cluster, a single rbd pool with 4096 PGs. If for expansion or other reasons we need to increase the count to 8192, we might choose to increment pg_num and pgp_num by steps of just 128 at a time, allow the cluster to adjust before proceeding to the next round. You may notice that this means that for a time the number of PGs in the subject pool will sub-optimally not be a power of 2, but since this is a temporary situation we can tolerate the imbalances until we reach the final power of value 2.

With the BlueStore backend that's the default in the new Luminous release of Ceph, the impact of splitting large numbers of PGs throughout a pool will nearly be a non-issue. BlueStore stores everything, including both data and metadata, in a key-value database, avoiding the limitations and overhead of an XFS-type filesystem. The metadata is partitioned into multiple database namespaces, which are equivalent to a table in SQL-based data stores. These include Object metadata, collection metadata, stats, **Object Map** (**omap**), and so on. PGs are mapped to collections and as a result splitting a PG will be a relatively quick operation that will only affect parts of the collection namespace without impacting any other metadata namespaces or actual object data. Thus, it becomes a relatively lightweight operation with minimal overhead, unlike the current and fairly expensive process when using FileStore.

The value of `pgp_num` controls how many PGs out of the total should be targeted by CRUSH to hold data; naturally, `pg_num` must at all times be less than or equal to `pgp_num`. Increasing `pgp_num` will result in rebalancing of the pool's PG distribution and data will move within the cluster. The more data the PGs hold, the more that will need to move. For this reason, it can be advantageous to stay on top of these values, adjusting them sooner rather than later to minimize disruption. Normally when we increase `pg_num` we increase `pgp_num` to the same value in lockstep. It's important to remember before changing these values for a pool that we can only increase the `pg_num` (and thus `pgp_num`); we cannot reduce their values. In other words, we can split PGs, but we can't merge them. Ceph's FileStore is adept at splitting PGs, but there is no mechanism yet available to merge them.

Let's practice adjusting these values in our sandbox cluster. We use the custom pool named `my_pool` that we created at the start of this chapter:

```
root@ceph-client0:~# ceph osd pool get my_poolpg_num
pg_num: 64
root@ceph-client0:~# ceph osd pool get my_poolpgp_num
pgp_num: 64
```

Let's evaluate these numbers to see if these are appropriate choices. We will use the same formula that we used in the *PG Calculations* section previously. We will need the following information:

- Total number of OSDs used by this pool
- Replication factor of the pool
- Speculative value of the ratio of PGs:OSDs

We can see the total number of OSDs in this cluster is 6 by running the following command:

```
root@ceph-client0:~# ceph osd stat
osdmap e12577: 6 osds: 6 up, 6 in
               flags sortbitwise,require_jewel_osds
```

We have a total of six OSDs (and fortunately all are *in* and *up*). Since it's a simple PoC cluster we have not segregated OSDs into separate pools. Thus we can consider the value of total number of OSDs in the cluster that we get from `ceph osd stat` to be used exclusively by our pool. This might not be the case for your production cluster depending on how you have set it up.

Let's see what replication factor we have set for this pool.

```
root@ceph-client0:~# ceph osd pool get my_pool size
size: 3
```

We will use 3 as the replication factor. The only parameter we are left with is a speculative value that we need to specify for PG to OSD ratio. Since these OSDs are running on virtual machines on emulated disks and thus are not particularly speedy, we will choose a value of 100 for now. Thus, our final set of values follows:

Number of OSDs used for this pool	6
Replication factor of the pool	3
Speculative ratio of PGs per OSD	100

Substituting into our *PG Calculations* formula, we get:

$$(Total\ OSDs\ *\ PGPerOSD)\ /\ Replication\ factor => Total\ PGs$$
$$(6 * 100)\ /\ 3 => 200$$
$$ceil\_power\_of\_(200) => \mathbf{256}$$

The desirable number of PGs for this pool is therefore 256. We have picked this value without checking whether there are other pools or not and thus without knowing what the current overall PG to OSD ratio is. In our sandbox environment where we test dummy use-cases, this value doesn't matter as much as it does in a production environment. In practice, it is highly recommended to survey all existing pools and calculate the PG to OSD ratio before deciding the best value for a new pool. But now let's adjust our PoC pool:

```
root@ceph-client0:~# ceph osd pool set my_poolpg_num 256
set pool 1 pg_num to 256
root@ceph-client0:~# ceph osd pool set my_poolpgp_num 256
set pool 1 pgp_num to 256
```

That's it! Your PG count on your pool (and hence your cluster) should now be increased. We increased the PG count directly to its final value in a single step because these operations are performed on a sandbox cluster with very little data and no sensitive paying customers. In a production environment, however, you would need to progress towards the final value in multiple steps, gradually increasing the value in each step. Increasing `pg_num` and `pgp_num` in a large step directly to their final values can precipitate intense change within your cluster, temporarily degrading health and client operations until the OSDs can catch up. Monitor the health of your cluster before you increase `pgp_num` while also taking care that `pg_num` is increased slowly and incrementally in lockstep to the final value. As with other Ceph maintenance, during PG splitting it's suggested to run `ceph -w` or `watch ceph status` in a dedicated window to keep a close eye on the cluster's health during the process. If each step precipitates excessive data movement, or especially slow/blocked requests, that's a good sign to decrease the increment.

PG peering

Client write and read requests issued against RADOS objects from a client are sent to the PG to which the object belongs before being persisted to OSDs. If the replication factor (denoted by the size attribute) of the pool is greater than 1, then writes must be persisted on multiple OSDs. For example, if the size of a pool is 3, then we have three copies of each Object present in the pool spread across 3 disjoint OSDs. Any write issued by a client however must to be completed on all three OSDs before the client gets an acknowledgement. Every PG denotes one OSD designated as the *primary* (or *lead*) OSD. All additional OSDs that hold a given PG are known as *secondary* OSDs within the context of that PG. The primary OSD is responsible for serving client requests for a given PG and ensuring writes complete successfully on all secondary OSDs before replying to the client. The primary OSD is also responsible for serving all the reads of Objects that belong to PGs for which it is primary. A single OSD will be primary for many PGs while secondary for others. However, at any given time, each PG will designate only a single primary OSD. The OSD designated as primary of a given PG most likely will, however, not remain primary for that PG throughout its lifetime. Events that may change a PG's primary OSD include the following:

- Adding or removing OSDs permanently
- OSD or host crashes
- Ceph or host upgrades and other maintenance
- Splitting PGs

The primary OSD for each PG is responsible for conducting a periodic status check operation, a process we call *peering*. Peering is essential in maintaining the consistency of each PG's contents across all its OSDs. The goal is to check if any of the PGs replicas are missing necessary data or are not fully caught up with changes. Peering simplifies recovery from cluster events and changes by allowing the system to reliably detect disparities and helps peer PGs catch up and return to a consistent state. When a cluster's topology changes as drives or entire servers are removed or added, each OSD receives an updated cluster map (also known as CRUSH map). The CRUSH algorithm helps minimize changes to the CRUSH map, but any PGs whose OSD mapping changes will need to re-peer.

If an OSD is removed and later added to the cluster — or even if it is down for a time — client operations in the interim may have changed the contents of the PGs that it hosts. The primary OSD of each PG at various times asks all the PG's peers to send their latest information including most recent update, PG log boundary, and the PG map epoch at which they last peered. An **epoch** is a unique identifier for each version of Ceph's maps, a logical timestamp if you will. The latest value of an epoch is usually denoted with a prefix distinguishing different types of cluster maps (there are separate epochs for PG map, mon map, OSD map, CRUSH map, and so on) with an integer appended. Every time a map is changed, its epoch is incremented. With this state information, each OSD generates a list of missing log fragments for any replicas whose latest information does not match the primary OSD's. It then sends these fragments to peer OSDs to help each replicas catch up, issuing background recovery operations while still serving clients. If all of a PG's replicas have caught up already, then it marks a new epoch for the completion of successful peering and moves on.

PG Up and Acting sets

Each PG has an attribute called **Acting Set**, comprising the current primary OSD and presently active replicas. This set of OSDs is responsible for actively serving I/O at the given moment in time. When the cluster topology changes, a PG may be updated to span a different set of OSDs. This new set of OSDs might or might not overlap with the previous set and is known as the **Up Set** of each PG. The OSDs in the Up Set are responsible for transferring data over from the current Acting Set's OSDs because they are now responsible for the PG that was adjusted. Once the data is current on all OSDs in the Up Set, the Acting Set will be the same as the Up Set and the PG should be in an active state.

Thus these sets are stable and identical most of the time as the cluster conducts business as usual.

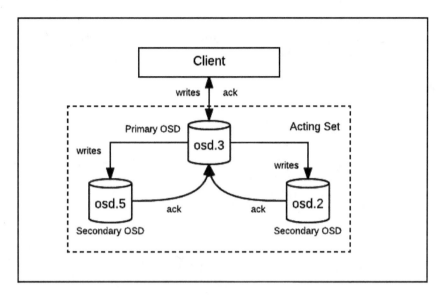

PG states

Every PG is assigned a set of states at any given time. In a day-to-day operation, a healthy PG shows `active+clean`. The active state indicates that the PG has no problems serving client I/O and clean implies that it fulfills other requirements including distributing its copies across a sufficient number of devices as dictated by the size attribute of the pool.

An unhealthy or degraded PG is denoted by a change in its states; for example, it has either stopped serving I/O, has lost communication with peers, or has fewer than required copies of its Objects. Each PG's states can include one or more of those described here. Ceph endeavors to return unhealthy PGs back to their healthy states and rebalances data to fulfill the constraints applied to it by CRUSH rules.

We will discuss some important PG states as follows:

- **Active**
  The PG is marked active once the peering operation completes. Once a PG is in the active state, client I/O should be able to proceed without issues on the primary and secondary OSDs.

- **Clean**
  Primary and secondary OSDs have successfully completed peering and all Objects are replicated the correct number of times. PGs are also pointing to their original locations and have not incurred any movement.

- **Peering**
  All OSDs that host a PG must remain in agreement about the state of all their Objects. Peering is the process of bringing each PG's set of OSDs to that agreement. Once peering completes, the OSDs mark their PGs as `clean` or with other states, say if recovery/backfill are needed.

- **Degraded**
  When an OSD gets marked down, all PGs assigned to it are marked degraded. Once the OSD is restarted it has to re-peer in order to return degraded PGs to the clean state. If the OSD stays marked down for more than 5 minutes (the default in Jewel), then it is marked out and Ceph kicks off recovery on the degraded PGs. Client I/O can be performed on a degraded PG as long as it remains active. PGs can also be marked as degraded when Objects inside them become unavailable or silent corruption is discovered in a replica. Ceph initiates recovery from the authoritative copy for those objects to ensure they are safely replicated the proper amount of times before marking the PG clean.

- **Stale**
  Every OSD is responsible for periodically reporting to the MONs the latest statistics of all PGs for which it is primary. If for some reason a primary OSD fails to send this report to the MONs or if other OSDs report that the primary OSD for a PG is down, that PG will immediately be marked as stale.

- **Undersized**
  PGs that have fewer replicas than the specified pool's replication size attribute are marked as undersized. Recovery and backfill are initiated for PGs that are undersizedto restore the proper number of copies.

- **Scrubbing**

  OSDs are responsible for periodically checking that their replicas exhibit no change in their stored content. This *scrubbing* process ensures that stored data's checksums are consistent across peers. The scrubbing state is applied to PGs while they perform these checks, which we call l*ight scrubs, shallow scrubs,* or simply *scrubs*. PGs also undergo less frequent *deep scrubs* that scan all data bits and make sure all replicas match. The state set on PGs during deep scrubs is scrubbing+deep.

- **Recovering**

  When adding a new OSD to the cluster or when an existing OSD goes down, PGs end up with a subset of OSD peers that have the new context before the rest haven't caught up. A PG enters a recovering state to catch up the replicas with the OSDs that have latest content.

- **Backfilling**

  Ceph is prompted to rebalance data when new OSDs are added to the cluster. It performs the rebalancing operation by moving some PGs from other OSDs to the new OSDs in the background. This operation is called *backfill*. Once rebalancing completes on an OSD it can participate in I/O.

A full list of PG states may be found at:
http://docs.ceph.com/docs/master/rados/operations/pg-states/

CRUSH

Ceph is a highly distributed data storage system designed not just to store massive amounts of data, but also to guarantee reliability, scalability, and performance. Instead of constraining I/O to be performed only in fixed-size blocks like traditional file systems, it provides a simple interface for reading and writing data in variable-sized units called objects. These objects are then replicated and distributed throughout the cluster to provide effective fault-tolerance and parallel access.

Distributing objects throughout the cluster arbitrarily improves aggregate write performance but complicates read operations. How should we allocate objects in the cluster? What gets us uniform distribution despite cluster topology changes? What should we do when drives die or hosts fail? If we relocate data to a new location, how will clients know about the new location? In the past, these issues have been addressed by storing an allocation list of all Objects that is updated when objects are recovered or moved to a new server. Reads were then fulfilled by accessing this list.

There are several pitfalls to this approach, especially the allocation list being both a potential performance bottleneck and a single point of failure. Moreover, the requirement of a distribution algorithm that optimizes globally balanced placement when new storage is added also remains.

Enter CRUSH! **Controlled Replication Under Scalable Hashing** (**CRUSH**) is a pseudo-random data distribution algorithm that optimizes placement of data replicas across a heterogeneous cluster and handles intentional (and unintentional) changes over its lifetime. It does not rely on any external per-Object metadata index or directory to route reads or writes. Instead it leverages a hierarchical description of the cluster's topology and a deterministic function that maps input values (Object name and replication factor) to compute a list of devices on which objects are stored. This computation to determine the location each Object enables Ceph's scalability and performance by decentralizing placement knowledge, as any client can independently and unilaterally calculate each Object's location. The cluster information required to compute Object locations is retrieved from Ceph infrequently (usually only when cluster topology changes and those changes affect the PG for our Object), which minimizes overhead on clients.

The CRUSH Hierarchy

Ceph **Monitor Nodes** (**MONs**) stores the cluster's state in the form of a map. This map is composed of devices and buckets. Each device and bucket is assigned a unique identifier and weight. The collected set of devices and buckets is known as the cluster map or CRUSH map. Buckets are hierarchical. They contain devices or other buckets, allowing them to act as interior nodes in the storage hierarchy while devices are always leaves, with the top bucket of the hierarchy known as the *root*. As OSDs are deployed Ceph assigns an initial weight to each OSD, typically based on the capacity of the drive on which it lives. Bucket weights are calculated as the sum of the weights of all the internal buckets or devices they contain. Administrators can later adjust the relative weights of devices or buckets as needed.

The CRUSH map is topology aware and is user configurable. A bucket can be associated with a host, rack, row, switch, PDU, room, datacenter or any other type of component. It is typical and useful for the CRUSH topology to represent the physical layout of cluster components as much as possible, as this allows Ceph to optimally place PGs in the cluster for RAS (Reliability, Availability, and Serviceability). As buckets are simple collection of devices and/or other buckets it is possible to construct a CRUSH map that does not match a physical topology, but this is not recommended unless you really know what you are doing and few Ceph admins will have a reason to do so.

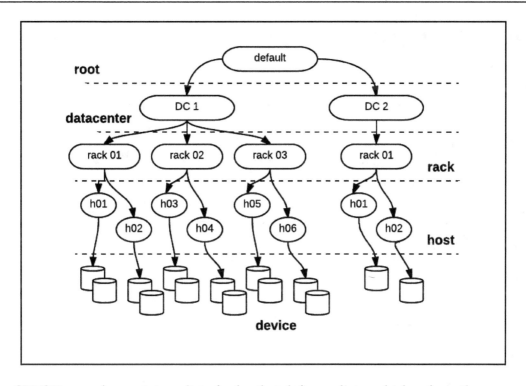

The CRUSH map also contains a list of rules that define policies which enforce the placement of Object replicas within their pool to ensure the required level of data durability and availability. Admins can define these rules to distribute replicas across multiple failure domains or to enforce other constraints. A failure domain could be anything that you deem to be susceptible to failure in your setup. The failure domains are most often of concern when planning Ceph clusters, they are entire OSD nodes and each entire logical rack. If your data center racks are subject to power failures (or have a single ToR switch that can cause unreachability to the entire rack when it's down) then you should also consider enforcing a rack failure domain.

Your set up can have multiple failure domains and you should plan your replica placement such that you never place any two copies in a single failure domain. That means if you have a pool with replication factor of 3, and you have at least 3 racks (with multiple hosts in each), you should distribute your data such that each copy is in a different rack. If you have fewer than 3 racks, but more than 3 hosts, you should distribute your copies across distinct hosts. CRUSH will try to spread Objects across the cluster in a balanced manner, with all devices participating proportionally based on their weights.

CRUSH Lookup

Any client that intends to issue reads or writes to the cluster needs to perform a lookup operation to know where the objects in question belong.

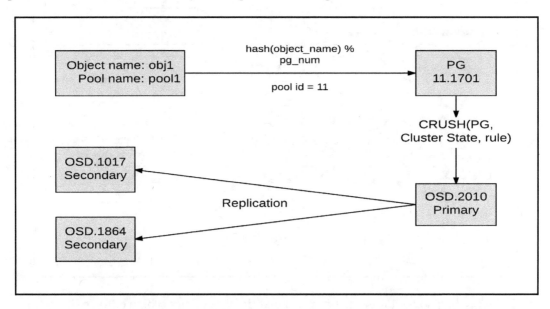

If the client doesn't have a current CRUSH map, for example when performing the first operations of a new run, it connects to one of the cluster's monitor nodes to request the latest CRUSH map. This map contains the state, topology, and configuration of the cluster. Each object is run through a fast hashing function then a bitmask is applied to ensure that the mapping function's range aligns with the key space dictated by the number of PGs in the pool. This is essentially a modulo operation. By concatenating the pool's ID with the computed hash, we get the unique identifier of the PG to which the Object should be written.

Placement group names or IDs thus always begin with the number of the pool to which they belong. This is handy when navigating Ceph status, logs, and forensics and adds valuable context especially when a cluster contains many pools, for example OpenStack and RGW deployments.

CRUSH provides us with the set of OSDs onto which each PG is mapped, including the designation of the primary OSD, to which the client directs operations. Since the computation is performed wholly on the client side, the Ceph cluster does not contribute to or suffer from any performance hit incurred by the lookup. This decentralized mechanism helps truly parallelize and scale Ceph clusters across a very large number of clients.

Backfill, Recovery, and Rebalancing

When any component within a cluster fails, be it a single OSD device, a host's worth of OSDs, or a larger bucket like a rack, Ceph waits for a short grace period before it marks the failed OSDs *out*. This state is then updated in the CRUSH map. As soon an OSD is marked out, Ceph initiates recovery operations. This grace period before marking OSDs out is set by the optional `ceph.conf` tunable `mon_osd_down_out_interval`, which defaults to 300 seconds (5 minutes). During recovery Ceph moves or copies all data that was hosted on the OSD devices that failed.

Since CRUSH replicates data to multiple OSDs, replicated copies survive and are read during recovery. As CRUSH develops the requisite new mapping of PGs to OSDs to populate the CRUSH map it minimizes the amount of data that must move to other, still-functioning hosts and OSD devices to complete recovery. This helps degraded objects (those that lost their copies due to failures), and thus the cluster as a whole becomes healthy once again as the replication demanded by the configured CRUSH rule policy is restored.

Once a new disk is added to a Ceph cluster, CRUSH will start renewing the cluster state, identify how the new PG placement should take place for all existing PGs and move the new disk to Up Set (and subsequently Acting Set) of the new disk. Once a disk is added newly to the Up Set, Ceph will start rebalancing data on the new disk for the PGs it's supposed to hold. The data is moved from older hosts or disks into our new disk. Rebalancing operation is necessary to keep all the disks equally utilized and thus the placement and workload uniform. For instance, if a Ceph cluster contains 2000 OSDs and a new server is added with 20 OSDs in it, CRUSH will attempt to change the placement assignment of only 1% of thePGs. Multiple OSDs might be employed for pulling relevant data out for the PGs they own, but they will work in parallel to quickly move the data over.

For Ceph clusters running with a high utilization is paramount to take care before adding new disks. The amount of data movement a new disk or a new server can cause is directly proportional to the percentage of the ratio of its CRUSH weight to the original CRUSH weight of the rest of the cluster. Typically for larger clusters, the preferred methodology to add new disks or servers is to add them with CRUSH weight of 0 to the cluster CRUSH map and gradually increase their weights. This lets you control the rate of data movement and speed it up or slow it down depending on your use-case and workloads. Another technique you can use is, when you are adding new servers you can add them to a separate, dummy, CRUSH root when you provision the OSDs on them, so they don't incur any I/O even though Ceph processes are running on the host. And then move the servers one by one into the respective buckets within the CRUSH root that your pools' CRUSH rules are using.

Customizing CRUSH

In this section, we will cover steps on how to tailor a CRUSH map to reflect local topology and requirements. Ceph provides us two ways to update a cluster's CRUSH map. One is to extract the current CRUSH map in binary form, *decompile* it to text, edit the file like any other, then compile and re-inject. In many cases though, with recent Ceph versions we can use subcommands of the familiar `ceph` utility including `ceph osd crush` to make changes in a safer and far more convenient way. In this section, we will demonstrate both methods.

For this exercise, we will again practice on the sandbox cluster used earlier in this chapter. If you do not have a sandbox Ceph cluster running, please refer to `Chapter 5`, *Deploying a Virtual Sandbox Cluster* to set one up.

Let's log into our client virtual machine as before.

```
$ vagrant ssh client0
vagrant@ceph-client0:~$sudo -i
root@ceph-client0:~#
```

Verify the cluster is healthy.

```
root@ceph-client0:~# ceph health
HEALTH_OK
```

Customizing a CRUSH map is a necessary step for building a robust and reliable Ceph storage cluster. Ceph's defaults are not aware of your physical topology and thus is also unaware of your specific fault domains. Using the techniques in this section we will provide Ceph information about your setup that will improve resiliency and help achieve optimal fault tolerance.

Before changing the CRUSH map, let's examine the current topology.

```
root@ceph-client0:~# ceph osd tree
ID WEIGHT    TYPE NAME          UP/DOWN REWEIGHT PRIMARY-AFFINITY
-1 0.06235 root default
-2 0.02078     host ceph-osd1
 6 0.01039         osd.6         up     1.00000          1.00000
10 0.01039         osd.10        up     1.00000          1.00000
-3 0.02078     host ceph-osd0
 7 0.01039         osd.7         up     1.00000          1.00000
11 0.01039         osd.11        up     1.00000          1.00000
-4 0.02078     host ceph-osd2
 8 0.01039         osd.8         up     1.00000          1.00000
 9 0.01039         osd.9         up     1.00000          1.00000
```

On running `ceph osd tree` we see that our cluster has six OSDs, three hosts and one root. The six OSDs are named osd.6, osd.7, osd.8, osd.9, osd.10 and osd.11. Your sandbox cluster might have different numbers or IDs for the OSDs which is just smurfy — remember that Ceph assigns newly-created OSDs the first unused number, which can vary over time as OSDs and hosts move through their lifecycles.We see that our three hosts are named ceph-osd0, `ceph-osd1`, and `ceph-osd2`. The root bucket that encompasses all three hosts is cleverly named `default`.

Now let's add three virtual racks to our CRUSH map. Imagine that each of our hosts live in a rack by itself, which we wish to reflect in the logical CRUSH topology. Since our sandbox cluster (and hence our datacenter) is running on a single host machine we have the luxury of stretching the limits of our imagination when it comes to designing the layout. In a production setup, it is strongly recommended to arrange the CRUSH map so that it models your physical hardware layout as closely as possible.

```
root@ceph-client0:~# ceph osd crush add-bucket rack01 rack
added bucket rack01 type rack to crush map
root@ceph-client0:~# ceph osd crush add-bucket rack02 rack
added bucket rack02 type rack to crush map
root@ceph-client0:~# ceph osd crush add-bucket rack03 rack
added bucket rack03 type rack to crush map
```

The above commands will create three new buckets of type `rack`. It is important to note that these racks will not initially be in the `default` root, but instead float in the dark and lonely limbo of CRUSH aether. They won't be allocated any data until they are moved to the default root.

We can see the new topology by again running `ceph osd tree`.

```
root@ceph-client0:~# ceph osd tree
ID WEIGHT  TYPE NAME            UP/DOWN REWEIGHT PRIMARY-AFFINITY
-7       0 rack rack03
-6       0 rack rack02
-5       0 rack rack01
-1 0.06235 root default
-2 0.02078     host ceph-osd1
 6 0.01039         osd.6         up   1.00000          1.00000
10 0.01039         osd.10        up   1.00000          1.00000
-3 0.02078     host ceph-osd0
 7 0.01039         osd.7         up   1.00000          1.00000
11 0.01039         osd.11        up   1.00000          1.00000
-4 0.02078     host ceph-osd2
 8 0.01039         osd.8         up   1.00000          1.00000
 9 0.01039         osd.9         up   1.00000          1.00000
```

We can see the new logical racks clustered at the top as expected, outside of the root. Now let's move them in from the cold to the `default` root. However, before we move them we ensure that their CRUSH weight is changed to 0. If their CRUSH weight is non-zero then Ceph will attempt to place PGs on them, which will not work since they don't yet contain any OSD devices, and our cluster state will be degraded. In the above command trace, we can easily see in the second column (labeled WEIGHT) that their CRUSH weight is indeed 0. Use the below commands to now move them into their rightful place in the CRUSH hierarchy.

```
root@ceph-client0:~# ceph osd crush move rack01 root=default
moved item id -5 name 'rack01' to location {root=default} in crush
map
root@ceph-client0:~# ceph osd crush move rack02 root=default
moved item id -6 name 'rack02' to location {root=default} in crush
map
root@ceph-client0:~# ceph osd crush move rack03 root=default
moved item id -7 name 'rack03' to location {root=default} in crush
map
```

If the cluster was in a healthy state when we started this process, it should be in a healthy state now too. This is because we haven't yet done anything to cause any data movement. As a final step, let us proceed to move the new hosts to their respective racks.

This will potentially cause data movement, so in production these steps must be executed gradually and carefully. However, because we are doing this on our lightly-utilized sandbox environment, we can safely do it all at once.

```
root@ceph-client0:~# ceph osd crush move ceph-osd0 rack=rack01
moved item id -3 name 'ceph-osd0' to location {rack=rack01} in
crush map
root@ceph-client0:~# ceph osd crush move ceph-osd1 rack=rack02
moved item id -2 name 'ceph-osd1' to location {rack=rack02} in
crush map
root@ceph-client0:~# ceph osd crush move ceph-osd2 rack=rack03
moved item id -4 name 'ceph-osd2' to location {rack=rack03} in
crush map
```

This action will temporarily degrade your cluster as the CRUSH map is updated and the PG distribution and placement are adjusted. Data on certain PGs may be very briefly unavailable but no data loss should occur and generally normal operation is restored quickly enough that users do not notice. That said, these operations are very infrequent once a cluster has entered production. After the Object copies the move to their new locations, the cluster should go back to its healthy state.

It is critically important to note here that we must not reverse the last two steps. If we were to move the hosts into the racks first, before the racks are positioned in the same root, all our PGs would be rendered inactive. This would not only render all the cluster data unavailable to clients but it could potentially precipitate data loss if the cluster were to remain in that unhappy state for long. It is imperative that any movement we perform in a production cluster of non-empty hosts or racks always be performed in their current CRUSH root.

Now that we have moved the hosts into our new virtual racks, let's check the new layout.

```
root@ceph-client0:~# ceph osd tree
ID WEIGHT   TYPE NAME              UP/DOWN REWEIGHT PRIMARY-AFFINITY
-1 0.06235 root default
-5 0.02078     rack rack01
-3 0.02078         host ceph-osd0
 7 0.01039             osd.7          up    1.00000          1.00000
11 0.01039             osd.11         up    1.00000          1.00000
-6 0.02078     rack rack02
-2 0.02078         host ceph-osd1
 6 0.01039             osd.6          up    1.00000          1.00000
10 0.01039             osd.10         up    1.00000          1.00000
-7 0.02078     rack rack03
-4 0.02078         host ceph-osd2
 8 0.01039             osd.8          up    1.00000          1.00000
 9 0.01039             osd.9          up    1.00000          1.00000
```

Devices within hosts within racks within the root. Perfect!

Now let's exploit our new layout to architect improved fault tolerance, availability, and durability for the data stored in the cluster. By default, when creating a replicated (vs. erasure coded) pool, Ceph will enforce the distribution of the copies across disjoint OSDs. Distribution of data across any hosts, racks, rows, etc. present will not be enforced.Thus, if we have a pool with replication factor (size) of 2, both copies of some objects will be assigned to two distinct OSDs found on the same host. That means, host failure or other downtime will not only prevent all access to all objects with all copies on that host, but we could potentially end up permanently losing data if the failure is severe. In other words, don't put all your objects in one basket (or bucket).

However, we can easily prevent this disastrous scenario by tailoring the CRUSH map to local topology and requirements. CRUSH offers flexible capabilities that allow us to override the default distribution by specifying rules for placing copies throughout the cluster. We can choose to direct each copy to a separate host or even a separate rack depending on our reliability and performance goals. In advanced complex scenarios we can also force data onto specific hosts or racks for specialized purposes.

We'll next modify the default placement strategy of our sandbox Ceph cluster to strictly distribute object replicas across the fancy new racks that we magically conjured up and installed in no time as part of the previous exercise.

We begin by first retrieving the CRUSH map from the MONs.

```
root@ceph-client0:~# ceph osd getcrushmap -o /tmp/crushmap.bin
got crush map from osdmap epoch 1234
```

The above command connects to the MON cluster, downloads the CRUSH map in binary form, and saves it in the /tmp directory.

The CRUSH map's binary representation is natural for Ceph's code but not convenient for humans, so we'll convert it to text form so that we can example and modify it readily.

```
root@ceph-client0:~# crushtool -d /tmp/crushmap.bin -o
/tmp/crushmap.txt
```

The CRUSH map is now expressed in a format we can open in our favorite text editor. Edit the file named /tmp/crushmap.txt and navigate to the end of the file. The last few lines should look like the below.

```
# rules
rule replicated_ruleset {
        ruleset 0
        type replicated
```

```
min_size 1
max_size 10
        step take default
        step chooseleaffirstn 0 type host
        step emit
}
```

This section holds the *CRUSH rules*. A CRUSH map can have multiple rules, although at any given time only a single rule can be applied to each Ceph pool. We will explain the components of the rule in more detail below:

- This rule is named `replicated_ruleset`. The name of the rule is followed by curly braces that delimit the actual specifications.
- The first field of the rule specification is the *ruleset ID*. This is the number that is stored as the `crush_ruleset` attribute of any pool to which the rule applies. We can see our `replicated_ruleset` has the ruleset ID of 0.
- The rule is of type `replicated`. Ceph currently supports just two types of rules: `replicated` and `erasure-coded`.
- The `min_size` and `max_size` settings define the minimum and maximum replication factor that may be set on pools to which this rule is applied. If these limits are violated by a pool's attributes then this CRUSH rule will not be applied. This allows flexibility when configuring multiple pools with differing characteristics within a single cluster. Note that `min_size` here is distinct from the `min_size` attribute of the pool itself; the term is unfortunately overloaded and easily confused.
- The `step` directives define a sequence of steps to follow to select an appropriate bucket (rack, host, OSD, etc.) for our objects. The last three lines of the default rule define the following sequence:
    - First we select the root `default` and proceed down its topology tree. All copies of objects will be sent only to this root.
    - Then we select a set of buckets of type `host` and pick a leaf node, which is the OSD device, from the subtree under each. The number of buckets in the set is usually the replication factor of the pool.
    - The `firstn` rule specifies how many copies of an object we can greedily choose to direct to the same bucket. Because the number is 0 and we are truly at the leaf node, it will only pick one host per copy.
    - The final `emit` step completes this process and empties the stack.

In order to distribute one copy per rack, as we favored in Chapter 4, *Planning Your Deployment,* we will need to change the second to last line that says:

```
step chooseleaffirstn 0 type host
```

And change host to rack:

```
step chooseleaffirstn 0 type rack
```

This will ensure that we choose a rack as the leaf for the distribution of our copies, and the OSDs within a rack can be picked at random (modulo weights) for uniform utilization within the rack.

Let's make that change in the file now, so the replicated_ruleset looks like follows:

```
# rules
rule replicated_ruleset {
        ruleset 0
        type replicated
min_size 1
max_size 10
        step take default
step chooseleaffirstn 0 type rack
        step emit
}
```

Now save the file and exit. We will compile the file to binary form and send it back, duly chastened, to our Ceph MONs from whence it came.

Note: This will temporarily degrade our cluster. Note that whenever we make changes to our CRUSH map there is always a potential of incurring a small to massive amount of data movement and thus impact to the ongoing client I/O. Ideally such changes should therefore be executed during a maintenance window or off hours.

```
root@ceph-client0:~# crushtool -c /tmp/crushmap.txt -o
/tmp/crushmap.bin
root@ceph-client0:~# ceph osd setcrushmap -i /tmp/crushmap.bin
set crush map
```

Your cluster will briefly report degradation but will soon return to health. This concludes the final step of manually changing the CRUSH map configuration.

Ceph pools

The concept of *pool* is not novel in storage systems. Enterprise storage systems are often divided into several pools to facilitate management. A Ceph pool is a logical partition of PGs and by extension Objects. Each pool in Ceph holds a number of PGs, which in turn holds a number of Objects that are mapped to OSDs throughout the cluster. This distribution across cluster nodes helps ensure the required level of RAS. In versions prior to Luminous, the initial Ceph deployment creates by default a pool named `rbd`; with Luminous or later you will need to create this yourself if you plan on providing block service. This might not be sufficient for all use-cases and it is recommended to create your own when needed. Deploying RGW or CephFS for your cluster will create the required pools automatically.

A pool guarantees data availability by defining and maintaining a desired number of copies of every object. The type of pool (replicated or erasure coded) determines how many copies of objects will be maintained. Ceph supports **Erasure Coding** (**EC**) strategies that allows data resiliency and fault tolerance by breaking data into fragments and storing them in a distributed manner with redundancy baked in.

At the time of pool creation, we define the replication factor (or *size*) of the pool; the default is 3. A replicated pool is very flexible and the replication factor can be changed at any time. However, increasing replication factor immediately updates PGs to make new copies of all Objects within the cluster. This can be quite expensive depending on the size of the cluster and its usage, so it has to be planned carefully. A pool can also be erasure coded. This provides less flexibility than replicated pools because the number of data copies within an erasure coded pool cannot be changed as flexibly. To change EC strategy a new pool must be provisioned with the desired EC profile and data move over, versus the update-in-place that is possible with a replicated pool.

A Ceph pool is mapped to a CRUSH ruleset when data is written. The CRUSH ruleset controls the placement of object replicas within the cluster. The ruleset enables sophisticated behavior for Ceph pools. For example, it is possible to create a fast cache pool out of SSD or NVMe drives, or a hybrid pool mixing of SSD and SAS or SATA disk drives. With care, one may even construct a pool where lead OSDs are on SSD devices for fast reads while safety replicas reside on less expensive HDD drives.

Ceph pools also support snapshot features. We can use `ceph osd pool mksnap` to take a snapshot of an entire pool in one operation. We can also restore a complete pool when necessary. Ceph pools also allows us to set ownership and access permissions to Objects. A user ID can be assigned as the owner of the pool. This is very useful in scenarios where we need to restrict access to certain pools.

Pool operations

Ceph pool operations are one of the day-to-day tasks of a Ceph administrator. Ceph provides rich CLI tools for pool creation and management. We will learn about Ceph pool operations in the following section:

Creating and listing pools

When creating a Ceph pool we must a specify a name, PG count, and a pool type of either `replicated` or `erasure-coded`. We'll begin by creating a replicated pool. We don't specify the type because `replicated` is the default. We will use our trusty sandbox cluster again in this exercise.

1. Create a pool named `web-services` with a `pg_num` value of 128. The pool's `pgp_num` is implicitly set to match the `pg_num` we specify.

```
root@ceph-client0:~# ceph osd pool create web-services 128
pool 'web-services' created
```

2. Listing existing pools can be done in three ways. The first two list only the names of the pools, while the third displays more information including numeric pool ID, replication size, CRUSH ruleset and PG count.

```
root@ceph-client0:~# ceph osd lspools
1 rbd, 2 my_pool, 3 web-services
root@ceph-client0:~# rados lspools
rbd
my_pool
web-services
root@ceph-client0:~# ceph osd pool ls detail
pool 1 'rbd' replicated size 3 min_size 2 crush_ruleset 0
object_hashrjenkinspg_num 64 pgp_num 64 last_change 5205 flags
hashpspoolstripe_width 0
pool 2 'my_pool' replicated size 3 min_size 2 crush_ruleset 0
object_hashrjenkinspg_num 256 pgp_num 256 last_change 12580 flags
hashpspoolstripe_width 0
pool 3 'web-services' replicated size 3 min_size 2
crush_ruleset 0
object_hashrjenkinspg_num 128 pgp_num 128 last_change 12656 flags
hashpspoolstripe_width 0
```

3. The default replication size for a pool is 3 when created using Ceph Jewel. This value is also the default in the new Luminous release. We can change the replication size if needed using the following command. Remember that we can get away with this in our sandbox, but that in production, this would result in considerable movement of data, which might contend with or overwhelm client operations.

```
root@ceph-client0:~#ceph osd pool set web-services size 3
set pool 3 size to 3
```

4. Our Principal architect demands a different name for our pool, so we'll rename it.

```
root@ceph-client0:~# ceph osd pool rename web-services frontend-
services pool 'web-services' renamed to 'frontend-services'
root@ceph-client0:~# rados lspools
rbd
my_pool
frontend-services
```

5. Ceph pools support snapshots. We can restore Objects from a snapshot in event of failure. In the following example we will create an Object then take a snapshot of the pool. We will then proceed to remove the Object from the pool then restore the deleted Object from our pool snapshot.

```
root@ceph-client0:~# echo "somedata" > object01.txt
root@ceph-client0:~# rados -p frontend-services put object01
object01.txt
root@ceph-client0:~# rados -p frontend-services ls
object01

root@ceph-client0:~# rados mksnap snapshot01 -p frontend-services
       created pool frontend-services snap snapshot01
root@ceph-client0:~# rados lssnap -p frontend-services
       1     snapshot01    2017.09.04 18:02:24
       1 snaps
root@ceph-client0:~# rados -p frontend-services rm object01
root@ceph-client0:~# rados -p frontend-services
       listsnaps object01 object01:
       cloneid      snaps size   overlap
             1       1     9       []
root@ceph-client0:~# rados rollback -p frontend-services object01
       snapshot01
       rolled back pool frontend-services to snapshot
       snapshot01
root@ceph-client0:~# rados -p frontend-services ls
       object01
```

6. Removing a pool will also remove its snapshots. After permanently removing a pool it is good practice to delete any associated custom CRUSH rulesets if you won't be re-using them. If you created users with permissions strictly for a pool that is no more, you can delete those too later.

```
root@ceph-client0:~# ceph osd pool delete frontend-services
                        frontend-
services —yes-i-really-really-mean-it
pool 'frontend-services' removed
```

Ceph data flow

The management of data as it flows through a Ceph cluster involves each of the components we have discussed so far. Coordination among these components empowers Ceph to provide a reliable and robust storage system. Data management begins with clients writing data to pools. When a client writes data to a Ceph pool, the data is sent to the primary OSD. The primary OSD commits the data locally and sends an immediate acknowledgement to the client if replication factor is 1. If the replication factor is greater than 1 (as it should be in any serious deployment) the primary OSD issues write subops to each subsidiary (secondary, tertiary, etc) OSD and awaits a response. Since we always have exactly one primary OSD, the number of subsidiary OSDs is the replication size - 1. Once all responses have arrived, depending on success, it sends acknowledgement (or failure) back to the client.

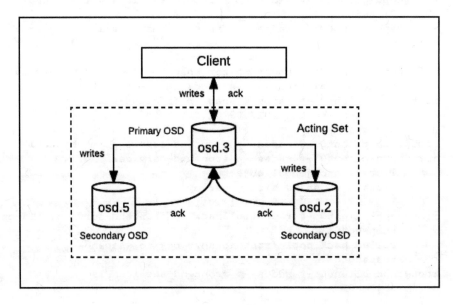

In this way Ceph carefully persists each client write operation to ensure strong consistency across replicas. Let's see how the data is actually stored in a Ceph cluster.

1. We will create a test file, and a pool and set its replication factor to 3.

```
root@ceph-client0:~# echo "Ceph, you are awesome!" >
                /tmp/helloceph
root@ceph-client0:~# cepho osd pool create HPC_Pool 128 128
                pool 'HPC_Pool' created
root@ceph-client0:~# ceph osd pool set HPC_Pool size 3
                set pool 4 size to 3
```

2. Now let's store the test data file we created in that pool and check the pool's contents.

```
root@ceph-client0:~# rados -p HPC_Pool put object1 /tmp/helloceph
root@ceph-client0:~# rados -p HPC_Pool ls
object1
```

3. The file is now stored in a Ceph pool. As you have seen, everything in Ceph gets stored in the form of objects, where each object belongs to a unique Placement Group that points to one or more OSDs. Now let's actually see how this mapping looks from within Ceph:

```
root@ceph-client0:~# ceph osd map HPC_Pool object1
osdmap e12664 pool 'HPC_Pool' (4) object 'object1' -
    >pg4.bac5debc (4.3c)
    -> up ([8,7,6], p8) acting ([8,7,6], p8)
```

Let's discuss the output of the above command:

- `osdmap e12664`: This is the OSD map version ID, indicating that we are at the 12664th epoch. Epochs are monotonically incremented when an OSD map changes.
- `pool 'HPC_Pool' (4)`: This is Ceph's pool name with the ID in parentheses.
- `object 'object1'`: This contains the name of the Object.
- `pg4.bac5debc (4.3c)`: This contains the long and short form ID of the PG to which object1 belongs. The short form i.e. 4.3c is used in most places.

- up ([8,7,6], p8): This shows the Up Set of OSDs, those that host the PG to which the object belongs (and hence the object). With our pool's size set to 3 data is replicated on three OSDs: osd.8, osd.7 and osd.6. The p8 tells us that osd.8 is the primary or lead OSD for this PG.
- acting ([8,7,6], p8): This shows the Acting Set, along with the acting primary OSD for the PG. We see that Acting Set in our case is exactly same as Up Set. This might not always be true, especially if the cluster is undergoing backfill / recovery and some PGs are queued for relocation.

4. To see how the object appears in FileStore, let's find the physical host of the primary OSD. We shall use the ceph osd find <osd-id> command to get the parent buckets of the OSD.

```
root@ceph-client0:~# ceph osd find 8
{
      "osd": 8,
      "ip": "192.168.42.102:6802\/3515",
      "crush_location": {
                  "host": "ceph-osd2",
                  "rack": "rack03",
                  "root": "default"
                            }
    }
```

This OSD resides on the host ceph-osd2 which is found in rack rack03.

5. Let's log into the ceph-osd2 host. In order to do so, we will need to exit from our client virtual machine and log back in from our host machine.

```
root@ceph-client0:~# logout
vagrant@ceph-client0:~$ exit
Connection to 127.0.0.1 closed.
$ vagrant ssh osd2
vagrant@ceph-osd2:~$ sudo -i
root@ceph-osd2:~#
```

6. Let's find where our Ceph data directory is located from the list of our file-system mounts. We will then jump in and find our object. Remember the PG ID we found in the `ceph osd map` command above (it was 4.3c)? We will need this now. The series of steps to do so follows.

```
root@ceph-osd2:~# df -h | grep ceph-8
/dev/sdb1    11G   84M   11G   1% /var/lib/ceph/osd/ceph-8
root@ceph-osd2:~# cd /var/lib/ceph/osd/ceph-8/current/
root@ceph-osd2:/var/lib/ceph/osd/ceph-8/current# cd 4.3c_head
root@ceph-osd2:/var/lib/ceph/osd/ceph-8/current/4.3c_head# ls -l
total 4
-rw-r—r— 1 cephceph  0 Sep  4 18:20 __head_0000003C__10
-rw-r—r— 1 cephceph 36 Sep  4 18:22 object1__head_BAC5DEBC__10
```

We can see that our beloved `object1` is stored in a file prefixed with the name of our object.

BlueStore (a significant enhancement over FileStore) is supported and default as Ceph's Luminous release. With BlueStore objects are not stored as files on a traditional Unix / Linux filesystem, rather they are stored within an embedded database that exploits each OSD block device directly. This is directly analogous to the traditional relational database option of using a raw partition to hold tables instead of files on a filesystem, or the way that Highwinds' Cyclone and Typhoon Usenet products gained substantial performance gains over traditional C news and INN. In all cases the application gains performance by bypassing the overhead of the filesystem layer. By implementing an underlying data store tailored to its specific needs — versus contorting itself to fit within the limits and semantics of filesystem designed for other purposes—Ceph is able to manage data much more efficiently. And who doesn't like efficiency and speed?

The tradeoff though with BlueStore's raw embedded database approach is that, we no longer have a traditional filesystem that we can traverse and inspect with familiar tools including `ls`, `cd`, `cat`, and `du`. As BlueStore is very new on the scene and the code has not yet been fully proven itself with conservative Ceph admins, deployment has not yet become widespread. BlueStore encapsulates an internal RocksDB metadata store that requires specialized techniques and tooling to pry open, ones that are still evolving as this chapter is written. We can expect though that like FileStore we will rarely have cause to delve this deep into the innards of an OSD in production.

Erasure coding

In this and other chapters we've discussed Ceph's replication strategy for data protection. Ceph also offers EC as an alternative. EC has its roots in data transmission, where it is not uncommon for portions of the signal to drop out or suffer *erasure* (hence the name). Unlike protocols (like TCP) that merely detect lost data and arrange for retransmission, erasure codes are designed to mix replication right in with payload data. Thus, missing sections can be regenerated computationally at the receiving end, unilaterally without having to contact the sender. The Voyager planetary probes, notably exploited a type of erasure code for their transmissions. At Neptune, the round trip time to send a signal back to Earth and receive a response was more than five *hours*, a delay quite successfully avoided by the Reed-Solomon encoding that the technology of the day enabled.

Another, more terrestrial example of erasure coding is the **Parchive (PAR)** encoding used by Usenet and other online communities to allow the reconstruction of large, fragmented binary files even if a number of segments were not retrieved. This implementation is perhaps more directly comparable to Ceph, where data loss due to component or network failure is still a concern even though network RTT generally isn't.

Thus erasure coding as implemented by Ceph is akin in some ways to familiar RAID5, RAID6, or RAIDZ3 data protection. Recall that we can select either erasure coding or replication at the pool level, which means that a single cluster can implement different data protection strategies on individual datasets according to their requirements and economics.

While Ceph replicated pools are almost always provisioned with a size (replication factor) of 3, erasure coding presents dozens of parameter combinations that vary in their overhead and resilience. With Ceph's present default erasure code algorithm (jerasure) we must consider two parameters, K and M. At the RADOS level,Ceph will split each Object into K separate chunks, from which M additional chunks are computed as a function of the input object's data. These original data chunks together with the computed (aka *encoded* or *parity*) chunks are called *shards*, which are independently written to underlying RADOS objects. These are distributed according to assigned CRUSH rules to ensure that they are spread across hosts, racks, or other failure domains. Each additional shard of data that we compute allows the reconstruction of the entire object if single shard out of the set is unavailable or lost. Thus, when properly distributed across failure domains, M represents the number of shards out of the set that can fail without compromising data availability. While jerasure is more flexible, this dynamic is congruent with parity RAID. RAID5 for example can tolerate the loss of any one device and in this fashion, is like an erasure code with M=1. Similarly, RAID6 is comparable to an erasure code with M=2, since any two devices out of each parity group can be lost without losing data.

The selection of a specific data protection strategy is always a tradeoff between resilience and overhead, especially the cost of acquiring and running storage devices. As storage deployments grow larger, to hundreds or thousands of individual devices, we increasingly are compelled to explore data protection strategies that tolerate the loss of a greater number of components and/or offer finer granularity of the efficiency tradeoff.

This is where Ceph's `jerasure` encoding choices of K and M come into play. We choose the values for a given EC pool based on factors including the number of failures we're required to tolerate, the encoding overhead we're willing to incur, and logistical factors including the number of hosts, racks, and other failure domains across which we'll deploy. The choice must be made carefully, as unlike replicated pools, we cannot adjust an EC pool after the fact that if we change our mind — the only option would be to create a new pool and move data over, which is possible but slow, complex, and disruptive.

We define the overhead of a pool with given replication factor or erasure code (K,M) values as the ratio of the raw to usable capacities. For example, a default replicated Ceph pool with size=3 results in a ratio of 3:1, or simply an overhead factor of 3. A conventional RAID 0 stripe volume has no redundancy and thus presents a ratio of 1:1, or an overhead factor of 1. Extending this concept to Ceph's jerasure encoding, the overhead factor is calculated by

$$\frac{(K + M)}{K}$$

k: data chunks
m: parity chunks

For example, an EC pool with K=4 and M=2 achieves an overhead ratio of 4:2, or 1.5. It is ideally spread across 6 failure domains, any 2 of which can drop without impacting data availability. While a pool with K=8 and M=4 might seem prima facie identical to this (4,2) pool, it differs in the way that the loss of any 4 out of each 12 failure domains can be tolerated, covering a somewhat larger constellation of faults.

In practice very large values of K and M become unwieldy, so let's calculate the overhead profile of each combination.

		M				
		1	2	3	4	5
	1	2.00	3.00	4.00	5.00	6.00
	2	1.50	2.00	2.50	3.00	3.50
	3	1.33	1.67	2.00	2.33	2.67
	4	1.25	1.50	1.75	2.0	2.25
K	5	1.20	1.40	1.60	1.80	2.0
	6	1.17	1.33	1.50	1.67	1.83
	7	1.14	1.29	1.43	1.57	1.71
	8	1.13	1.25	1.38	1.50	1.63
	9	1.11	1.22	1.33	1.44	1.56
	10	1.10	1.20	1.30	1.40	1.50

In practice, the degenerate choice of K=1 rarely makes sense, as it approximates simple replication (mirroring), without the utilization ratio advantages of better EC profiles. Such profiles are inefficient in the way that they require more CPU resources for reconstruction of lost data or parity chunks. Network traffic is amplified since there is no sharding of data. In other words, even partial erasures require the system to act as though the entire chunk of data is lost, contrasted with a better profile where small erasures affect only one of multiple shards, and thus only a fraction of the data must be restored.One might think that the choice of (K,M) is driven by the desired efficiency ratio, but it's more complex than that.

EC profiles where K is a larger number and M=1 also are not ideal. The effectiveness of sharding is limited, and the system can only tolerate a single drive failure without losing data.

EC profiles where K<M are not favorable. The additional parity shards beget poor efficiency ratios and add computational overhead without much benefit.

Applying these constraints to the table above, we can limit our decision to the shaded profiles. Columns for larger values of M are plausible for correspondingly larger values of K, with two caveats:

1. With larger numbers of shards, proper alignment with DC racks for fault tolerance becomes complicated.
2. That would make the table really wide for e-reader users

 Here's another example of the value of the Ceph community. This informative ceph-users mailing list thread discusses EC profile decisions for a specific use-case: https://www.mail-archive.com/ceph-users@lists.ceph.com/msg40452.html

Let's consider now an example of a Ceph erasure coded pool with (K=3, M=2) and explore what happens as data is written and read.

With these parameters, each Object will be split into 3 shards, from which 2 additional shards are computed with redundancy information, for a total of 5 shards. The shards need to be of exactly the same size, so padding will be added if necessary. Each shard is written to a separate OSD, which ideally our rack layout and CRUSH rules house in a separate rack, or at the very least on a separate server.

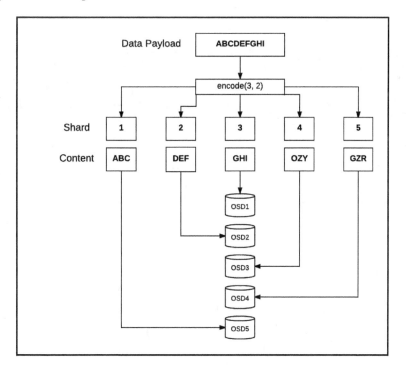

When it's time to read this Object, reads for each shard 1 through 5 are issued. To illustrate the value of erasure coding for data protection, let's say that OSD2 is being sluggish and OSD4 was struck by lightning and caught on fire. Since the pool and thus our erasure code defines K=2, we still have enough information to reconstitute all of each Object's data. The shards are fed into the erasure code's decoding function, which spits out our intact original data, which is then sent to the client.

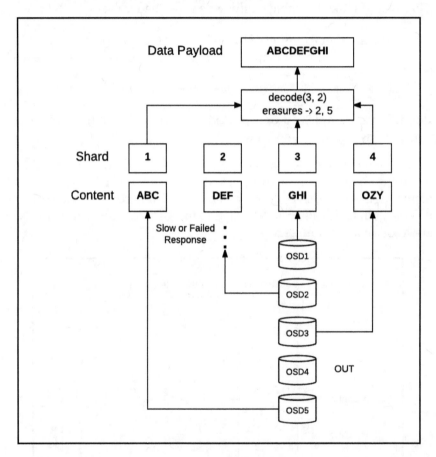

As we've detailed elsewhere in this book, Ceph has offered erasure coded RADOS GateWay pools for years, but support for RBD pools comes only with the Luminous release. EC has considerable appeal in the efficient use of raw storage capacity. Depending on the parameters selected, fault tolerance can even exceed that of replication in certain scenarios. The tradeoff however is decreased performance with higher latency. A strategy known as Cache Tiering is described in some references as mitigating the performance impact of EC, especially when implemented on HDD drives, though in practice this has proven tricky to get right. The added management complexity and the cost of additional hardware and fast drives to provision as a cache tier also narrows the financial gap when compared to replication.

> A deep dive into the guts of Erasure Coding can be a bit of a rabbit hole, even for those of us with Applied Math degrees. For those so inclined, however, a wealth of information and pretty diagrams can be found on the below pages.

```
http://docs.ceph.com/docs/master/architecture/#erasure-coding
http://ceph.com/geen-categorie/ceph-erasure-coding-overhead-in-a
-nutshell/
https://software.intel.com/en-us/blogs/2015/04/06/ceph-erasure-c
oding-introduction
http://smahesh.com/blog/2012/07/01/dummies-guide-to-erasure-codi
ng/
https://www.snia.org/sites/default/files/JasonResch_Erasure_Code
s_SDC_2013.pdf
http://static.usenix.org/events/fast/tech/full_papers/Khan.pdf
```

With either strategy, replication or erasure coding, Ceph stores each data object in a replicated manner across multiple failure domains. This intelligence is at the core of Ceph's data management.

Summary

In this chapter we learned about Ceph's internal components including Objects, the CRUSH algorithm, Placement Groups and pools and how they interact with each other to provide a highly reliable and scalable distributed storage cluster. We also harnessed our sandbox cluster to gain experience with interacting with these components. We also explored how data is stored within the cluster right from the point it entered in as a write request until it reached the correct OSD and was written on a storage device in the form of an Object file. We recommend that you try to repeat these examples on your test cluster to get a better idea of how Ceph replicates and stores data in a highly available fashion. If you are a system administrator, you should focus more on understanding how Ceph pools and CRUSH works as mentioned in this chapter. In the next chapter, we will learn how to provision a working Ceph Storage system.

9
Storage Provisioning with Ceph

Provisioning storage is an important task of a storage system administrator. Ceph provides us with multiple abstractions to access data stored in various forms as we have seen in the previous chapters. We can store data within a block device attached to our machine, on a locally mounted filesystem, or remotely accessible object storage using those abstractions.

In this chapter, we will cover the following topics:

- Setting up Ceph Block Devices
- Setting up the Ceph Filesystem
- Setting up Ceph Object Storage using RADOS Gateway
- Configuring S3 and Swift with RADOS Gateway

Client Services

As we discussed in `Chapter 2`, *Ceph Components and Services*, Ceph clients can be categorized under three distinct interfaces, each of which we'll explore in this chapter:

- RBD
- CephFS
- RGW

In order to interact with Ceph we will first need to create a cluster to be at our disposal. Chapter 5, *Deploying a Virtual Sandbox Cluster* covers the process of setting up a working Ceph cluster. Please go through that step-by-step process if you haven't gone through it yet and don't have a working cluster.

Ceph Block Device (RADOS Block Device)

Many deployments using platforms such as OpenStack or DigitalOcean manage and attach RBD images at the virtualization layer, so they appear to the guest operating system through SCSI or Virtio drivers. Here we'll also explore the use of the Linux kernel driver on arbitrary, even bare metal, systems.

The **RADOS Block Device (RBD)**—formerly known as the Ceph Block Device—provides block-based persistent storage to Ceph clients. The block device is presented as a traditional drive on the client machine. Such a drive can be used in various ways. It can be used as a raw block device or as a filesystem by partitioning, formatting, and subsequently mounting it.

RBD makes use of the librbd library and stores blocks of data striped over multiple OSDs in a Ceph cluster. RBD is built on the fundamental RADOS layer of Ceph. Thus every block device is spread over multiple Ceph nodes and delivers high performance and excellent reliability.

RBD is rich with enterprise-class features including thin provisioning, live resize, **Copy-on-Write (CoW)** snapshots and client-side caching. The RBD protocol is fully supported within Linux via a mainline kernel driver; it is also exploited by virtualization platforms including KVM, QEMU, and libvirt to allow virtual machines to take advantage of Ceph Block Devices. These features make RBD an ideal solution for cloud platforms such as OpenStack and CloudStack. We will now learn how to create and utilize a Ceph Block Device.

Creating and Provisioning RADOS Block Devices

We will assume that you have a working Ceph cluster sandbox configured with one or more MON nodes, one or more OSD nodes, and at least one client node. These nodes can be virtual machines if you are running the cluster that we created in Chapter 5, *Deploying a Virtual Sandbox Cluster,* or they can be physical instances if you already have a cluster running. Most of the actions below will be performed on the client node, but if we need to run a command on an OSD or MON node we'll be sure to note so.

Let's start by logging into the client node and switching to the root user:

```
$ vagrant ssh client0
vagrant@ceph-client0:~$ sudo -i
root@ceph-client0:~#
```

We can now create a RADOS block device named `ceph-client1-rbd1`. We will need to specify a size, which for our example will be 10240 MB (or 10 GB). We will use the `rbd` command-line tool to interact with Ceph. This command should already be available on the client node via the package installation we performed in `Chapter 5`, *Deploying a Virtual Sandbox Cluster*:

```
root@ceph-client0:~# rbd create ceph-client1-rbd1 --size 10240
```

If the above command fails with a permission error, we will need to enable client node to access our Ceph cluster. This requires the addition of a `keyring` for a user that has read-write access to the cluster, placed alongside the Ceph configuration file. The user will be authenticated via the `keyring` and if deemed to be a valid user with an appropriate set of permissions they will be allowed to perform read-write operations on the cluster. For security reasons, we should be careful to not distribute `keyrings` with read/write privileges to hosts that do not require it. If a host needs only read access to the cluster then we can create a separate user with just read privileges.

If using the client from our Virtual Sandbox, we already have the proper configuration and user `keyring` set up to talk to the cluster. The files can be seen under the default directory: `/etc/ceph`:

```
root@ceph-client0:~# ls -l /etc/ceph/
total 16
-rw------- 1 ceph ceph 63 Aug 19 02:49 ceph.client.admin.keyring
-rw-r--r-- 1 ceph ceph 1208 Aug 19 02:49 ceph.conf
```

Once the `rbd create` command succeeds we should now have a single RBD image in our cluster. Let's list all the images belonging to all users in our cluster, which should show the image that we just created:

```
root@ceph-client0:~# rbd ls
ceph-client1-rbd1
```

We can use the `info` subcommand to find more information about the image we just created, which can be thought of as attributes or metadata:

```
root@ceph-client0:~# rbd info ceph-client1-rbd1
rbd image 'ceph-client1-rbd1':
size 10240 MB in 2560 objects
order 22 (4096 kB objects)
block_name_prefix: rbd_data.ac9c238e1f29
format: 2
features: layering, exclusive-lock, object-map, fast-diff, deep-flatten
flags:
```

By default, RBD images are created within a pool named `rbd`. You can specify a different pool by supplying a pool parameter to the `rbd` command with the `-p` switch. The following command will return the same output as the previous command, but we manually specify the pool name. Similarly, you can create RBD images within other pools by using the `-p` switch:

```
root@ceph-client0:~# rbd -p rbd info ceph-client1-rbd1
rbd image 'ceph-client1-rbd1':
size 10240 MB in 2560 objects
order 22 (4096 kB objects)
block_name_prefix: rbd_data.ac9c238e1f29
format: 2
features: layering, exclusive-lock, object-map, fast-diff, deep-flatten
flags:
```

Now that we have created a block device we will walk through the steps to access it. To use the volume we will need to map it to a kernel block device on our client operating system. Once mapped the device should show up as `/dev/rbd0` on the client node.

 RBD block devices are also known as *volumes* or less commonly *images* or *allocations*. The terms are mostly interchangeable and you'll see all of them used out in the wild. The great thing about standards is that there are so many of them from which to choose.

Mapping the RBD image to a virtual disk using the RBD kernel driver requires a Linux kernel of at least version 2.6.32. If you are using the virtual sandbox, the kernel version on the client should at least be 4.4.0 and thus is more than sufficient for this exercise. Before proceeding we will first need to load the `rbd` kernel module:

```
root@ceph-client0:~# uname -r
4.4.0-92-generic
root@ceph-client0:~# modprobe rbd
```

We can now verify that the rbd module loaded correctly. The `lsmod` command shows the current set of loaded modules. Note that modules loaded on the fly with `modprobe` do not persist across reboots. That means if you were to reboot this machine, you'd need to again reload this module manually or via an operating system startup script. If you wish to load the `rbd` module with every operating system boot, you will need to add it to the `/etc/modules` file and ensure that all its dependencies are present:

```
root@ceph-client0:~# lsmod | grep rbd
rbd 69632 0
libceph 245760 1 rbd
```

We now have everything we need to use the RBD image we have created. The next step is to map the image to a kernel device on our client node that we can treat just like a local disk or other block device. We will again use the `rbd` command-line utility to create this device:

```
root@ceph-client0:~# rbd map ceph-client1-rbd1
/dev/rbd0
```

This command might fail if the kernel you are using does not provide support for certain image features (or *attributes*) that newer `librbd` images might possess. The features that the kernel driver supports are slightly behind compared to the mainstream `librbd` client driver because it is maintained and managed independently. A failure might look like this:

```
root@ceph-client0:~# rbd map ceph-client1-rbd1
rbd: sysfs write failed
RBD image feature set mismatch. You can disable features unsupported by the
kernel with "rbd feature disable".
```

An expedient workaround is to disable certain image features that the kernel doesn't support. If you are using kernel version 4.4.0 or below, you might need to disable at least the following image features:

- exclusive-lock
- object-map
- fast-diff
- deep-flatten

We can use the feature subcommand of the `rbd` utility to update the set of features (attributes) that we want the image to possess:

```
root@ceph-client0:~# rbd info ceph-client1-rbd1
rbd image 'ceph-client1-rbd1':
size 10240 MB in 2560 objects
order 22 (4096 kB objects)
block_name_prefix: rbd_data.ac9c238e1f29
```

```
format: 2
features: layering, exclusive-lock, object-map, fast-diff, deep-flatten
flags:
root@ceph-client0:~# rbd feature disable ceph-client1-rbd1 exclusive-
lock,object-map,fast-diff,deep-flatten
root@ceph-client0:~# rbd info ceph-client1-rbd1
rbd image 'ceph-client1-rbd1':
size 10240 MB in 2560 objects
order 22 (4096 kB objects)
block_name_prefix: rbd_data.ac9c238e1f29
format: 2
features: layering
flags:
root@ceph-client0:~# rbd map ceph-client1-rbd1
/dev/rbd0
```

We can now see all images that we have mapped onto the local devices using the `showmapped` subcommand:

```
root@ceph-client0:~# rbd showmapped
id pool image snap device
0 rbd ceph-client1-rbd1 - /dev/rbd0
```

Mapping the image to an operating system device (aka *device node*) helps us access the image as a traditional block device. We now format the drive with a filesystem type of our choice, for example, XFS, EXT4, or even ZFS. We can then perform conventional file-oriented operations on the device once we mount it on an arbitrary `mountpoint` directory on our system.

```
root@ceph-client0:~# fdisk -l /dev/rbd0
Disk /dev/rbd0: 10 GiB, 10737418240 bytes, 20971520 sectors
Units: sectors of 1 * 512 = 512 bytes
Sector size (logical/physical): 512 bytes / 512 bytes
I/O size (minimum/optimal): 4194304 bytes / 4194304 bytes

root@ceph-client0:~# mkfs.xfs /dev/rbd0
meta-data=/dev/rbd0
isize=512 agcount=17, agsize=162816 blks
sectsz=512 attr=2, projid32bit=1
crc=1 finobt=1, sparse=0
bsize=4096 blocks=2621440, imaxpct=25
sunit=1024 swidth=1024 blks
naming =version 2 bsize=4096 ascii-ci=0 ftype=1
log =internal log bsize=4096 blocks=2560, version=2
sectsz=512 sunit=8 blks, lazy-count=1
realtime =none extsz=4096 blocks=0, rtextents=0
```

```
root@ceph-client0:~# mkdir /mnt/ceph-vol01
root@ceph-client0:~# mount /dev/rbd0 /mnt/ceph-vol01
root@ceph-client0:~# echo "it works!" > /mnt/ceph-vol01/rbd.txt
root@ceph-client0:~# cat /mnt/ceph-vol01/rbd.txt
it works!
```

Congrats! You have provisioned your first Ceph storage volume and are already accessing files on it like a champ.

Your data is persistently written to and managed by your Ceph cluster. If for some unfortunate reason your client crashes and refuses to come back up, your precious data will remain intact thanks to Ceph's commitment to strong consistency. The sandbox environment we are using for this exercise is built only to conveniently demo several ways to access Ceph's abstractions. It is important to note that it is not designed to achieve high fault tolerance since your entire Ceph environment is running on a single physical machine. For production-quality storage with full data durability and availability you will need to deploy Ceph clusters separately from your clients, in different racks and perhaps a dedicated subnet. The OSD and MON nodes that in our sandbox are realized as virtual instances will be architected as separate physical servers in a production deployment.

Resizing RADOS Block Devices

Ceph RBD block devices are thin-provisioned volumes, which means that the underlying physical storage on Ceph clusters (provided by OSDs) is not fully written or allocated until the user actually writes data to the device. For example, say we provision a 5 TB volume—something that the author's users do daily on local disks, all 5 terabytes are allocated immediately and the available capacity is immediately reduced by 5 TB. This holds true whether the user writes 5 TB of data, just 1 GB, or none at all. With thin provisioning, almost no space is immediately allocated on the underlying storage, and the available capacity is not significantly reduced. Thus there is an important distinction between *provisioned* and *allocated* data.

There are many advantages to thin-provisioning volumes. Create operations are very fast since only new metadata (header, ID and/or journal) objects are written to the the cluster regardless of the provisioned size of the image. Resizing existing images is similarly fast, and as easy as updating the volume's metadata. This allows product managers to overprovision (also known as oversell) the cluster's capacity with the assumption that not every client or user will fill or *allocate* data on volumes to 100% or even 50% of their *provisioned* capacity. In the worst-case scenario of users actually filling their volumes, transparently scaling Ceph's capacity to match is as easy as adding more OSD nodes or drives to the cluster, as described in Chapter 6, *Hardware Selection*.

As we write, the authors recently found certain users writing (allocating) 8 TB of data per day to a certain cluster that initially provided 330 TB of usable space. We addressed this rapid growth by transparently doubling the available storage in just two days. We incrementally added new OSDs on new nodes, without users being impacted or even knowing about the expansion. Several years ago this author performed a similar yet much smaller expansion on a traditional HBA-based (RAID card) volume. The entire server, which was collecting and processing billing data, locked up for a full seven hours, which cost the company significant bill-lables and the author no small measure of embarrassment. The management flexibility of a Ceph-based storage solution is invaluable, especially when compared to traditional scenarios like this.

- A valuable but less obvious advantage of thin provisioning is that as data is moved, deleted, or truncated the space it occupied can be reclaimed. With a traditional *thick-provisioned* strategy, once you create a 100GB volume it consumes the entire 100GB of underlying storage all the time, even if it's filled with nothing but zeros.
- With proper client OS support, Ceph RBD images can release unused data back to the underlying storage cluster for reuse. Visit the below resources to learn about the SSD-inspired fstrim utility:
  `http://manpages.ubuntu.com/manpages/trusty/man8/fstrim.8.html`

Resizing the Ceph RBD block device is, however, only half of the story. If the filesystem which is laid out on the block device or one of its partitions does not support resizing, then growing the underlying volume is futile. Fortunately all common modern filesystems including XFS, EXT4, Btrfs, and ZFS support resizing the installed filesystem after the size of underlying block device has changed. Please refer to the documentation for your filesystem of choice on how to resize your volumes, which in most cases can be performed live and with little or no disruption.

For EXT4 or XFS filesystems, use `resize2fs` or `xfs_growfs` as described on these pages:

- https://access.redhat.com/documentation/en-US/Red_Hat_Enterprise_Linux/7/html/Storage_Administration_Guide/xfsgrow.html
- http://www.jesusamieiro.com/increase-an-ext4-partition-with-gparted/
- https://www.nonamehosts.com/blog/how-to-extend-ext4-root-partition-without-reboot/
- http://positon.org/resize-an-ext3-ext4-partition

We can both expand and shrink the size of a Ceph RBD image. Expanding an RBD image is simpler and less impactful than shrinking one, especially if an image has a significant amount of data allocated or written to it. Shrinking an image is tricky: if not done carefully can discard legitimate blocks on your block device. If they have any valuable information written to them, that will be lost forever when those blocks are discarded. Always proceed with caution when shrinking an image. Ideally you should never reduce the size of an image that's been written to, especially if the data on it is at all important.

Changing the size of an RBD image can be done by using the resize subcommand to `rbd` or by GUI or CLI tools such as Openstack's Horizon and Cinder and DigitalOcean's `doctl` or droplet control panel. We will use the—size argument to specify a new size that is double than that previously provisioned. We will operate on the same image we created, formatted, and mounted above:

```
root@ceph-client0:~# rbd resize ceph-client1-rbd1 --size 20480
Resizing image: 100% complete...done.
root@ceph-client0:~# rbd info ceph-client1-rbd1
rbd image 'ceph-client1-rbd1':
size 20480 MB in 5120 objects
order 22 (4096 kB objects)
block_name_prefix: rbd_data.ac9c238e1f29
format: 2
features: layering
flags:
```

You can see in the output of the info command above that the image now reflects the provisioned size increase to 20 GB. Another way to validate that this change was made to the underlying block device is to check the size reported by the client operating system for the mapped block device. We will use the `lsblk` utility that is installed by default on most Linux systems. This tool conveniently displays information about all block devices presently found on the system:

```
root@ceph-client0:~# lsblk | grep ceph-vol01
rbd0 251:0 0 20G 0 disk /mnt/ceph-vol01
```

The size in the 4th column of the output is now `20G` as expected. However, since we haven't updated the size of the filesystem we see that `df` still shows only as 10 GB even though the RBD image has grown to twice that size:

```
root@ceph-client0:~# df -h | grep ceph-vol01
/dev/rbd0 10G 33M 10G 1% /mnt/ceph-vol01
```

The reason for that is most filesystems don't automatically change their structure until we explicitly tell them to. In most cases you want the filesystem to also grow to fill the block device, and now need to instruct it to do so. We have formatted our block device with XFS so we will run an XFS-specific command:

```
root@ceph-client0:~# xfs_growfs -d /mnt/ceph-vol01
meta-data=/dev/rbd0 isize=512 agcount=17, agsize=162816 blks
sectsz=512 attr=2, projid32bit=1
crc=1 finobt=1 spinodes=0
data =bsize=4096 blocks=2621440, imaxpct=25
sunit=1024 swidth=1024 blks
naming =version 2 bsize=4096 ascii-ci=0 ftype=1
log =internal bsize=4096 blocks=2560, version=2
sectsz=512 sunit=8 blks, lazy-count=1
realtime =none extsz=4096 blocks=0, rtextents=0
data blocks changed from 2621440 to 5242880
root@ceph-client0:~# df -h | grep ceph-vol01
/dev/rbd0 20G 34M 20G 1% /mnt/ceph-vol01
```

If you are using a different filesystem you will need to use an analogous command that the associated documentation specifies. It's important to note that not all filesystems support online resizing. If you are using one that does not, you will need to unmount your image, perform your resize and then mount it again. Covering resize procedures for less-common filesystems is out of scope for this chapter.

RADOS Block Device Snapshots

Ceph supports the ability to take snapshots of RBD images and then use them at a later time. RBD snapshots are point-in-time, read-only copies of their respective RBD images. They are very useful if you wanted to go back in history to a time where you know your image was in a desirable state. A typical use-case for snapshots is backing up an image's state before running an application that has a chance of corrupting data. If the new application destroys your data, you can roll back time by reverting to the snapshot that you took before the destruction took place.

In order to see how a Ceph snapshot works and how to harness its functionality, let us create a file on our currently mounted RBD image and write some data into it:

```
root@ceph-client0:~# ls -l /mnt/ceph-vol01/
total 4
-rw-r--r-- 1 root root 10 Aug 19 15:43 rbd.txt
root@ceph-client0:~# echo "Hello Ceph This is snapshot test" /mnt/ceph-
vol01/snaptest_file
root@ceph-client0:~# sync
root@ceph-client0:~# cat /mnt/ceph-vol01/snaptest_file
Hello Ceph This is snapshot test
```

Now we will create a snapshot of this image and call it snap1. After taking the snapshot, we will delete the file we just created to simulate the loss or corruption of data. We will then take the volume to its original state where the file we created still existed — by rolling the image back to snap1 snapshot.

```
root@ceph-client0:~# rbd snap create rbd/ceph-client1-rbd1@snap1
root@ceph-client0:~# rm -f /mnt/ceph-vol01/snaptest_file
root@ceph-client0:~# cat /mnt/ceph-vol01/snaptest_file
cat: /mnt/ceph-vol01/snaptest_file: No such file or directory
```

The command-line syntax for creating a snapshot is:

```
rbd snap create <pool>/<image>@<snap>
```

The pool and image parameters select the existing resources on which to operate and *snap* is the name of the new snapshot to create. The name of the pool where all RBD images are stored by default is rbd. Our image was named ceph-client1-rbd1 and we created a snapshot named snap1.

After creating the snapshot, we delete the file we created on the mounted filesystem and ensure that it does not exist anymore.

Now we will use our RBD snapshot to restore the filesystem to its original state with our `snaptest_file` back in place with all its data. Before we initiate a rollback we have to first unmount the filesystem. And after we are done rolling back we mount it back to the same location and *voila!* Our file is back in its original place with all its data intact. It is almost like it was never deleted from the system:

```
root@ceph-client0:~# umount /mnt/ceph-vol01
root@ceph-client0:~# rbd snap rollback rbd/ceph-client1-rbd1@snap1
Rolling back to snapshot: 100% complete...done.
root@ceph-client0:~# mount /dev/rbd0 /mnt/ceph-vol01
root@ceph-client0:~# cat /mnt/ceph-vol01/snaptest_file
Hello Ceph This is snapshot test
```

Here we pass the arguments to `rbd snap rollback` in the same way that we did for `rbd snap create`. The pool name, image name, and snap name are all needed in order to roll back to the snapshot correctly.

Once we are done with using a snapshot we can choose to delete it if we don't intend to use it again. This reclaims any additional space your snapshot was consuming on the Ceph cluster. Ceph implements CoW snapshots, so any objects (or blocks) that are not modified on the parent image of the snapshot aren't duplicated. In other words, the snapshot only allocates additional storage for existing blocks that are updated by new writes. Internally, a new copy of the original block is created. The original block is at the same time modified with the new incoming writes, and the snapshot pointer is updated to now point to the copy instead of the parent block. Thus deleting a snapshot when it's no longer needed helps free up space that was occupied by such copies.

We use the `rbd snap rm` command to delete an existing snapshot:

```
root@ceph-client0:~# rbd snap rm rbd/ceph-client1-rbd1@snap1
```

An image can have more than one snapshot present at any given time. If we want to delete all snapshots of an image, we can make use of the purge subcommand:

```
root@ceph-client0:~# rbd snap purge rbd/ceph-client1-rbd1
```

RADOS Block Device Clones

Ceph has an ability to create CoW *clones* from RBD snapshots. This mechanism is known as *snapshot layering*. The layering feature allows Ceph to create multiple clones of an RBD image. This feature is extremely useful to private cloud and virtualization platforms such as OpenStack, CloudStack, and Qemu/KVM. These platforms allow the use of snapshots to protect RBD images that contain OS/VM images. The OS images can then be cloned to spin up new VM instances. Ceph snapshots are read-only but image clones are writeable.

Every cloned image stores a reference to its parent snapshot. It is thus important that the parent snapshot be protected before it can be used for cloning. The protection is necessary to prevent deletion of the snapshot while the cloning is in progress. Since the objects that comprise a clone can only ever point to their parent snapshots, if the snapshot copy of those objects are deleted, then the clones can end up in an orphaned state with some objects left with no parents.

Clones are similar to RBD images. They are writeable, resizable, and can have snapshots and even clones of their own. Not all RBD images support clones. In Ceph, there are two types of RBD images: *format-1* and *format-2*. The RBD snapshot feature is available on both *format-1* and *format-2* RBD images. However, the layering feature that provides CoW behavior necessary for clones is only available for RBD images with *format-2*. Recent Ceph releases create all new images with *format-2* by default.

For demonstration purposes, we will create a new image named `ceph-client1-rbd2` and take a snapshot. Once that goes well, we will create a clone of that snapshot:

```
root@ceph-client0:~# rbd create ceph-client1-rbd2 --size 10240 --image-
feature layering
root@ceph-client0:~# rbd info ceph-client1-rbd2
rbd image 'ceph-client1-rbd2':
size 10240 MB in 2560 objects
order 22 (4096 kB objects)
block_name_prefix: rbd_data.dd832ae8944a
format: 2
features: layering
flags:
root@ceph-client0:~# rbd snap create ceph-client1-rbd2@snap1
root@ceph-client0:~# rbd snap ls ceph-client1-rbd2
SNAPID NAME SIZE
15 snap1 10240 MB
```

We will now start the process of creating a clone from this snapshot. Protecting the snapshot that will act as a parent of the clone is essential because deleting the snapshot by accident will render the clone unusable:

```
root@ceph-client0:~# rbd snap protect ceph-client1-rbd2@snap1
```

Next, we will create a clone from this snapshot. Let's name this cloned image ceph-client1-rbd3. Notice the changed rbd3 suffix at the end:

```
root@ceph-client0:~# rbd clone ceph-client1-rbd2@snap1 ceph-client1-rbd3
```

We can verify that the clone was created as expected by checking the attributes of the cloned image with the rbd info command.

```
root@ceph-client0:~# rbd info ceph-client1-rbd3
rbd image 'ceph-client1-rbd3':
size 10240 MB in 2560 objects
order 22 (4096 kB objects)
block_name_prefix: rbd_data.dd872eb141f2
format: 2
features: layering
flags:
parent: rbd/ceph-client1-rbd2@snap1
overlap: 10240 MB
```

The last two lines are of importance here and are an extension to the general output of info run against a normal image. The parent field specifies which snapshot is the parent of the given clone. It also implies that the clone still has references to the parent snapshot and thus needs it to handle reads and writes correctly for the volume's objects. The overlap field shows how much data overlap the child clone has with its parent snapshot. At the initial stage when a new clone is created the overlap is equal to the size of the snapshot; this is expected as the two are identical. However, as data is written, the overlap decreases. If a clone is overwritten entirely from the beginning to its full provisioned size, it will end up with no overlap relative to its parent snapshot.

As we see above, even if we have a cloned image that we can read from and write to (unlike snapshots which we can only read from), it still holds references to a snapshot in the cluster. Deleting the snapshot will either not be possible or will end up removing the clone as well if we proceed. Sometimes this might not be desirable and you might want to delete the snapshot and treat the clone as a standalone image. Ceph gives us the ability to do exactly that by using a process called *flattening*. Flattening a clone removes all the references to its parent and creates independent copies of all of its objects. This consumes extra space on the cluster but it also means that we can now delete the original snapshot from which we spawned this clone without losing any data.

Here's how we flatten a cloned image. Since the data from parent snapshot will need to be copied to the child image, the process will take the amount of time proportional to the size of the image. Once the flattening process completes there is no dependency between the cloned image and its parent snapshot.

We will use the `flatten` subcommand to perform flattening of a clone:

```
root@ceph-client0:~# rbd flatten ceph-client1-rbd3
Image flatten: 100% complete...done.
root@ceph-client0:~# rbd info ceph-client1-rbd3
rbd image 'ceph-client1-rbd3':
size 10240 MB in 2560 objects
order 22 (4096 kB objects)
block_name_prefix: rbd_data.dd872eb141f2
format: 2
features: layering
flags:
```

As a result of flattening the clone, we can see that references to its parent have been removed. The clone now exists as an independent, standalone image and the parent snapshot or image can be deleted when required.

Once we are done processing a clone of a snapshot or we have detached it from its parent, we need to unprotect the snapshot to allow deletion. Unprotecting the snapshot is a necessary step for deletion, but you don't need to delete all unprotected snapshots. One does need to ensure, though, that a snapshot has no clones before it can be unprotected:

```
root@ceph-client0:~# rbd snap unprotect ceph-client1-rbd2@snap1
```

If we want to delete the unprotected snapshot, we can do that as well:

```
root@ceph-client0:~# rbd snap rm ceph-client1-rbd2@snap1
```

You should now know how to use Ceph snapshots and clones of an RBD image to your advantage.

The Ceph Filesystem (CephFS)

The Ceph Filesystem is also known as CephFS. It is a POSIX-compliant distributed filesystem built upon the RADOS layer. In order to provision CephFS filesystem storage, we need at least one **MetaData Server** (**MDS**) instance running alongside the rest of the Ceph cluster. In order to demonstrate mounting and using a CephFS filesystem we will again use the virtual sandbox cluster we created in `Chapter 5`, *Deploying a Virtual Sandbox Cluster*. We will demonstrate two different ways of using the filesystem:

- Mounting using the kernel driver
- Mounting using the FUSE user-space driver

Let's start by first spinning up a new virtual machine for our MDS. This process should now be familiar given how we spun up MON, OSD and Client virtual machines in `Chapter 5`, *Deploying a Virtual Sandbox Cluster*. First let's check whether our sandbox cluster is running or not. If not, let's start it up:

```
$ vagrant status
Current machine states:
client0 poweroff (virtualbox)
mon0 poweroff (virtualbox)
osd0 poweroff (virtualbox)
osd1 poweroff (virtualbox)
osd2 poweroff (virtualbox)
$ vagrant up --no-provision --provider=virtualbox
...
$ vagrant status
Current machine states:
client0 running (virtualbox)
mon0 running (virtualbox)
osd0 running (virtualbox)
osd1 running (virtualbox)
osd2 running (virtualbox)
```

It is important to run the above commands from within the `ceph-ansible` directory that we cloned in `Chapter 5`, *Deploying a Virtual Sandbox Cluster*. The `vagrant` status command will not work as expected if we are running it from a different location. Now that we have our existing cluster up and running again, let's create a new MDS virtual machine and make it a part of this cluster. Open the file named `vagrant_variables.yml` in your favorite text editor and then change the value of the field `mds_vms` to 1. The saved and changed file should appear as follows: Let's again issue the `vagrant up` command to spin up the new MDS virtual machine instance. Remember that the value specified on each line denotes how many virtual machines of that type to build and run. If we increase it to 2 then we will have 2 new virtual machines created for MDS and so on.

Since our cluster is only for proof of concept use we only need one MDS, but when running this service in production you will need additional MDS instances to avoid a single point of failure. Once the vagrant run completes we should see the MDS node come up in the status. Let's provision this node to start CephFS related services. This is important to start the correct processes and create necessary Ceph pools before we start using Ceph's Filesystem. After the provisioner run completes, we should have a fully configured MDS server running. Let's verify this by logging into our pre-existing client node. We can see that we now have an MDS server named `ceph-mds0` as a part of the cluster. The state of that node is also shown as *active* as desired for a healthy cluster.

CephFS with Kernel Driver

Now let's attempt to interact with the CephFS system using the Linux kernel driver. Linux kernels older than v2.6.34 did not support CephFS but most likely you are using a reasonably modern distribution of Linux. Our sandbox uses the Linux kernel version 4.4.0 that contains better CephFS support than earlier releases.

Before we mount the CephFS system on our client machine, we will need two pieces of information:

- The IP address of a MON node
- The key for `client.admin` user

The IP addresses of the MON nodes may be extracted from the `ceph.conf` file on our client virtual node. The IP address is explicitly present in the mon host entry which we can retrieve as follows:

```
root@ceph-client0:~# cat /etc/ceph/ceph.conf | grep 'mon host'
mon host = 192.168.42.10
```

On the author's system the IP address of the current MON node is `192.168.42.10`. It likely will be different for your cluster. Make a note of the value that you get by running the above command. We will use that value when mounting the CephFS filesystem.

Next, we look for the path for the admin `keyring`. By default it should be placed within your `/etc/ceph` directory on the client:

```
root@ceph-client0:~# ls -l /etc/ceph/ceph.client.admin.keyring
/etc/ceph/ceph.client.admin.keyring -rw ------- 1 ceph ceph 63 Aug 19 02:49
/etc/ceph/ceph.client.admin.keyring
```

We will need to extract the value for the key that we will use as the *secret* to pass to the mount command:

```
root@ceph-client0:~# cat /etc/ceph/ceph.client.admin.keyring
[client.admin]
      key = AQBtuoRZRWixMhAAfVIRFj5fY3nhmfotLHZrmQ==
```

Make a note of the value of the key field above. Let's use these values now to mount the CephFS filesystem locally on the client system. Before mounting we will need to create a directory mountpoint, as with any other type of Linux filesystem. Let's create it under /mnt path and call it kernel_cephfs:

```
root@ceph-client0:~# mkdir /mnt/kernel_cephfs
```

Now that we have our mountpoint, let's mount our filesystem on it. The mount command's syntax is as shwon in the following command:

```
mount -t ceph <ip address of mon>:6789/ <mount-point>
      -o <options including name= and secret=>"

root@ceph-client0:~# mount -t ceph 192.168.42.10:6789:/ /mnt/kernel_cephfs
-o name=admin,secret=AQBtuoRZRWixMhAAfVIRFj5fY3nhmfotLHZrmQ==
```

We now see that our mount command worked by checking all mounts on the system:

```
root@ceph-client0:~# mount | grep kernel_cephfs
192.168.42.10:6789:/ on /mnt/kernel_cephfs type ceph
(rw,relatime,name=admin,secret=<hidden>,acl)
```

Perfect! You should be able to use the /mnt/kernel_cephfs directory to store all your files that will automatically find their way onto your Ceph cluster with strong durability and fault tolerance guarantees.

Passing in the *secret* string in command-line is not ideally secure given that the commands we run might be captured in shell history, displayed by the ps command, or logged remotely. A safer way to perform mounts is to write the key to a file and then pass the filename to the mount command. We will need to save only the key we extracted from the admin keyring in a new file, and supply the file's path to a new mount option called secretfile instead of specifying the secret in the clear in the CLI.

CephFS with the FUSE Driver

It might not be feasible to use the kernel driver if you are running an older version of the Linux kernel. There could also be a case where you need to exploit new CephFS features that the kernel driver might not have incorporated yet. In such cases, you can use the CephFS FUSE driver.

 FUSE stands for Filesystem in USErspace—technology that allows unprivileged users to operate filesystem types not offered natively by their running kernel. For more information visit: https://en.wikipedia.org/wiki/Filesystem_in_Userspace

Before accessing CephFS via the FUSE driver we will need to first install it. Check your OS distribution or other repos for a package named `ceph-fuse` and install it. Our sandbox environment comes with `ceph-fuse` already installed for our purposes, so we don't need to do anything here. Isn't that great?

Let's create a separate mountpoint for the filesystem:

```
root@ceph-client0:~# mkdir /mnt/cephfs
```

That's all we need to do! We are ready to mount the filesystem now:

```
root@ceph-client0:~# ceph-fuse -m 192.168.42.10:6789 /mnt/cephfs
ceph-fuse[6773]: starting ceph client
ceph-fuse[6773]: starting fuse
```

Notice that we used the same MON IP address that we previously used for mounting the filesystem via the kernel driver, and that it picks the default admin user and credentials automatically. We should be able to see our filesystem mounted in the intended location now.

```
root@ceph-client0:/mnt/cephfs# mount | grep cephfs
ceph-fuse on /mnt/cephfs type fuse.ceph-fuse
(rw,nosuid,nodev,relatime,user_id=0,group_id=0,default_permissions,allow_ot
her)
```

The downside of the FUSE approach is that it tends to be significantly slower than the native kernel driver. Feel free to create files and a directory and start using CephFS for all your file storage needs!

Ceph Object Storage (RADOS Gateway)

Ceph provides us more abstractions other than RBD images and CephFS to store and access data. One of the most widely used is the object storage system. An object storage system is one where files can be uploaded to and downloaded from storage servers using simple and conventional protocols such as HTTP.

Ceph's **RADOS Gateway** (**RGW**) storage service aims to fill this need by presenting Amazon S3-compatible and OpenStack Swift-compatible interfaces atop RADOS objects. There are abundant GUI clients, command line clients, and SDKs for every major programming language that supports Amazon S3. Clients talking to object storage systems need only to know how to leverage these widely-available tools to store and retrieve files.

In order to show how to provision an RGW service, we will again use the sandbox cluster we created in Chapter 5, *Deploying a Virtual Sandbox Cluster*. When deploying in production you most likely will want to configure the RGW service on dedicated physical machines, depending on expected workload. First ensure we have a Ceph cluster running in our sandbox environment on our local machine, by running the following command:

```
$ vagrant status
Current machine states:
client0                    running (virtualbox)
mon0                    running (virtualbox)
osd0                    running (virtualbox)
osd1                    running (virtualbox)
osd2                    running (virtualbox)
```

If you don't have a Ceph cluster running on your local machine in a sandbox environment, make sure you follow the steps in Chapter 5, *Deploying a Virtual Sandbox Cluster* to create one. This is a prerequisite for provisioning the RGW service that we will use in this chapter. If you did previously create a Ceph cluster sandbox environment, you can simply run vagrant status from within the directory ceph-ansible that you had cloned.

Now that we have verified we have the existing Ceph cluster sandbox environment running, we need to add a new virtual machine for the RGW service. In order to do this, again open the vagrant_variables.yml file in your favorite text editor and change the value of rgw_vms from 1 to 0.

```
# DEFINE THE NUMBER OF VMS TO RUN
mon_vms: 1
osd_vms: 3
mds_vms: 0
rgw_vms: 1
nfs_vms: 0
```

```
rbd_mirror_vms: 0
client_vms: 1
```

The values of all other fields can be kept as they are. After the value is updated, save the file and exit the editor. Now run `vagrant up` again as follows to create a new RGW instance.

```
$ vagrant up --no-provision --provider=virtualbox
```

This will create a new virtual machine for RGW and connect it automatically to the rest of the existing cluster without the need to do any additional network configuration. After the RGW instance creation completes, we need to configure the RGW instance to create the necessary user, `keyring` and storage pools dedicated to object storage. This is accomplished by running the provisioner again on the cluster:

```
$ vagrant provision
```

The RGW instance is now ready for configuration and use.

Before we modify the RGW instance to work for our specific use-case, we log into it and verify that the initial connection to Ceph cluster is set up properly. All commands we execute on the RGW instance will be done as the root user:

```
$ vagrant ssh rgw0
vagrant@ceph-rgw0:~$ sudo -i
root@ceph-rgw0:~# ceph --keyring /var/lib/ceph/radosgw/ceph-rgw.ceph
rgw0/keyring --id rgw.ceph-rgw0 -s
    cluster e6d4e4ab-f59f-470d-bb76-511deebc8de3
     health HEALTH_OK
     monmap e1: 1 mons at {ceph-mon0=192.168.42.10:6789/0}
            election epoch 8, quorum 0 ceph-mon0
     osdmap e6914: 6 osds: 6 up, 6 in
            flags sortbitwise,require_jewel_osds
      pgmap v20156: 144 pgs, 11 pools, 17246 kB data, 2842 objects
            645 MB used, 64687 MB / 65333 MB avail
                 144 active+clean
root@ceph-rgw0:~# pidof radosgw
13969
```

The `keyring` and `id` for the user of the configured instance need to be specified so that Ceph command-line tools are able to authenticate to the cluster and access its state. The user that we will use to access the cluster has the ID `rgw.ceph-rgw0`. The keyring is stored under `/var/lib/ceph/radosgw/ceph-<id>/`. Using the ever-handy `pidof` command we verify that RGW process is indeed running as expected.

Now that we are able to access the cluster, let's configure our RGW instance to enable S3 protocol access. To do so we will need to perform the following steps:

- Customize the Ceph and system configuration for RGW
- Enable S3 object operations using s3cmd
- Enable object operations using Swift API

Configuration for the RGW Service

The RGW process that runs on the rgw0 virtual machine by default reads /etc/ceph/ceph.conf for configuration settings as it starts up, as do other Ceph daemons. We need to update configuration parameters in this file to customize the RGW settings for our use-case. It is important to note that the values of the configuration options we choose will only be applicable to our sandbox environment and might differ somewhat from those needed for production environments.

First open the Ceph configuration file /etc/ceph/ceph.conf in your favorite text editor and go to the section beginning with [client.rgw.ceph-rgw0]. Before changes it should look like the following:

```
...
[client.rgw.ceph-rgw0]
host = ceph-rgw0
keyring = /var/lib/ceph/radosgw/ceph-rgw.ceph-rgw0/keyring
rgw socket path = /tmp/radosgw-ceph-rgw0.sock
log file = /var/log/ceph/ceph-rgw-ceph-rgw0.log
rgw data = /var/lib/ceph/radosgw/ceph-rgw.ceph-rgw0
rgw frontends = civetweb port=10.0.2.15:8080 num_threads=50
rgw resolve cname = False
```

We need to make three changes to this section:

1. The value of rgw frontends is modified to listen on the default HTTP port tcp/80.
2. The field rgw resolve cname is not required and can be removed.
3. We will add a new entry rgw dns name and give it the value that we want to use to access our object storage.

Now change the aforementioned section to look like this:

```
...
[client.rgw.ceph-rgw0]
host = ceph-rgw0
keyring = /var/lib/ceph/radosgw/ceph-rgw.ceph-rgw0/keyring
rgw socket path = /tmp/radosgw-ceph-rgw0.sock
log file = /var/log/ceph/ceph-rgw-ceph-rgw0.log
rgw data = /var/lib/ceph/radosgw/ceph-rgw.ceph-rgw0
rgw frontends = civetweb port=80 num_threads=50
rgw dns name = ceph-rgw.objectstorage.example.com
```

As you can see we have changed only the port field of the `rgw frontends` line and replaced the *host:port* pair with `port=80`. The rest of the line is untouched.

For demo purposes, we have chosen the DNS name `ceph-rgw.objectstorage.example.com` for the cluster. Feel free to change this name to anything else that you find is more convenient and appropriate for your setup, especially if you are deploying this in a non-sandbox environment. If you are not using this configuration in production, you can leave the value as it is.

Once these changes are complete save the file and restart the `radosgw` daemon. This is necessary for the daemon to pick up our changes, as it reads `ceph.conf` only at startup. The RGW daemon (`radosgw`) is a lightweight and largely stateless process, so restarting is not problematic especially as it's not presently serving any traffic:

```
root@ceph-rgw0:~# systemctl restart ceph-radosgw@rgw.ceph-rgw0.service
root@ceph-rgw0:~# pidof radosgw
14119
```

After restarting, we always verify that the process has actually started running again using `pidof` to display the current process ID. It's possible that the `radosgw` process could fail to start properly. In such cases doublecheck `ceph.conf` to see whether it contains anything odd. A malformed `ceph.conf` can prevent `radosgw` from starting up correctly.There are additional steps to perform before utilizing our RGW as an S3 object storage solution. We need to create a user with its own set of S3 credentials, which include an S3 access key and a secret key pair. A user can have additional access-secret key pairs if needed but we will start with one. We will access the Object Storage as though it lives on a remote machine using a DNS name, even though in the context of this chapter it is co-located on the same physical system. Simulating remote DNS access should provide a clear idea of how RGW accesses work in a production-like setup.

User creation is an administrative task for which we cannot use any of the tools that we have previously used. We will use a new tool named `radosgw-admin` that is designed to perform all administrative tasks on the cluster. This tool is pre-installed on your `rgw0` virtual machine. Run the following `radosgw-admin` command to get an insight into types of operations you can perform against a Ceph object storage system:

```
$ radosgw-admin help
```

Before creating a user, execute a shortcut command that will help us going forward. As mentioned in the previous section of this chapter, when accessing a Ceph cluster from an RGW node we always need to pass in the keyring and ID of the user we need to authenticate to Ceph before running any commands. `radosgw-admin` is no exception and it also needs both parameters to be passed in every time we run it.

However, Ceph provides a shortcut we can exploit to avoid typing the same parameters repeatedly to every command. For every command we run, it reads the `CEPH_ARGS` environment variable for any common arguments to interpolate. Any value we add to the above environment variable will always be included in subsequent commands we run. This helps keep the commands concise and reduces clutter and improves readability. We will add our keyring and ID to the `CEPH_ARGS` environment variable, keeping our succession of Ceph commands clean:

```
root@ceph-rgw0:~# export CEPH_ARGS='--keyring /var/lib/ceph/radosgw/ceph-rgw.ceph-rgw0/keyring --id rgw.ceph-rgw0'
```

Now we initiate the user creation process with the `user create` subcommand of `radosgw-admin`:

```
root@ceph-rgw0:~# radosgw-admin user create --uid=harshita --display-name='Harshita Bhembre'
{
    "user_id": "harshita",
    "display_name": "Harshita Bhembre",
    "email": "",
    "suspended": 0,
    "max_buckets": 1000,
    "auid": 0,
    "subusers": [],
    "keys": [

        {
            "user": "harshita",
            "access_key": "C24PQKGQ01504JAFQE5L",
            "secret_key": "LCyKZPr7rHqtxqD586d6Y1Zs38lzyIwNpql6IRN9"
        }
```

```
    ],
    "swift_keys": [],
    "caps": [],
    "op_mask": "read, write, delete",
    "default_placement": "",
    "placement_tags": [],
    "bucket_quota": {
    "enabled": false,
          "max_size_kb": -1,
          "max_objects": -1
          },
       "user_quota": {
       "enabled": false,
       "max_size_kb": -1,
       "max_objects": -1
          },
    "temp_url_keys": []
}
```

The two command-line parameters we need to supply are uid and display-name. We can pass in other values including email or max-buckets but they are not mandatory. The output of the user create subcommand is all the data about the user that Ceph has stored. This is presented in a stable, structured JSON format that it is straightforward to parse by humans with a command line JSON tool or by applications via a JSON client library. Once the user is created, we can use the S3 credentials of that user to access RGW object storage. The credentials are extracted from the section of the JSON user object titled *keys*. We will explore how to use those keys using a tool like s3cmd in the next section. Until then please stash a copy of the keys section or at least the access_key and secret_key.

Before we perform S3 operations against the cluster, we next ensure that the DNS name we have chosen for the cluster is resolvable by our S3 client and points to our RGW instance. A typical way of doing this is buying a domain name for your service from a registrar, engaging a **Virtual Private Server** (**VPS**) provider like DigitalOcean to provide a server to host your service on, then pointing the domain name to the location of the server. However, as we are deploying our service on a local virtual machine, we don't need to worry about buying a domain; we can simply make one up and use it locally.

To do so we will need to setup a local DNS server to answer our queries. S3 URLs can be formatted in 2 different ways: path-based or domain-based. Path-based URLs use the same domain name as the host, but domain-based URL's prefix the hostname with a bucket name, thus changing the host component of the URL.

To explain it more clearly, let's say we are accessing an S3 endpoint named `ceph-rgw.objectstorage.example.com`. Assuming that we are using HTTP (and not HTTPS) the complete URL will look like this:

`http://ceph-rgw.objectstorage.example.com/`

To access a bucket named `childhood-videos` via the above endpoint, we construct a path-based S3 URL as follows:

`http://ceph-rgw.objectstorage.example.com/childhood-videos/`

However, if we wish to access the same bucket using a domain-based S3 URL, that will look slightly different:

`http://childhood-videos.ceph-rgw.objectstorage.example.com/`

Thus, the A record (or AAAA if you are using IPv6) we add to our DNS server should include not only an entry for the original domain name, but also for a wildcard prefix. The two entries should thus look like this, exploiting the local loopback address:

```
ceph-rgw.objectstorage.example.com          A        127.0.0.1
*.ceph-rgw.objectstorage.example.com        A        127.0.0.1
```

Fortunately, we will not be adding these exact entries manually to a remote DNS server but instead a nifty local resolver to serve these for us behind the scenes. We use a server called `dnsmasq` that can be quickly installed on our RGW virtual machine. Let's install and configure it to enable us to interact with our RGW instance using our custom DNS name:

```
root@ceph-rgw0:~# apt-get install -y dnsmasq
```

Now open its configuration file located at `/etc/dnsmasq.conf` and change the commented out line that specifies the DNS domain we want to point to `localhost`. Change the last line in the above section so that the domain becomes `ceph-rgw.objectstorage.example.com` but still pointing to `localhost`:

```
# Add domains which you want to force to an IP address here.
# The example below send any host in ceph-rgw.objectstorage.example.com to a local
# web-server.
address=/.ceph-rgw.objectstorage.example.com/127.0.0.1
```

Notice, the . in front of the domain. That adds a DNS entry for the wildcard domain and is necessary for dnsmasqto know that all requests using the domain-based format for accesses should return the same location. After editing that file, save it and restart the dnsmasq service.

```
root@ceph-rgw0:~# systemctl restart dnsmasq.service
```

We should now be able to talk to our RGW instance using the domain name we specified. Verify that the access works as expected by trying out the following command:

```
root@ceph-rgw0:~# nslookup ceph-rgw.objectstorage.example.com
Server:        127.0.0.1
Address:   127.0.0.1#53
Name:      ceph-rgw.objectstorage.example.com
Address: 127.0.0.1
root@ceph-rgw0:~# nc -vz ceph-rgw.objectstorage.example.com 80
Connection to ceph-rgw.objectstorage.example.com 80 port [tcp/http]
succeeded!
```

The output of the command shows that the communication to the port on the host succeeds. If the above command fails for some reason please ensure that you have performed all the preceding steps from the beginning of this chapter and in the order they are presented.

Congrats! You now have your RGW server up and running and ready to respond to any and all object storage operations.

Performing S3 Object Operations Using s3cmd

We now use the working Ceph cluster along with the RGW instance that you set up to perform various types of object storage operations. We will walk through setting up the open source client utility s3cmd to give an idea of how to interface with the cluster. The configuration that we do to enable S3 utilities or SDKs to talk to Ceph will also translate across other clients and tools.

First let's install the s3cmd tool on the rgw0 virtual machine instance.

```
root@ceph-rgw0:~# apt-get install -y s3cmd
```

Now let's configure the s3cmd utility. This command line tool provides a nice little wizard that walks us through setting the necessary configuration parameters. After we complete this initial configuration there are additional changes we need to make. We will use the -- configure switch in order to invoke the configuration process.

Note: for this step we will need the previously stashed *access_key* and *secret_key* of your user that were created using by radosgw-admin.

```
root@ceph-rgw0:~# s3cmd --configure
```

You'll be prompted for the following values. Make sure you pass the responses that are stated to the side of each question/field for which you need to fill in a value:

- Access Key:*<copy-paste your access key for your user>*
- Secret Key: *<copy-paste your secret key for your user>*
- Default Region [US]: *<leave blank, press enter/return>*
- Encryption password:*<leave blank, press enter/return>*
- Path to GPG program [/usr/bin/gpg]: *<leave blank, press enter/return>*
- Use HTTPS protocol [Yes]: no
- HTTP Proxy server name: *<leave blank, press enter/return>*
- Test access with supplied credentials? [Y/n]: n
- Save settings? [y/N]: y

Make sure you avoid testing with the configuration until we have completed additional configuration. Once you complete this process, you will have a file called .s3cfg in your home directory. Let's open this file in our favorite text editor and navigate to the following lines:

```
host_base = s3.amazonaws.com
host_bucket = %(bucket)s.s3.amazonaws.com
...
```

The host_ endpoints default to Amazon's S3 service. We need to adjust them to now point to our local instance. Recall that our local instance can be reached at the ceph-rgw.objectstorage.example.com DNS name that we configured our local dnsmasq to serve. Let's update the above two fields to reflect our custom domain:

```
host_base = ceph-rgw.objectstorage.example.com
host_bucket = %(bucket)s.ceph-rgw.objectstorage.example.com
...
```

For the host_bucket line we leave the %(bucket)s. prefix as-is. Now save the file and exit your editor. We are now set to send object storage queries to Ceph.

Let's start by creating a first bucket on our freshly created object storage cluster:

```
root@ceph-rgw0:~# s3cmd mb s3://first-bucket
Bucket 's3://first-bucket/' created
root@ceph-rgw0:~# s3cmd ls
2017-08-20 20:34   s3://first-bucket
```

Buckets are no fun without storing actual files in them. In order to play with files, let's create a sample file and then place it in the new bucket we made above:

```
root@ceph-rgw0:~# echo "RGW works!" > new-file.txt
root@ceph-rgw0:~# s3cmd put new-file.txt s3://first-bucket
upload:'new-file.txt'->'s3://first-bucket/new-file.txt'[1 of 1]
11 of 11   100% in   1s     7.66 B/s   done
```

As a final step, let's download the file we just pushed onto Ceph and ensure that the content is intact. Before we do that, let's remove the local copy of the file we just created so we don't mistake it for the copy from the object storage service, in case the download fails.

```
root@ceph-rgw0:~# rm new-file.txt
root@ceph-rgw0:~# s3cmd get s3://first-bucket/new-file.txt new-file.txt
download:'s3://first-bucket/new-file.txt'->'new-file.txt'[1 of 1]
 11 of 11   100% in   0s   280.71 B/s   done
root@ceph-rgw0:~# cat new-file.txt
RGW works!
```

This is great! Congrats on working through everything it takes to set up a new RGW instance and S3 Object Storage! You now have a shiny new object storage service ready to store all your files in a robust and reliable way.

Enabling the Swift API

Ceph's RGW also offers a RESTful API that is compatible with OpenStack's Swift. However, unlike S3, we need to create a separate user for Swift. In Ceph's nomenclature, such a user is a *subuser*. The new subuser we create for our original RGW user will give us access to the same objects and buckets that we have created via S3 but using the Swift interface.

Creation of the subuser will be done from the RGW virtual machine itself, the same node we used to run all the above commands. We will use the familiar `radosgw-admin` utility to create a subuser for making calls through the Swift API:

```
root@ceph-rgw0:~# radosgw-admin subuser create --uid=harshita --
subuser=harshita:swift --key-type=swift
{
    "user_id": "harshita",
```

```
    "display_name": "Harshita Bhembre",
    "email": "",
    "suspended": 0,
    "max_buckets": 1000,
    "auid": 0,
    "subusers": [
        {
            "id": "harshita:swift",
            "permissions": "<none>"
        }
    ],
    "keys": [
        {
                    "user": "harshita",
            "access_key": "C24PQKGQD15O4JAFQE5L",
            "secret_key": "LCyKZPr7rHCtxqD586d6YlZs38lzyIwNpql6IRN9"
        }
    ],
    "swift_keys": [
        {
            "user": "harshita:swift",
            "secret_key": "m38OvpnOMf8ILNZyfDuKTDTWKC7YCEUH9v4Te64o"
        }
    ],
    "caps": [],
    "op_mask": "read, write, delete",
    "default_placement": "",
    "placement_tags": [],
    "bucket_quota": {
        "enabled": false,
        "max_size_kb": -1,
        "max_objects": -1
    },
    "user_quota": {
        "enabled": false,
        "max_size_kb": -1,
        "max_objects": -1
    },
    "temp_url_keys": []
}
```

We see here two new fields, swift_keys and subusers, which have been populated with new information. We will use the secret key from swift_keys to interact with the Ceph cluster using the Swift interface.

In order to talk Swift to Ceph, we use a command line tool similar to the s3cmd utility used for talking to Ceph via the S3 API. For the purposes of this demonstration we will use the popular `python-swiftclient` but you can use any of the alternatives available online. Let's download and install the Swift client so it's ready for use:

```
root@ceph-rgw0:~# apt install python-pip
root@ceph-rgw0:~# pip install python-swiftclient
```

Performing Object Operations using the Swift API

Now that we have the Swift client installed, let's use it to create a new bucket on our Ceph object storage. We will cleverly name our new bucket `example-bucket`. Once the bucket creation completes we'll list all buckets our user has access to and verify that the previously created buckets are visible:

```
root@ceph-rgw0:~# swift -V 1.0 -A
http://ceph-rgw.objectstorage.example.com/auth -U harshita:swift -K
m38OvpnOMf8ILNZyfDuKTDTWKC7YCEUH9v4Te64o post example-bucket

root@ceph-rgw0:~# swift -V 1.0 -A
http://ceph-rgw.objectstorage.example.com/auth -U harshita:swift -K
m38OvpnOMf8ILNZyfDuKTDTWKC7YCEUH9v4Te64o list
example-bucket
first-bucket
```

Swift commands are constructed using the following syntax:

```
swift -V <version> -A <auth-url> -U <subuser> -K <secret-key> <calls>
```

We can see above that the post operation to create a new container worked as expected, and so did listing all the user's existing buckets. The S3 bucket shows up because it is also a bucket that the user owns and has access to. Remember that the S3 and Swift API's are two different ways of interacting with the same service, and the buckets and objects we create are compatible with both.

Summary

Storage provisioning is the most important operation an administrator performs on their systems. Unlike clunky traditional enterprise storage systems, we don't have to procure, manage, maintain, and support multiple storage systems for different storage modalities. Ceph uniquely delivers object, block, and file storage from a single unified back end. So far we have learned how to configure and provision RADOS block devices, CephFS filesystems, and Ceph object storage. The familiar block device and filesystem storage abstractions have existed for decades now; object storage however is relatively new and is gaining momentum due to the popularity and flexibility of the Amazon S3 and OpenStack Swift services which Ceph supports right out of the box.

10
Integrating Ceph with OpenStack

In this chapter we look at how Ceph is used with OpenStack. We will cover the following topics:

- Introduction to OpenStack
- Ceph is the best choice for OpenStack storage
- Integrating Ceph and OpenStack
- Guest Operating System Presentation
- Virtual OpenStack sandbox deployment

Every cloud platform requires a robust, reliable, scalable, and feature-rich storage solution. Ceph is very common in OpenStack deployments, 60% or more exploit it for base image and instance volumes. Ceph's unique, unified, and distributed architecture makes it the right choice for today's and tomorrow's cloud storage backend.

Introduction to OpenStack

OpenStack is an open source platform for multitenant-capable private or public cloud deployments, providing components to build a flexible and scalable **Infrastructure as a Service (IaaS)** solution. As free open source software, OpenStack offers a rich suite of capabilities without vendor lock-in or expensive licensing. OpenStack is governed by the non-profit OpenStack Foundation and backed by prominent companies including Red Hat, Mirantis, Dell, Cisco, IBM, and Rackspace. There are also myriad individual contributors.

OpenStack's components are too numerous to list in full, so here we'll concentrate on those that leverage Ceph most prominently. Here's a diagram showing how these interact with Ceph.

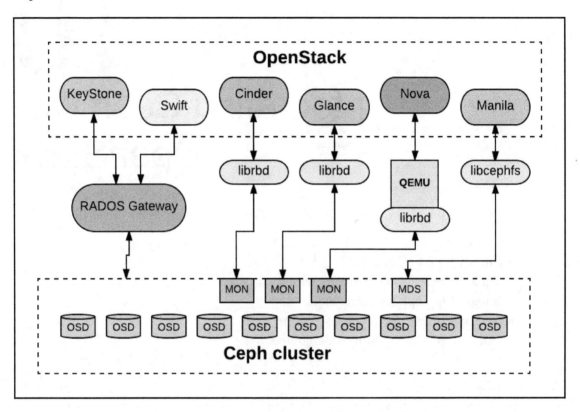

Nova

Nova is the heart of OpenStack: it creates and manages virtual machine instances usually leveraging QEMU/KVM but other guest virtualization technologies are also available via the libvirt system including Xen, Hyper-V, VMware, and even bare metal. Nova assorts instances across hypervisor systems according to need, availability, and policies, and arranges for the attachment of network and storage resources.

Glance

Glance provides and manages a library of base images -- ready-to-wear operating system installations that can be instantiated as new instances in minutes or seconds. More than a simple file retrieval system, Glance also allows users to create and manage image snapshots and upload and share their own customized operating system templates or software appliances. Glance can cache images locally on hypervisor nodes, but needs a backing central storage solution.

Cinder

Cinder provides an API for OpenStack instances to create and manage block devices, both as boot drives and supplemental volumes. Volumes are persistent and can be detached from one instance and attached to another as needed. Like Glance it also supports snapshots and enforces quotas. Cinder abstracts one or more storage backends so that the user does not need to know the specifics of the storage solution(s) in use.

Swift

Swift is OpenStack's object storage system. It includes both a storage back end of redundant account, proxy, controller, and object storage nodes and an access API similiar to Amazon's S3. One can build a scalable object store with Swift, but if you also need block or filesystem service, you will have provision and separately manage additional solutions. Ceph's RADOS Gateway service offers a Swift-compatible API for those who need it while also supporting block and file service against a single back-end.

Ganesha / Manila

These components provide traditional shared file-oriented storage via NFS, CIFS, and potentially other protocols.

Horizon

Horizon is a web-based dashboard interface that tenants can use to create and manage OpenStack resources, including storage volumes. It does not directly interact with user storage but rather brokers calls to other OpenStack components.

Keystone

Keystone is OpenStack's **Identity Management** (**IM**) that provides service endpoint discovery, client authentication, and multitenant authorization services. The name reflects the central, crucial role that Keystone plays with other OpenStack components.

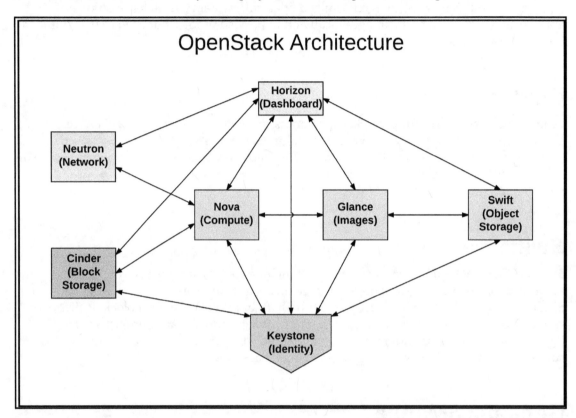

Within an OpenStack deployment Ceph leverages Keystone by providing a mapping between RADOS Gateway users and OpenStack tenants and roles. Keystone is also used to register the RGW and other service endpoint URLs.

For more information on OpenStack, visit http://www.openstack.org

The Best Choice for OpenStack storage

Anyone who has attended the increasingly popular OpenStack Summit conference can attest to the growing enthusiasm for and adoption of OpenStack as the framework for open cloud deployments. This author helped deploy and manage over a dozen OpenStack regions around the world.

Cloud infrastructures need a fast, robust, and especially scalable bulk storage solution without bottlenecks. Here are some of the reasons why Ceph is the best choice for OpenStack clouds:

- Ceph provides a single back-end for block, file, and object storage. You do not need to manage three disparate and disjoint storage systems.
- Ceph offers advanced block storage functionality that enables fast creation, backup / snapshotting and cloning of volumes and virtual machine instances.
- Ceph's thin-provisioning and **copy-on-write** (**COW**) abilities facilitate fast parallel instance creation without the penalty of serially writing each volume's full space up-front.
- Ceph provides persistent volumes that unlike Nova's native disk system can outlive instances and which enable fast and seamless live migration between hypervisors.
- Ceph provides featureful, enterprise class storage at a low cost per TB, which helps minimize operating costs both the providers and tenants.
- Ceph provides rich API's both for the popular S3 object interface and OpenStack's native Swift interface.
- The Ceph and OpenStack communities work closely to continually improve features, performance, and reliability. Red Hat is a major contributor to both OpenStack and Ceph; their acquisition of InkTank has accelerated the -- dare I say synergy—of their mutual development.

Integrating Ceph and OpenStack

OpenStack is complex and evolving, so an accurate yet full accounting of configuring OpenStack for Ceph is difficult within the scope of this book.

At a high level, one creates Cinder, Glance, and RGW pools then installs Ceph packages, credentials, and configuration on OpenStack Nova hypervisors as well as Cinder and Glance controllers. See the following references for full details, but briefly:

```
# ceph-deploy install <name of OpenStack node>
# ceph-deploy admin <name of OpenStack node>
```

One also needs to manage a basic configuration file under /etc/ceph on each OpenStack node so that the cluster can be contacted and accessed. Each OpenStack service also needs configuration to leverage your Ceph clusters. For example:

```
glance-api.conf:
[glance_store]
 stores = rbd
 default_store = rbd
 rbd_store_pool = images
 rbd_store_user = glance-user
 rbd_store_ceph_conf = /etc/ceph/ceph.conf
 rbd_store_chunk_size = 8

cinder.conf:
[DEFAULT]
 enabled_backends = ceph

 [ceph]
 volume_driver = cinder.volume.drivers.rbd.RBDDriver
 volume_backend_name = ceph
 rbd_pool = cinder-pool
 rbd_ceph_conf = /etc/ceph/ceph.conf
 rbd_flatten_volume_from_snapshot = false
 rbd_max_clone_depth = 3
 rbd_store_chunk_size = 4
 rados_connect_timeout = -1
 glance_api_version = 2
rbd_user = rbd-user
rbd_secret-uuid=xxxx-xxxxxx
backup_driver = cinder.backup.drivers.ceph
 backup_ceph_conf = /etc/ceph/ceph.conf
 backup_ceph_user = cinder-backup
 backup_ceph_chunk_size = 134217728
 backup_ceph_pool = backups
 backup_ceph_stripe_unit = 0
 backup_ceph_stripe_count = 0
 restore_discard_excess_bytes = true

nova.conf:
 [libvirt]
```

```
images_type = rbd
images_rbd_pool = cinder-pool
images_rbd_ceph_conf = /etc/ceph/ceph.conf
rbd_user = rbd-user
rbd_secret_uuid = 457ec676-34da-4bec-938c-9291138d545c337
disk_cachemodes="network=writeback"
hw_disk_discard = unmap # enable discard support
live_migration_flag=
"VIR_MIGRATE_UNDEFINE_SOURCE,VIR_MIGRATE_PEER2PEER,VIR_MIGRATE_LIVE,VIR_MIG
RATE_PERSIST_DEST,VIR_MIGRATE_TUNNELLED"
```

Most OpenStack deployments have their own mechanisms for populating and managing packages and configuration using Ansible, Puppet, Chef, or other tools. Chances are that your deployment already has the ability to manage these for you.

Once configured, users and services are able to locate service endpoints by querying the Keystone DB, and the Nova service through `libvirt` is able to create and use Ceph RBD volumes.

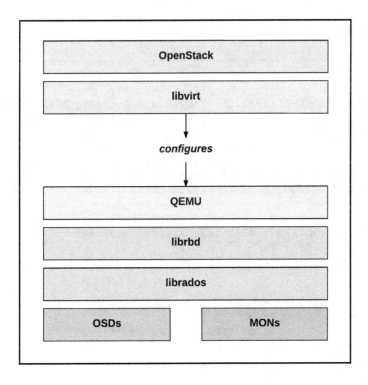

Guest Operating System Presentation

OpenStack clouds are usually configured to present virtual drives to guest operating system instances through `libvirt` via the `virtio` drivers, which avoid the baggage and performance limitations of emulating traditional IDE/ATA drives. On Linux clients these volumes will often be presented as `/dev/vda`, `/dev/vdb`, and so forth if the older `virtio-blk` driver is used and `/dev/sda`, `/dev/sdb`, etc. if the newer `virtio-scsi` driver is configured. In either event one can also reference devices by UUID as shown in the preceding example.

Guest operating systems can thus install and use Ceph-backed volumes as they would a traditional physical disk, for boot or supplementary data drives. The guest operating system via the `cloud-init` utility will typically resize itself on the first boot to match the provisioned size.

Here's an example of creating a 500GB volume and attaching it to an existing Nova instance as a supplementary drive:

```
$ cinder create --display_name MyVolume 500
$ cinder list
+-------------------------------+-----------+-------------+----+------------+
|              ID               |  Status   |Display Name|Size|Volume Type|
+-------------------------------+-----------+-------------+----+------------+
|19a9f901-ba9d-45e1-8622-a5466673ae76 |available|MyVolume 500|            |
+-------------------------------+-----------+-------------+----+------------+
$ nova list
+-------------------------------+-------+--------+------------------------+
|              ID               | Name  | Status |        Networks        |
+-------------------------------+-------+--------+------------------------+
| 842331c-ncc-n0-b100di-abcd    |eprise| ACTIVE | private=192.168.1.2    |
+-------------------------------+-------+--------+------------------------+
$ nova volume-attach 842331c-ncc-n0-b100di-abcd \
          19a9f901-ba9d-45e1-8622-a5466673ae76 auto
```

Then on the instance we can see, partition, format, and mount the volume.

```
instance$ ls /dev/vd*
/dev/vda /dev/vda1 /dev/vdb
instance$ lsblk
 NAME    MAJ:MIN RM   SIZE RO TYPE MOUNTPOINT
 vda     253:0    0    10G  0 disk
 └─vda1 253:1    0    10G  0 part /
 vdb     253:16   0   500G  0 disk

instance$ fdisk /dev/vdb
instance$ mkfs.xfs /dev/vdb1
```

```
instance$ mkdir /mountpoint
instance$ mount /dev/vdb1 /mountpoint
```

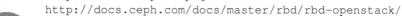

Resources for integrating Ceph with OpenStack

https://www.stratoscale.com/blog/storage/integrating-ceph-storage-openstack-step-step-guide/
http://docs.ceph.com/docs/master/rbd/rbd-openstack/
http://superuser.openstack.org/articles/ceph-as-storage-for-openstack/
http://ceph.com/geen-categorie/openstack-nova-configure-multiple-ceph-backends-on-one-hypervisor/
https://github.com/infn-bari-school/cloud-storage-tutorials/wiki/Mitaka-Openstack:-ceph-backend-configuration
http://docs.ceph.com/docs/master/radosgw/keystone/

Virtual OpenStack Deployment

OpenStack is evolving and complex; it is difficult for us to present here detailed steps for deploying a virtual OpenStack cluster in a way that will work and be relevant as you reach this chapter. There are however two popular packages to help you deploy a quick virtualized cluster that you can experiment with and even integrate with your virtual Ceph cluster from Chapter 5, *Deploying a Virtual Sandbox Cluster* .

DevStack:
https://wiki.openstack.org/wiki/DevStack
https://fedoraproject.org/wiki/OpenStack_devstack

Packstack:
https://wiki.openstack.org/wiki/Packstack
https://access.redhat.com/articles/1127153

Summary

In this chapter we've explored the key OpenStack services that leverage Ceph and resources for configuring and exploiting them. In the next chapter we'll explore ways to tune your Ceph deployment for stability and performance.

11
Performance and Stability Tuning

In this chapter, we look at getting the most out of your Ceph cluster. There are operating systems as well as Ceph settings, that we should look at to ensure smooth and performant operation.

Topics covered include:

- Kernel settings
- Network settings
- Ceph settings
- Ceph daemon osd|mon|radosgw perf dump
- Benchmarking

Ceph performance overview

It has long been said that data expands to fill available space, a phenomenon quite familiar to Ceph admins. As your constellation of Ceph clients continues to change and grow, it becomes increasingly vital to plan for sustained performance. Many factors at the operating system and Ceph architectural levels become increasingly important as Ceph clusters grow in capacity and workload.

Fortunately, Ceph is up to the challenge, and we will explore a number of ways to measure and optimize your deployments in this final chapter.

As we've explored in earlier chapters, many traditional and commercial storage systems exhibit performance that is limited by a single SAS, Fiber Channel, or network interface. As they are scaled for capacity, throughput may remain constant, or at best grow at a lower rate than capacity. Among Ceph's strengths is the ability to avoid data-plane choke points so that we are able to scale capacity and throughput together as we add additional storage nodes and take advantage of improved networking technologies.

Kernel settings

The Linux kernel adapts to the system on which it runs in a number of ways, scaling buffers and pools according to the number of CPU cores present and the amount of RAM provisioned. However, since the kernel and other operating system components must be usable on both heavily-equipped servers and modest consumer systems, there's only so much it can do out of the box.

Experience with Ceph has taught us a number of ways to ensure operational stability and continued performance as the workload grows. Some are common to most systems; others are highly dependent on your individual hardware and situation.

Many Linux kernel settings are persistently configured via the `sysctl` framework when the system boots. Historically, additions or changes were made within the `/etc/sysctl.conf` file, but with modern distributions it is advisable to instead exploit the drop-in directory `/etc/sysctl.d`. We can group related settings into individual files that can be conveniently managed separately within this directory. By convention Ceph-related settings would be entered in a file named something like `/etc/sysctl.d/60-ceph.conf`.

pid_max

Your Linux kernel manages traditional processes as threads and has a setting that limits how high a thread's numerical identifier may grow, and thus indirectly limits how many may exist system-wide at any given time. This `pid_max` setting defaults to `32768` as of the 3.19 kernel, a value more than sufficient for desktops or systems that host traditionally-architected applications. Ceph's daemons, however, are multi-threaded, and can spawn thousands of threads, especially during heavy recovery. As clusters become larger and busier, OSD nodes with multiple OSDs running can easily exceed this limit. If your OSD or system logs contain messages like *unable to fork* or *thread_create failed*, this is likely what's going on.

Since we know that Ceph behaves this way, we need to increase the limit. This can be done at boot time in the appropriate `sysctl` file:

```
kernel.pid_max = 4194303
```

It can also be done in the running state:

```
$ echo 4194303 > /proc/sys/kernel/pid_max
```

This value should suffice for even very dense OSD nodes. When deciding on values for this and other settings related to scale, consider that in the future your systems will be busier, more numerous, and likely denser. It pays to anticipate future resource needs to avoid service issues before they happen.

kernel.threads-max, vm.max_map_count

Space does not permit detailed descriptions of all settings, but we'll note here that raising these also helps to avoid thread/process creation problems.

```
kernel.threads-max=2097152
vm.max_map_count=524288
```

XFS filesystem settings

Busy XFS-based FileStore OSDs may find that these settings optimize performance, especially if you have the luxury of using SSDs. The XFS metadata sync operations have traditionally been intrusive and somewhat painful. When the sync thread awakens it may pre-empt the writes of all other processes (threads), which can interfere with Ceph's journal and data flushes. The `fs.xfs` settings here help to mitigate that effect.

The `fs.aio-max-nr` setting expands the queue for disk operations. Modest to moderate OSD nodes, say those with fewer than 20 OSDs, may do fine with the default value. As the per-host OSD density increases, it increasingly becomes a limiting factor. Throughput benefits from scaling this value proportionally to drive count; this value of 50 million should be ample for even the densest Ceph OSD nodes:

```
fs.xfs.xfssyncd_centisecs=720000
fs.xfs.xfsbufd_centisecs=3000          # pre-4.0 kernels only
fs.xfs.age_buffer_centisecs=720000     # pre-4.0 kernels only
fs.aio-max-nr=50000000
```

Virtual memory settings

These are perhaps the most controversial of the settings we list in this chapter: ones that affect the kernel's management of virtual memory. Research the latter five on the net before setting; your kernel and situation may have dynamics that favor different or default settings.

`vm.min_free_kbytes` sizes a pool of free memory that the kernel tries to maintain in order to service allocation requests. By raising the value, we can speed up memory allocation and avoid fragmentation that confounds larger request sizes.

At the very least, though, we recommend setting `vm.min_free_kbytes` to `1048576`, or even `2097152` unless your systems are provisioned with limited memory, in which case you should really consider getting more. Modern RAM is affordable, especially on the open market:

```
vm.min_free_kbytes=1048576
vm.vfs_cache_pressure=10
vm.zone_reclaim_mode=0
vm.dirty_ratio=80
vm.dirty_background_ratio=3
```

Network settings

Most operating systems are not prepared to efficiently handle very heavy network traffic out of the box. You will need to consult with your networking team on the right settings for your infrastructure and adapt to your kernel, Linux distribution, and network environment. In this section, we'll discuss several common changes that can benefit Ceph deployments.

Jumbo frames

We've mentioned before the value of Jumbo frames to increase performance by increasing network and protocol efficiency. A common raised MTU size is 9,000 bytes; this must be configured within your network infrastructure as well as your system's interface configuration. Depending on your distribution, you may configure this in `/etc/network/interfaces` or, interface-specific files like `/etc/sysconfig/network-scripts/ifcfg-eth0`.

To dive more deeply into Linux network optimization, including topics like increasing NIC ring buffers, we suggest this document:
`https://access.redhat.com/sites/default/files/attachments/`
`20150325_network_performance_tuning.pdf`

TCP and network core

Space does not allow us to discuss this group of settings in detail. Consider them food for thought and online research. Most mainstream Linux distributions come out of the box tuned to run on even modest hardware. Systems like Ceph that do heavy network traffic can benefit considerably from tuning.

```
net.ipv4.tcp_timestamps=0
net.ipv4.tcp_sack=1
net.core.netdev_max_backlog=250000
net.ipv4.tcp_max_syn_backlog=100000
net.ipv4.tcp_max_tw_buckets=2000000
net.ipv4.tcp_tw_reuse=1
net.core.rmem_max=4194304
net.core.wmem_max=4194304
net.core.rmem_default=4194304
net.core.wmem_default=4194304
net.core.optmem_max=4194304
net.ipv4.tcp_rmem="4096 87380 4194304"
net.ipv4.tcp_wmem="4096 65536 4194304"
net.ipv4.tcp_low_latency=1
net.ipv4.tcp_adv_win_scale=1
net.ipv4.tcp_slow_start_after_idle=0
net.ipv4.tcp_no_metrics_save=1
net.ipv4.tcp_syncookies=0
net.core.somaxconn=5000
net.ipv4.tcp_ecn=0
net.ipv4.conf.all.send_redirects=0
net.ipv4.conf.all.accept_source_route=0
net.ipv4.icmp_echo_ignore_broadcasts=1
net.ipv4.tcp_no_metrics_save=1
net.ipv4.tcp_slow_start_after_idle=0
net.ipv4.tcp_fin_timeout=10
```

iptables and nf_conntrack

These kernel modules are used to enhance network security by implementing a flexible kernel-level firewall. As with other aspects of the Linux kernel, default settings are often insufficient for a busy Ceph cluster. If your organization's policies permit it, you may blacklist these altogether to keep them from loading. It's still prudent to raise their limits as a fallback option, as even blacklisted modules have a way of slipping back in. There is a connection table maintained by `nf_conntrack` that may default to as low as 65536. We suggest half a million as an ample value for OSD nodes hosting 24 4TB OSDs. Extremely dense nodes may require an even larger setting:

```
net.netfilter.nf_conntrack_max=524288
net.nf_conntrack_max=524288
```

Your kernel may use one or both of these names. Raising these will consume megabytes of additional kernel memory; on modern systems, this is trivial.

Below is an Ansible playbook to unload and remove `iptables` and `nf_conntrack` along with their dependencies.

```
# Unload and blacklist kernel modules related to iptables and nf_conntrack
# ref: https://goo.gl/aQFI8d
#
# Usage: ansible-playbook -e target=hostname rmmod.yml
# It is ok for some of the modules to fail during removal if
# they are not loaded. these are ignored.
- name: ensure we are applying to ceph server nodes
  assert:
    that: "'ceph_mon' in group_names or 'ceph_osd' in group_names or
'ceph_rgw' in group_names or 'ceph_aio' in group_names"
- name: stop and disable iptables
  service:
    name: iptables
    enabled: no
    state: stopped
- name: remove nat, conntrack modules. order here is important.
  command: rmmod {{ item }}
  with_items:
   - iptable_nat- nf_nat_ipv4
   - nf_nat
   - nf_conntrack_ipv4
   - nf_defrag_ipv4
   - nf_conntrack_proto_gre
   - xt_CT
   - nf_conntrack
   - iptable_filter
```

```
      - iptable_raw
      - ip_tables
    ignore_errors: true
  - name: do not load conntrack on boot
    file: path=/etc/sysconfig/modules/ip_conntrack.modules state=absent
  - name: do not load conntrack_proto_gre on boot
    file: path=/etc/sysconfig/modules/nf_conntrack_proto_gre.modules
state=absent
  - name: blacklist the modules to ensure they are not loaded on reboot
    copy:
      owner: root
      mode: 0644
      dest: /etc/modprobe.d/conntrack.conf
      content: |
        blacklist nf_conntrack
        blacklist nf_conntrack_ipv6
        blacklist xt_conntrack
        blacklist nf_conntrack_ftp
        blacklist xt_state
        blacklist iptable_nat
        blacklist ipt_REDIRECT
        blacklist nf_nat
        blacklist nf_conntrack_ipv4
        blacklist nf_conntrack_proto_gre
        blacklist xt_CT
        blacklist iptable_raw
        blacklist ip_tables
```

This playbook was designed for RHEL7.2 systems using an Ansible inventory file with certain hostgroup definitions. Your site practices, Linux distribution, and kernel release version will require adjustments to the inventory file and the lists of modules.

This file may be downloaded from:
`https://learningceph2ed.nyc3.digitaloceanspaces.com/rmmod.yml`

Every Ceph admin (and every sysadmin) has a favorite set of tunables and values to set, and there can be controversy over best practice. The names and effects of settings, as well as their defaults vary by kernel and Linux distribution release. Those we present here are based on our experiences. Your mileage, as they say, may vary, and you are encouraged to research what's right for you. The archives of the `ceph-users` mailing list are an especially rich hunting ground.

`ceph-users` archives may be found at
http://lists.ceph.com/pipermail/ceph-users-ceph.com.

In `Chapter 6`, *Operations and Maintenance*, we learned mechanisms to configure myriad Ceph behavioral and tuning settings. We changed values both in the configuration file read at startup and dynamically in running daemons by injection. Those settings dovetail into those we describe in this chapter to maximize the stability and performance of your Ceph deployments.

Ceph settings

In earlier chapters, we discussed the hundreds of internal settings that may be tweaked to optimize Ceph performance or adapt to local needs. The vast majority of these are eldritch and arcane; you're likely to shoot yourself in the foot by tweaking them. In this section we will discuss a number that are conceptually accessible and which have clear benefits.

max_open_files

Earlier in this chapter, we discussed Ceph daemons' thirst for threads. On busy systems they can also run out of file handles. The proper way to increase this limit varies by operating system and Ceph release. Suggested values are a minimum of 131072, and potentially as high as 524288 on dense, busy servers. Recent versions of Ceph allow one to set this in `ceph.conf` and will raise it on your behalf. Yes, this an OS setting, but Ceph can manage it for us now:

```
[global]
max_open_files = 131072
```

If your system has `/etc/init/ceph-osd.conf`, you may raise the value, which may be as low as 32768 there. On other systems you may need to use `sysctl`:

```
fs.file-max=524288
```

Recovery

Among the most tweaked Ceph settings are those that limit the behavior of backfill and recovery. We explored these in Chapter 6, *Operations and Maintenance*. In summary: one trades off the speed of healing against disruption to ongoing client operations. Through the Hammer LTS release, the defaults were too aggressive for many deployments, especially those running on relatively slow LFF HDDs with colocated journals. The Jewel release brought significantly more conservative defaults; if you're running Jewel or later, you may do well without tweaks. If you're on an earlier release, revisit Chapter 6, *Operations and Maintenance*, and consider throttling these down.

OSD and FileStore settings

There are quite a few settings that may be tweaked for OSDs; optimal values vary depending on the speeds of your OSD and journal drives, your workload, and the number of CPU cores available. The suggestions here must be researched and tested in the context of your unique deployment:

```
[osd]
filestore_queue_max_bytes = 1048576000
filestore_queue_max_ops = 50000
```

The above settings work well for the authors to enhance performance of FileStore OSDs deployed on fast SSDs. Your mileage may vary, especially on HDD OSDs:

```
[osd]
osd_op_threads = 16
osd_disk_threads = 4
```

These thread settings are sometimes controversial; some hold that increasing them can benefit performance, others that they increase contention and can lead to thrashing. Their effects vary by Ceph release, as internal management of work queues has evolved. Kernel versions and I/O scheduler settings also affect what's best here. Tweak these carefully and benchmark before and after. If your systems have a larger number of OSD daemons but a small number of CPU cores, you may experience context switching overhead by setting them too high.

We discussed scrub settings in Chapter 6, *Operations and Maintenance* as well; you may wish to consider lengthening your osd_deep_scrub_interval to minimize contention, especially on HDD systems.

MON settings

In Ceph releases beginning with Jewel, the MONs do a pretty good job at managing their databases. This was not necessarily the case in older releases. MON DB size is a function of both the numbers of OSDs and PGs in your cluster and of how much topology churn is going on. During periods of heavy recovery or node maintenance, the `/var/lib/ceph/mon` DB can grow to tens of GBs. This can become problematic on systems that provision meager filesystem space, and in some cases it can impact MON responsiveness and thus overall cluster snappiness.

Even on Jewel and later releases, this setting is recommended; it directs MON daemons to sweep stale entries from their DBs at startup-time:

```
[mon]
mon_compact_on_start = true
```

Another valuable setting is the mouthful `mon_osd_down_out_subtree_limit`. This affects how Ceph behaves when components go down:

```
[mon]
mon_osd_down_out_subtree_limit = host
```

This behavior, like the name, is tricky. This is defined as the smallest CRUSH bucket type that will not automatically be marked out. What this means is that if everything underneath a CRUSH bucket of the specified type fails at once, those items will not have the out state applied to them. With the default value of rack, hosts and OSD buckets will be marked out if they enter the down state due to failure and the cluster will begin recovery to ensure replication policy.

If we change the value to host, this means that if an entire OSD node suddenly bites the dust, Ceph will not mark its OSDs down. If we have a replicated cluster with a failure domain of rack, the loss of an entire host at once will no longer trigger recovery. The idea is that most of the time a host can be brought back up quickly, say by a hard reset because it wedged during reboot. Or maybe we installed a bad kernel that we need to remove before a second reboot.

If the host is legitimately dead, then we have the ability to run backfill/recovery on our own terms at our own rate, say with the `ceph-gentle-reweight` script we used in Chapter 6, *Operations and Maintenance*.

This option is tricky and can be difficult to understand. If you aren't really sure it's right for you, you should stick with the default.

Many other settings are possible and may benefit your deployment. They may also drag you down. In this second edition of *Learning Ceph*, we're taking a conservative approach. We do not want to overwhelm you with a raft of settings that you aren't comfortable with and which may not be right for your installation's unique mix of hardware, versions, and use-cases. Once you are conversant with Ceph's components and the dynamics of your clusters, we suggest perusing the larger set of settings detailed at `http://docs.ceph.com` and the `ceph-users` mailing list archives.

Client settings

Ceph's RBD block service is heavily utilized by cloud platforms like OpenStack and other virtualization solutions. Effective caching in memory on the client side can significantly improve the performance that users experience:

```
[client.yourclientname]
rbd_cache = true
rbd_cache_size = 67108864
rbd_cache_max_dirty = 50331648
rbd_cache_target_dirty = 33554432
```

These values of 64MB, 48MB, and 32MB are double the default numerical values as of Luminous.

Settings must be selected so that
`rbd_cache_size` > `rbd_cache_max_dirty` > `rbd_cache_target_dirty`.

Some references suggest larger values, but consider that these cache buffers are allocated per attached volume. Consider a dense hypervisor node hosting 100 smaller VM instances, each mapping an RBD volume for its boot drive. With these values, the hypervisor node will dedicate more than 6 GB of RAM just for caching guest boot drives. You may be able to spare that much, but hypervisors are often limited by RAM, and this should be considered carefully within the context of the overall server memory budget and the capacity configured for scheduling.

Benchmarking

There are utilities built into Ceph to measure performance, as well as valuable external tools. We'll discuss both. It's important to remember that workloads that issue smaller requests will yield much lower numbers than those issuing larger requests.

RADOS bench

To use Ceph's built-in tool, first create a dedicated, disposable pool to scribble into. For this to be a legitimate test, it must have the same attributes as your production pool: PG count, replication factor, CRUSH rules, etc.

Options to rados bench include:

- `-p`: The name of our dedicated test pool
- `seconds`: Number of seconds the test should run
- `write|seq|rand`: Type of workload to present: write, sequential read, random read
- `-t`: Number of concurrent operations; the default is 16
- `--no-cleanup`: Don't clean up the objects created during the run

Let's run a 60 second write test against a small cluster with a pool named data. A dedicated pool should be used to ensure that user data is not clobbered. Longer tests are better than shorter, as they ensure that caching effects do not overly skew the results:

```
# rados bench -p data 60 write
Maintaining 16 concurrent writes of 4194304 bytes for up to 60 seconds or 0
objects
Object prefix: benchmark_data_ncc_1701
sec Cur ops started finished avg MB/s cur MB/s last lat avg lat
0 0 0 0 0 0 - 0
1 16 39 23 92.9777 93 0.627 0.56
2 16 67 50 98.853 109 0.523 0.59
3 16 97 80 105.234 119 0.267 0.55
4 16 126 109 107.843 114 0.231 0.54
5 16 152 135 106.111 103 0.301 0.52
6 16 181 164 108.334 114 0.714 0.56
7 16 209 192 108.945 110 0.843 0.59
8 16 237 220 108.238 111 0.133 0.53
9 16 266 249 109.934 113 0.780 0.53
10 15 292 276 109.364 111 0.822 0.51
...
```

Tests should be run multiple times and for longer periods and the results compared and averaged to validate the method.

CBT

The Ceph Benchmarking Tool is a sophisticated test harness that can leverage multiple data collection methods. Space does not permit a full exploration in this book. Those interested in serious repeatable quantitative data, say for testing different EC profiles or FileStore settings, will find this invaluable.

CBT can be found at `https://github.com/ceph/cbt`.

FIO

The Flexible I/O Tester is what it says: a highly configurable tool for testing a variety of storage systems. Many Linux distributions provide a bundled `fio` packages for easy installation.

 One may visit `https://github.com/axboe/fio` to grok all things FIO. Especially useful is the collection of example profiles at `https://github.com/axboe/fio/tree/master/examples`.
The FIO examples boxed below may be downloaded with these URLs:
`https://learningceph2ed.nyc3.digitaloceanspaces.com/random.1m.fio`
`https://learningceph2ed.nyc3.digitaloceanspaces.com/mix.fio`
`https://learningceph2ed.nyc3.digitaloceanspaces.com/random.small.fio`

Here are some example FIO profiles that the authors find useful for benchmarking Ceph RBD clusters. Instances are run from several virtual machine clients in parallel.

Fill volume, then random 1M writes for 96 hours, no read verification:

```
[global]
ioengine=libaio
direct=1
group_reporting
filename=/dev/sda
[sequential-fill]
description=Sequential fill phase
```

```
rw=write
iodepth=16
bs=4M
random-write-steady]
stonewall
description=Random write steady state phase
rw=randwrite
bs=1M
iodepth=32
numjobs=4
time_based
runtime=345600
write_bw_log=fio-write-bw
write_lat_log=fio-write-lat
write_iops_log=fio-write-iops
log_avg_msec=1000
```

Fill volume, then small block writes for 96 hours, no read verification:

```
[global]
ioengine=libaio
direct=1
group_reporting
filename=/dev/sda[sequential-fill]
description=Sequential fill phase
rw=write
iodepth=16
bs=4M
[random-write-steady]
stonewall
description=Random write steady state phase
rw=randwrite
bssplit=512b/10:1k/3:2k/3:4k/45:8k/15:16k/7:32k/5:64k/5:128k/7
time_based
runtime=345600
iodepth=32
numjobs=4
write_bw_log=fio-write-bw
write_lat_log=fio-write-lat
write_iops_log=fio-write-iops
log_avg_msec=1000
```

Fill volume, then 4k random writes for 96 hours, occasional read verification:

```
[global]
ioengine=libaio
direct=1group_reporting
filename=/dev/sda
[sequential-fill]
description=Sequential fill phase
rw=write
iodepth=16
bs=4M
[random-write-steady]
stonewall
description=Random write steady state with verification
rw=randwrite
bssplit=512b/10:4k/80:64k/5:1M/5
time_based
runtime=345600
iodepth=32
numjobs=4
write_bw_log=fio-write-bw
write_lat_log=fio-write-lat
write_iops_log=fio-write-iops
log_avg_msec=1000
verify=crc32c-intel
verify_dump=1
verify_backlog=1000000
```

Summary

The learning does not stop here; not for you, and not for your humble authors. Several companies in the Ceph community offer interactive classes and professional services. Ceph topics are popular at conferences, including the semiannual OpenStack Summits. As we mentioned in Chapter 2, *Ceph Components and Services* the community is an integral part of Ceph's evolution. The authors have contributed code, and you are welcome and encouraged to as well.

Whew! We've made it through eleven action-packed chapters exploring the conceptual and practical aspects of planning, deploying, and managing Ceph clusters. We hope that this second edition of *Learning Ceph* has helped you design, implement, and manage awesome distributed storage.

Index

Host Bus Adapters (HBA) 62

www.ingramcontent.com/pod-product-compliance
Lightning Source LLC
LaVergne TN
LVHW081515050326
832903LV00025B/1497